Moth Orchids

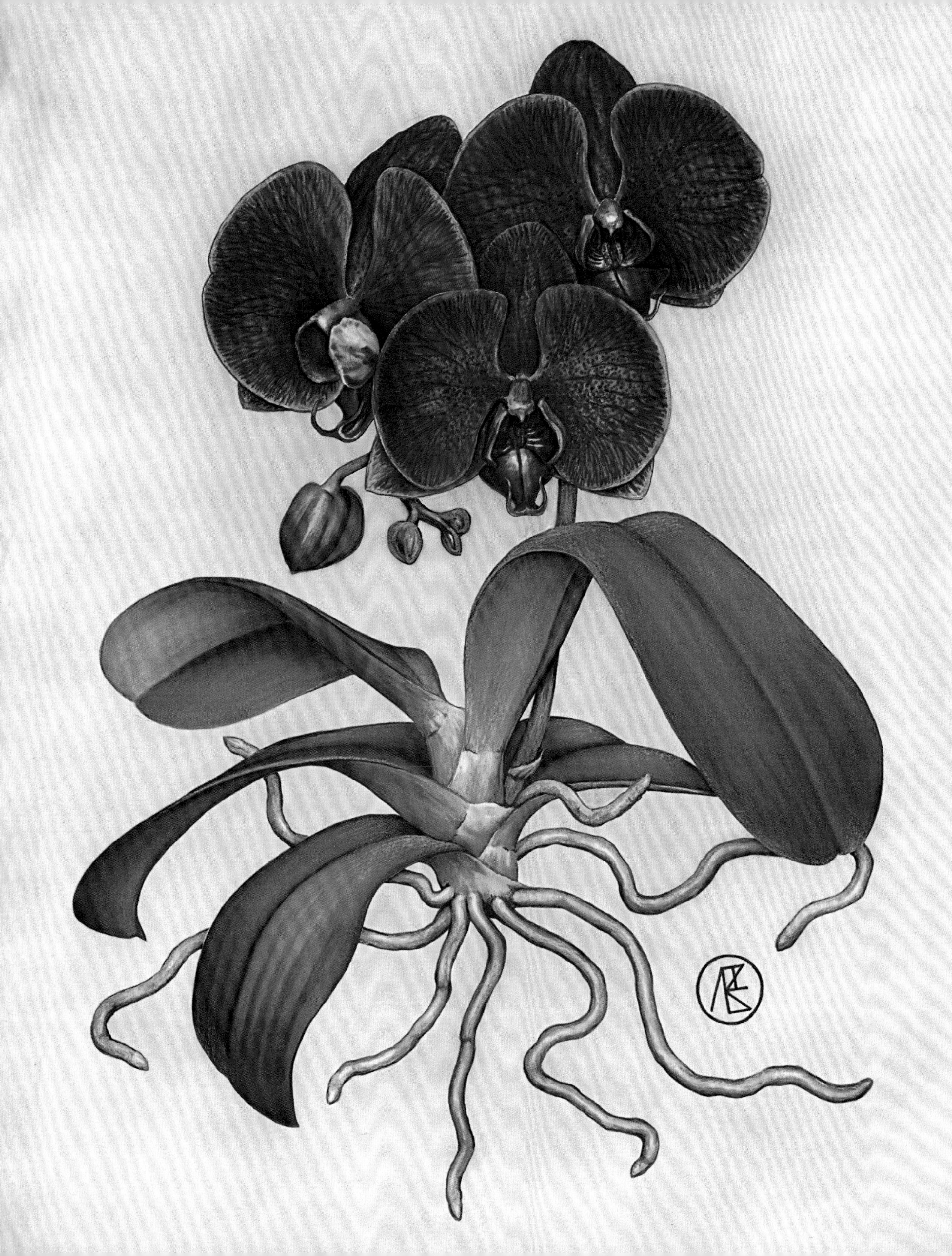

Moth Orchids

The Complete Guide to *Phalaenopsis*

STEVEN A. FROWINE

TIMBER PRESS
Portland • London

Frontispiece: *Doritaenopsis* Yu Pin Lover (*D.* Minho Princess × *D.* Minho Kingbeauty). Painting by Liena Dieck.

Mention of trademark, proprietary product, or vendor does not constitute a guarantee of warranty of the product by the publisher or author and does not imply its approval to the exclusion of other products or vendors.

Published in 2008 by
Timber Press, Inc.

The Haseltine Building
133 S.W. Second Avenue, Suite 450
Portland, Oregon 97204-3527
www.timberpress.com

2 The Quadrant
135 Salusbury Road
London NW6 6RJ
www.timberpress.co.uk

Printed in China

Library of Congress Cataloging-in-Publication Data

Frowine, Steven A.
Moth orchids : the complete guide to Phalaenopsis / Steven A. Frowine.
p. cm.
Includes bibliographical references and index.
ISBN-13: 978-0-88192-870-9
1. Phalaenopsis. I. Title.
SB409.8.P47F76 2008
584'.4—dc22
2007036186

A catalog record for this book is also available from the British Library.

To my wife, Sascha.
To my mother, Janet, and
deceased father, Samuel.
To phalaenopsis lovers
everywhere.

Contents

Preface

I started writing this book with the intention of describing and showing some of the new developments in breeding moth orchids. As I researched phalaenopsis, I found that few books that dealt with the many nuances of growing and enjoying these wonderful orchids were still in print by popular presses, so I felt compelled to expound on these issues. Over the years, many so-called mysteries and secrets have contributed to orchid growing lore. I have done my best to expose misconceptions and provide up-to-date information about how to grow and enjoy these elegant and popular orchids.

This book will appeal to the more serious phalaenopsis grower and collector as well as the casual grower. For the grower who wants details about parentage and histories of breeding developments in each color group, I have added information collected from many references and, in some cases, from the mouths of the breeders. For the casual reader, the book is densely populated with informative line drawings, paintings, and photos. For both groups, it contains an extensive section on culture. Hopefully, whatever your level of expertise, this book will prove helpful in your continuum of discovering the beauty and joy of growing phalaenopsis.

Various phalaenopsis hybrid categories are presented by flower color. Though color does not provide scientific information or exact characteristics, it is used by most people who buy phalaenopsis and by breeders and dealers in their catalog listings. For orchids with solid coloring, this categorization works fairly well. However, as many flowers are multicolored or striped, determining in which category they belong has proven difficult. In general, the "base" color of the flower is used to categorize it. For instance, if the orchid features a white flower with an overlay of various colors, it falls within the white category. This approach is particularly tricky with the red phalaenopsis, since many of them have a yellow base. In some cases, particular hybrids could be placed in more than one category. I made a few subjective decisions about where these "borderline" hybrids fit in, though I have no pretense that I have always made the "correct" decisions! In a few cases, references and images of the same grex will appear in more than one category, since it fits in more than one. Another challenging category is the "novelties." Chapter 7 is a catch-all chapter for novelty, miniature, and multiflora hybrids that do not clearly fall within the other categories.

As you can see, a color system of categorizing phalaenopsis is not an exact science. The most important objective of this book—the one in which I hope to be most successful—is to expose the wondrous variations of the phalaenopsis flowers so you can search out those that most attract you and enjoy the outstanding beauty they display.

Finally, this undertaking of describing the development of *Phalaenopsis* hybrids has been both fascinating and daunting, with so much information and opinions to sort through. "Orchid people" are passionate about their hobby or occupation and have strong beliefs that can conflict with those of others. I have done my best to sort fact from fiction.

Acknowledgments

Lucky for phalaenopsis lovers, a dedicated group of orchid breeders and growers continues to give us new and exciting varieties. Some are large commercial growers with acres of greenhouse production areas, while others are passionate hobbyists. I have consulted many of them while writing this book and am deeply grateful for their freely shared information and their determined breeding efforts. It is because of them that we are able to enjoy an unparalleled selection of moth orchids and can look forward to even more exciting offerings. I am particularly indebted to the following individuals for their time, expertise, and, in some cases, loaned images.

Liena Dieck has created the breathtakingly gorgeous silk paintings for this book. She also shows her impressive illustration skills with the various drawings that appear here. These contributions are immense and greatly appreciated. They add a quantum measure of beauty and information to this book. To find out more about her fine work, visit her web site at http://ld-art.com.

Eric Goo of Phoenix Orchids made substantial contributions in text and images to the chapters on red, yellow, and novelty phalaenopsis. His enthusiastic help, generous offer of his superb images, and his time and expertise have been invaluable.

Russ Vernon, owner of New Visions Orchids, has been my sounding board for much of the information in this book. He has a vast knowledge of orchids in general and phalaenopsis in particular. His unfailing willingness to help and understated manner made him a pleasure to work with.

Lisa Theobald, the editor of this book, has painstakingly worked to root out my errors and check details. I am deeply indebted to her for a job well done.

Marshall Ku gathered and photographed various images used in this book. He also shared with me some of the impressive contributions that the Taiwanese phalaenopsis breeders and growers have been and will be making. Taiwan is truly the Land of Phalaenopsis.

Hats off to the research team of Professors Yin-Tung Wang and Erik S. Runkle and graduate assistants Roberto Lopez and Matthew Blanchard of the Department of Horticulture at Michigan State University for their past and continuing work to inform the professional phalaenopsis growers of the world about the science of growing these lovely and popular orchids. I owe a special thanks to Dr. Runkle for his review and helpful comments and corrections for the chapter on culture.

Judy Becker continued to help with reviewing this book as she has done with most of my other books. I depend on her encyclopedic knowledge of orchids and eye for detail.

Doug Conkin, assistant editor of *Orchid Digest*, made very significant contributions to chapter 4 on standard yellow and orange phalaenopsis.

Tom Harper, phalaenopsis breeder and owner of Stones River Orchids in Franklin, Tennessee, offered his knowledge of *Phalaenopsis* species and their contributions to hybrids.

Meir Moses, owner of Orchid Konnection, added his cutting-edge knowledge and insight into the world of phalaenopsis breeding and offered the use of images of some of the newer hybrids. Thanks particularly for his contribution to the information on harlequins in chapter 6.

It is impossible to overestimate the value that the American Orchid Society, The Orchid Digest, International Phalaenopsis Alliance, *The Orchid Review*, and the many other fine orchid organizations and publications in the world contribute to the knowledge about and pleasure in growing orchids. Local chapters of these organizations, as well as all orchid societies or groups, are connected by a common thread of reverence for the grandeur of nature's floral masterpieces—orchids.

The Wonderful World of Moth Orchids

Moth orchids are by far the most popular type of orchid grown today. According to the American Orchid Society, they accounted for about 75 percent of all orchids purchased in the United States in 2002. Because they are easy to grow and their gorgeous flowers last for months, phalaenopsis are first choice orchids for beginners to orchidophiles, whether they are grown in greenhouses, on windowsills, or in light gardens.

It has not always been this way, however. In Victorian England, orchids were all the rage, but moth orchids were hardly grown. Because phalaenopsis have succulent leaves and no pseudobulbs, they were more perishable than some of the other available orchids and were very difficult to transport safely from their tropical climes to the greenhouses of Europe. During that time period, cattleyas, oncidiums, and other "tougher" orchids ruled in the orchid market.

With improved and speedier transportation and superior growing techniques that produce better quality plants faster, the tides have changed. According to R. J. Griesbach (2000), the number of potted phalaenopsis plants sold at the largest flower auction in the world, Aalsmeer in Holland, increased from 50,000 in 1983 to 3,150,000 in 1994. In the United States, according to the USDA Floriculture Crops Survey for 2005, more than 18,000,000 orchids were sold that year, a 5 percent increase over 2004. If we do the math, we know that if 75 percent of all orchids purchased are phalaenopsis, then about 13,500,000 phalaenopsis were sold in 2005 in the United States. Sales continue to grow. According to figures from the Taiwan Orchid Growers Association published in the May 2007 edition of the trade magazine *Floriculture International*, the export value of phalanopsis from Taiwan to the United States increased from $8 million in 2005 to $13 million in 2006. Worldwide sales of Taiwanese phalaenopsis increased from $27.5 million to $35.4 million from 2005 to 2006.

Why are these orchids so popular today? Here are some key reasons:

- Growing phalaenopsis is fun! That is the most important motive.
- Phalaenopsis are easy to grow. Any newcomer can be wildly successful by starting with standard hybrids.
- They cost less than ever.
- Some phalaenopsis emit delicious perfumes.
- They are available almost everywhere—from big-box stores and garden centers, to specialty growers, orchid shows, botanical gardens, orchid societies, and mail-order suppliers.
- Phalaenopsis are available in a diverse assortment of colors, varieties, and forms, so you will never tire of them and can always find new varieties to try and enjoy.
- They inspire the fanatical dedication of many collectors, who like to share information. Think about joining the International Phalaenopsis Alliance, The American Orchid Society, and your local orchid society. Subscribe to the *Orchid Digest* and *The Orchid Review*. These organizations provide great information and produce some of the best-quality orchid magazines in the world.

- Phalaenopsis happily grow on a windowsill or under artificial lights; they do not require an expensive greenhouse to thrive.
- They will beautify your home and life.
- Phalaenopsis can live almost forever.

Many of the newer hybrids have compact growth habits and are better suited for space-challenged orchid lovers who grow their plants in windowsills and under lights. These varieties, referred to as *multifloras*, are frequently characterized by having many flowers on branched spikes that produce a lot of flower power.

Phalaenopsis thrive in indoor climates that also suit humans. Their temperature, ventilation, humidity, and light requirements are easy to provide without making significant adjustments in human living conditions. A greenhouse is not required to grow these beauties to perfection, as many phalaenopsis are grown in windowsills and under lights.

Phalaenopsis have come to represent the ultimate in grace and glamour, often appearing as an elegant accessory in fashion and design magazine photo spreads, upscale restaurants, and shopping centers. In Europe as well as the United States, the "plain vanilla" varieties are so inexpensive (less costly than a bouquet of flowers) that they are sometimes purchased as a disposable *objet d'art* that can be discarded in a month or more, after the last blossoms have faded.

Because phalaenopsis are easy to grow, are reasonably priced, can be found in myriad and glorious colors and patterns, and are long-lasting, their popularity sees no signs of waning. In fact, with a flood of exciting new hybrids constantly being introduced, the phalaenopsis will continue as the favorite and most popular orchid for the foreseeable future.

Phalaenopsis display at the 2007 Orchid Show at the New York Botanical Garden

Chapter 1

What Makes an Orchid a Phalaenopsis?

Phalaenopsis (fal-en-OP-sis) is a genus of orchids whose distinctive characteristics make them unique. Foremost are their beautiful flowers, but these orchids also have attractive and sometimes strikingly handsome foliage (uncommon in the orchid world) and are sometimes scented.

The Wondrous Flower

The "typical" phalaenopsis flower is round and flat with petals resembling the wings of a moth—thus its common name, moth orchid. The genus name *Phalaenopsis* is essentially a compound Greek word: *phalaina* (moth) and *opsis* (appearance).

Knowing the name of each part of the phalaenopsis flower can be helpful in describing how one flower differs from another. Although I avoid using jargon in this book, sometimes these terms are necessary to describe flowers accurately. You can use the accompanying illustration as a reference.

Another interesting characteristic of phalaenopsis is the various ways the flowers are borne on the inflorescence (flower spike). The flowers can be borne opposite

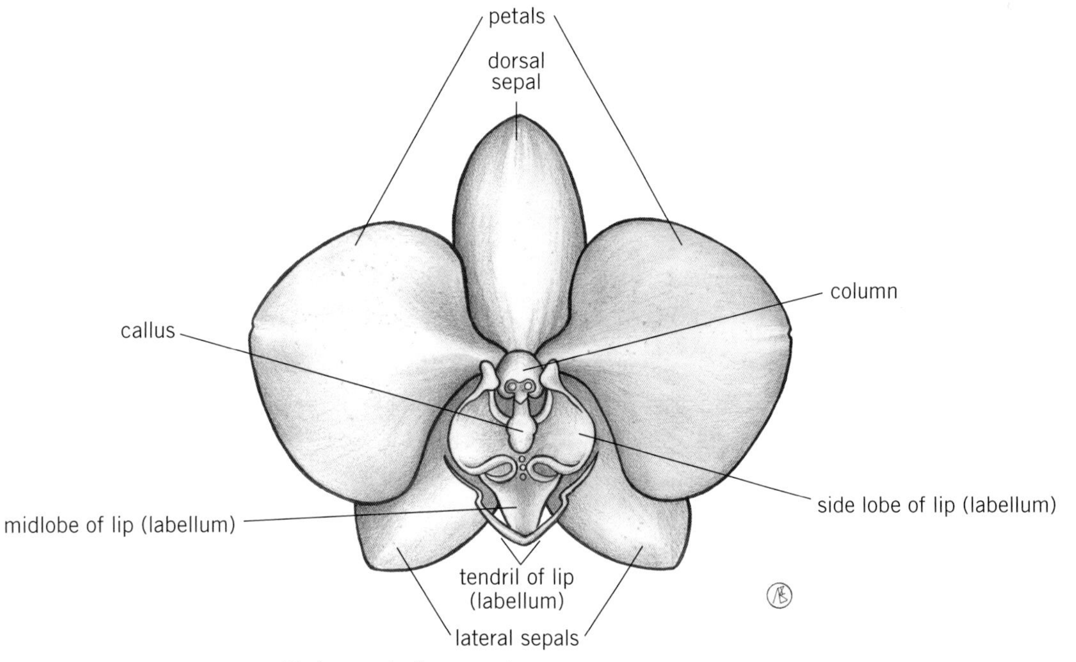

Phalaenopsis flower parts. Illustration by Liena Dieck.

Phalaenopsis inflorescence types. Illustrations by Liena Dieck.

on the inflorescence in double rows (raceme), as a branched inflorescence (panicle), or in an opposite pattern on a very short spike (raceme), typical of many of the species *Phalaenopsis.*

Importance of flowers in orchid judging

Various orchid judging systems have been devised by orchid societies around the world, and each has its own specific criteria for determining whether one phalaenopsis flower is superior to another. Point systems are used to determine which phalaenopsis are worthy of various honors or awards. Simplistically, phalaenopsis that are flat, round, and large, with strong color or patterning, heavy substance, high flower count, and good presentation on the inflorescence are favored. Vigor, ease of flowering, frequency of flowering, attractive foliage, and fragrance are not part of the usual award evaluation process.

If one of your goals is obtaining awards and ribbons at orchid shows, review the judging criteria from the appropriate governing orchid society to familiarize yourself with evaluation methods. For specific and detailed information on how phalaenopsis judging occurs in the United States, consult the *American Orchid Society Handbook on Judging and Exhibition* from the AOS web site (http://orchidweb.org/aos/publications/default.aspx).

Awarded phalaenopsis are considered by many as the crème de la crème of the orchid world. They've earned this distinction after evaluation by trained, discriminating orchid judges. At each accredited orchid show, a covey of judges carefully examine phalaenopsis that are exceptional and use special databases and Internet connections to check all existing records of the orchids being judged. They look for orchids of similar parentage to learn what has been awarded in the past to serve as a benchmark of excellence. These records reveal which parents have been awarded, the size and

Mutations: Peloric flowers and color breaks

A *peloric* flower has two normal petals that take on colors and markings that strongly resemble the lip. Some admire this mutation as a beautiful, albeit odd, gift from nature while others dismiss it as a freakish occurrence and discard such plants. The term *pelora* is derived from the Greek word *pelorus* (monstrous). According to A. Dean Stock (2005b), author and retired cytogeneticist, this mutation seems to occur when an entire plant or a portion of the plant has an odd number of chromosomes (termed an *aneuploid*) or abnormal chromosomes. Normal flowers can occur on the same inflorescence if the growing points gain or lose chromosomes. Although peloric flowers can sometimes develop from the cloning process or may be accentuated by cold stress, an odd number of chromosomes in the plant's makeup is usually the cause. Studies have determined that hybrids using *Phalaenopsis equestris* as a parent are more likely to produce peloric flowers.

Individual flowers can sometimes show *color breaks*, unusual, irregular color markings—for example, each half of the flower is a different color or has unusual and variable markings. Rarely will the same or even similar markings appear from flower to flower, and this unstable condition will not usually repeat itself in the next flowering. Stock (2005c) writes that this happens when pigment cells on part of the flower do not "turn on," due to a control gene malfunction during bud formation. Or the plant may have two pigment systems, and the dominant one is "shut off."

The intergeneric hybrid *Devereuxara* Hawaiian Delight (*Phalaenopsis* Barbara Moler × *Devereuxara* Hawaiian Rainbow) features a peloric flower. Painting by Liena Dieck.

Phalaenopsis flower with color break

number of flowers that appeared on the awarded plants, and other information. These criteria are then used to determine whether the new specimens are indeed superior to others of this type and whether they are worthy of awards.

Three common award categories are used by the American Orchid Society (from highest to lowest).

First Class Certificate (FCC): Only a handful of orchids (10 or 15) earn the coveted highest award every year.
Award of Merit (AM): Usually a few hundred orchids win this distinction every year.
Highly Commended Certificate (HCC): A few hundred orchids are assigned this level of award.

Phalaenopsis Breeding and Propagation

Although the all-familiar phalaenopsis come in elegant whites, pinks, and striped hybrids, a revolution in breeding has resulted in an entirely new, diverse, and wonderful array of moth orchids that display flower colors and patterns unimaginable only a few years ago. These sensuous flowers can be found in all shades of red, orange, yellow, dark purple, and even hues of blue. The harlequin types, with their unpredictable but usually delightful patterns, have opened a Pandora's box of colors with seemingly endless possibilities. As a bonus, some species *Phalaenopsis* are wonderfully fragrant, and these have been used as parents to produce an entirely new array of sweet-scented hybrids.

Cloning phalaenopsis

The process of cloning orchids, which began in the late 1950s, has made it possible to create award-quality plants that are made available at affordable prices. The growing point of the orchid, called the *meristem*, is excised and chopped into many microscopic, cell-size pieces that are placed in a sterile nutrient culture in a flask. After they reach a specific size, they can be removed from their "incubator" and planted in groups in community pots (in which many seedling are grown together) until they mature enough to be planted into individual pots. The entire process from test tube to mature plant takes a few years. The result is thousands of identical orchids, all of which are clones of a single parent plant.

A simpler method of cloning, called *stem propagation*, which is useful for producing a few plants at a

The importance of ploidy in phalaenopsis breeding

Every living cell has pairs of chromosomes. A *diploid* plant possesses two sets of chromosomes, and this condition is designated in scientific shorthand as *2N*. Sometimes in nature, but more often by chemical treatment by humans with a growth stimulant (such as colchicine), cells can be induced to increase their chromosomal numbers. The resulting cells and plants can have any multiple of the normal chromosomal number and are referred to as *polyploids*. If their cells have double the normal chromosome number (2×2) they are referred to a *tetraploids* (4N). If a diploid plant is bred with a tetraploid plant, the result is a *triploid* (3N) offspring.

This information may seem a bit arcane, but to a phalaenopsis breeder it is important stuff, because knowing the chromosome number of a phalaenopsis can be a strong indicator as to whether a plant can be successfully bred with another. Diploids are generally easy to breed to each other. They can also be bred with tetraploids, resulting in triploids that are usually sterile "dead ends" as far as future breeding goes.

Tetraploids can be bred with other tetraploids perfectly. Tetraploids are receiving a lot of attention these days in all fields of horticulture, because the doubling of chromosomes frequently produces desirable results. Among them can be a thickening of the substance of the flower parts, which usually means longer lasting flowers, larger flowers, more flowers, and increased plant vigor.

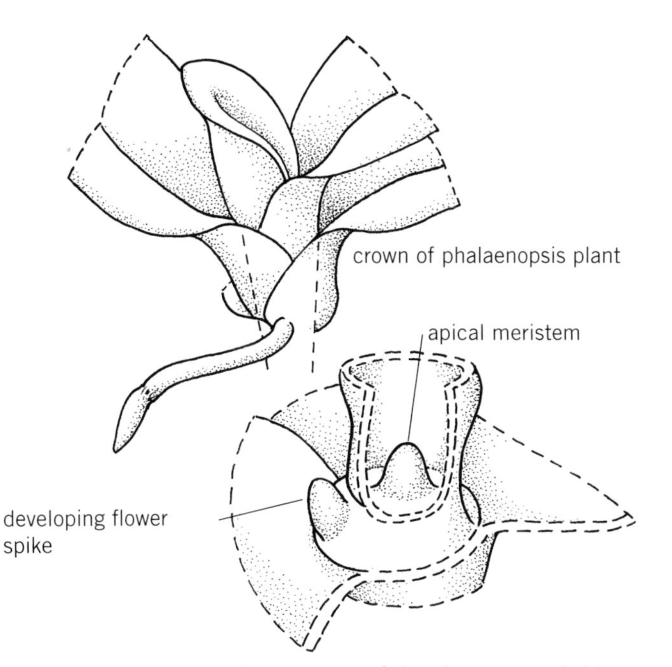

The apical meristem is in the center of the plant, concealed by the developing leaves. The flower spike grows nearby. Illustration by Liena Dieck.

time, can be accomplished by the hobbyist. Chapter 8 describes this method in detail.

Pollinating phalaenopsis

After a phalaenopsis breeder has carefully chosen superior parents with potential for producing superior offspring, the pollination process is ready to take place. One of the yellow, waxy clustered pollen masses called the *pollina* is removed from one parent (referred to as the *male* or *pollen* parent) and transferred, usually with a toothpick, to the stigmatic surface of the second plant (referred to as *female*, *pod*, or *capsule* parent). This process is very straightforward and decidedly low-tech. (For more detailed information on this process, see Bill Tippit's excellent two-part series in the November and December 1997 issues of *Orchids*.)

If the pollination is successful, a seed pod, which looks much like a green bean, will form. The miniscule seeds from this pod are sown in a flask containing a special nutrient culture. In about a year, the seedlings will be ready to transplant, eventually growing to flowering sized plants.

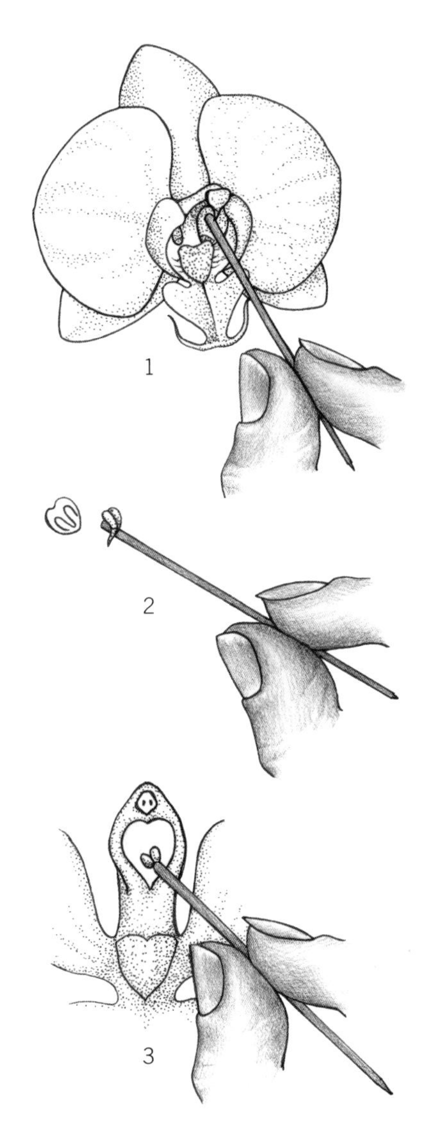

1. The anther cap is removed with a toothpick to obtain access to the pollina. 2. Then one of the two to four pollina is removed from the anther cap. 3. The pollina is placed on the backside of the second plant's stigmatic surface, located on the underside of the flower column. Illustration by Liena Dieck.

Growth Habit

Moth orchids' growth habit is called *monopodial*, which literally means one foot. This refers to the fact that the plant has one growing point that proceeds upward rather than multiple growths that "walk" sideways in the pot, as with cattleyas or oncidiums.

The leaf spread can vary from a few feet, as with

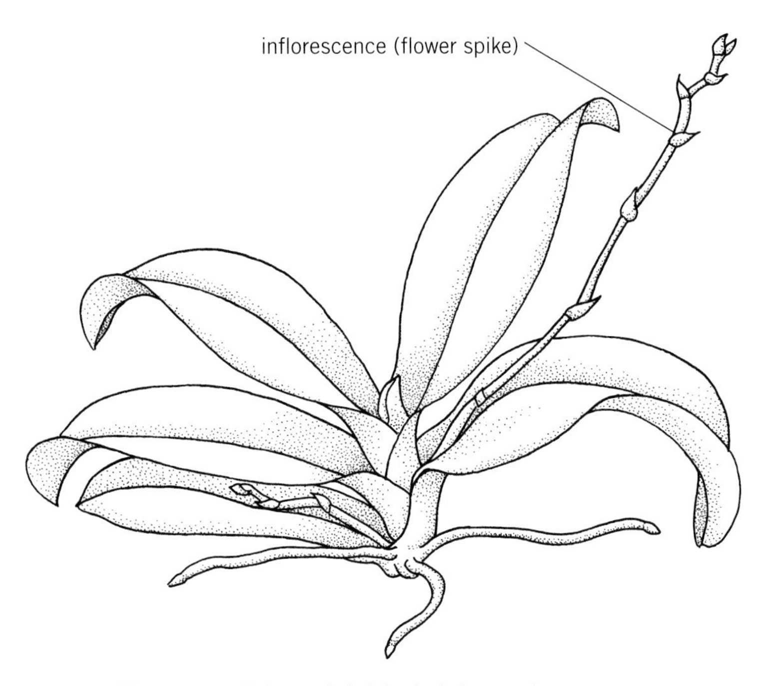

The monopodial growth habit of phalaenopsis. Illustration by Liena Dieck.

Some species and hybrids display striking foliage patterns.

Phalaenopsis gigantea or some of the white hybrids, to just a few inches in the miniature species, such as *P. lobbii*. The leaves themselves can display stunning patterns, especially in species such as *P. stuartiana* or *P. schilleriana* and some of their hybrids. Most moth orchids have waxy, bright to dark green, leathery or succulent, elongated oval-shaped leaves that are entire, or smooth-edged. The undersides of the leaves are often deep red to burgundy if the plant has dark flowers and is grown in adequate light.

Phalaenopsis leaves arise from the center of the plant, one at a time, in an alternating pattern. They are attached to a short stem, which makes the orchids relatively compact. Most plants in good health display several sets of dark green leaves, but a few of the lowest, oldest leaves often turn yellow and whither as new ones are produced (this is common and not a problem). These dead leaves will eventually separate themselves neatly from the stem along a line of cells called the *abscission layer*—this same process occurs in leaves of deciduous trees and shrubs in the autumn.

At the base of every leaf, where it attaches to the stem, is a bud. In the early stages of its development,

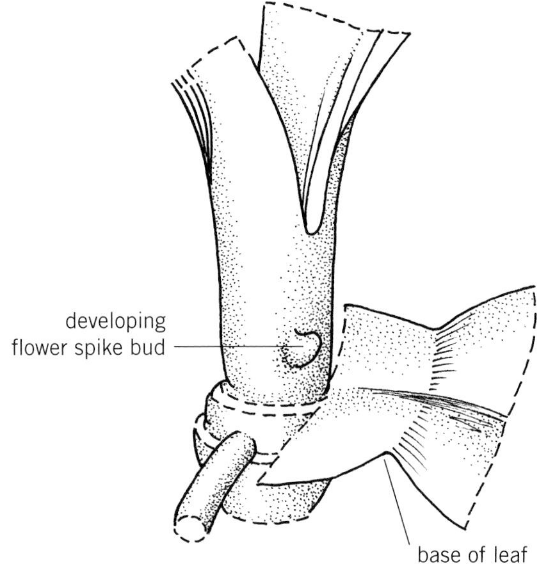

The developing flower spike bud. Illustration by Liena Dieck.

the bud is invisible to the naked eye, but when the orchid is ready to bloom, an upward pointing bump will appear from the base of the leaf. This is the flower bud, which will elongate and slowly develop into a flower spike.

Phalaenopsis roots are typical of most epiphytic orchids and similar to corn (to which all orchids are distantly related). The round or somewhat flat roots (depending on the species or hybrid) are about ⅛ to ¼ in. (3 to 5 mm) thick. The center of each root is cylindrical and wiry, surrounded by a spongelike layer

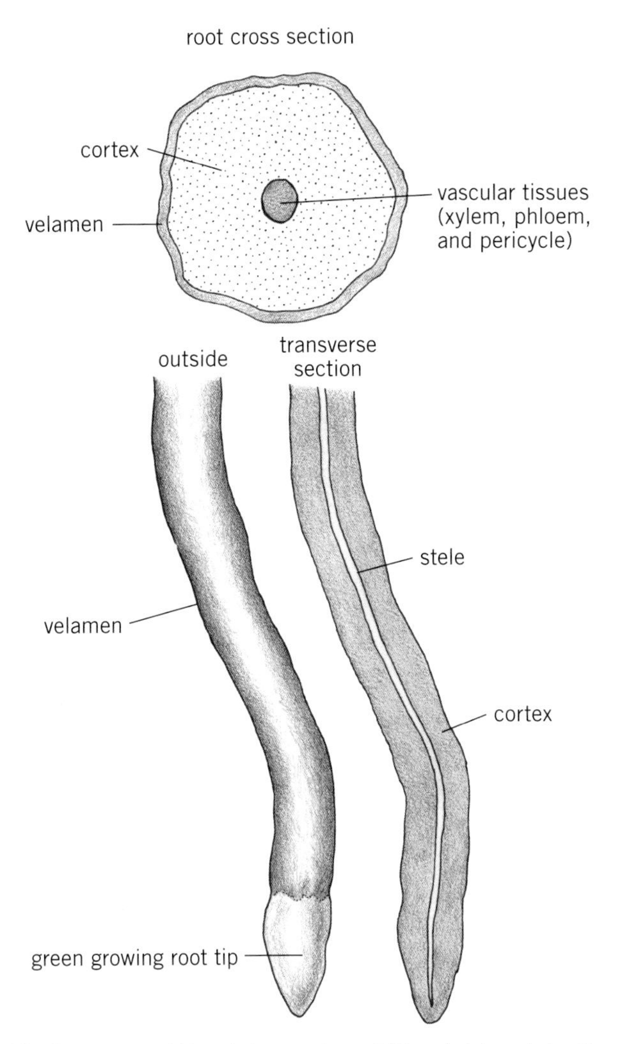

The inner core of the phalaenopsis root (the *stele*) contains the vascular tissues that transport water and nutrients, while the outside layer (the *velamen*) primarily serves as protection for the root. Most of the root consists of the *cortex* that stores starches and other substances in small amounts. Illustration by Liena Dieck.

called *velamen* that is silver-white when dry and green when wet. At one time, it was thought that the velamen absorbed and moved water and water vapor to the center of the root. Now, many plant scientists believe that the green root tips absorb water, which is then transported to the rest of the plant by the inner cylindrical portion of the root (the *stele*), although some moisture may still be absorbed through other root parts. Some phalaenopsis can go long periods of time, especially species that go dormant such as *P. lobbii*, without green roots tips, but they apparently are able to absorb moisture somehow. Instead of absorbing water, the spongy velamen is actually water resistant and serves as insulation or protection for the rest of the root. Velamen also attaches itself to the tree or other object on which a wild orchid is growing.

Genus, genera, generic?

A *genus* is the first half of the Latin binomial name of the orchid. It is the taxonomic subdivision between the family and species. The word *genera* is simply the plural form of *genus*. *Generic*, when used in reference to orchids, is a misnomer; there is no such thing as a generic orchid.

Moth Orchid Names

Probably one of the most intimidating hurdles faced by beginning phalaenopsis growers is the complex phalaenopsis naming scheme. Because of the immenseness of this group of plants, most orchid species are referred to by their Latin names rather than common names. In fact, very few *Phalaenopsis* species even have a common name. For the hybrids, most people use the grex and cultivar name, since it is understood that the genus is almost always *Phalaenopsis* or *Doritaenopsis*.

Species orchid names

Phalaenopsis, as they exist in the wild, untouched by human hybridizing efforts, are referred to as species *Phalaenopsis* and usually have only two names: the *genus* name is written first and is capitalized, and the *species* name is lowercase. Both names are in Latin and italicized in print (as foreign languages are usually treated). To understand the relationship between the genus and species names, you can think of genus names as being like our last names, and species names are like our first names. In other words, orchid naming is backward to the way most of us say our names. So if my name were written as an orchid name, I would be *Frowine steven*.

A third name, the botanical variety or form, can appear after the species name. This name is given to an orchid species that varies somewhat from the standard—it may have a larger flower or a slightly different coloration, for example. It is preceded by the letters *var.* (variety) or *f.* (form) and appears in lowercase and in Latin. A fine example of a species orchid variety is *Phalaenopsis equestris* var. *alba*.

Phalaenopsis equestris var. *alba*

Sometimes a particular plant of a species that is considered superior in some way—with better color or shape, for example—will have a cultivar name, which is usually set off in single quotation marks. For example, a blue flower selection of *Phalaenopsis violacea* is written like this: *Phalaenopsis violacea* 'Blue Chip'.

Grex and hybrid names

It would be so simple if naming stopped here, but hybrid and grex names add other layers of complexity. *Hybrids* are the result of crossing two species or hybrids (using the pollen from one orchid to pollinate another). A *grex* is all the siblings produced by the same cross. A marvelous thing happens when two different species or hybrids of orchids are crossed or mated: their progeny is usually stronger, easier to grow, and frequently produces larger flowers than either parent—which is why hybrids are desirable and popular. Finally, if a particular orchid (species or hybrid) wins an award or awards by the American Orchid Society (or another organization), its award(s) is apended to the end of its name. An awarded hybrid orchid name looks like this: *Phalaenopsis* Sogo Cock 'Oriental Princess' HCC/AOS.

The accompanying table shows a breakdown of this hybrid orchid's name and its various parts.

Phalaenopsis violacea 'Blue Chip'

Phalaenopsis Sogo Cock 'Oriental Princess' HCC/AOS

PART OF NAME	NAME	COMMENTS
Genus	*Phalaenopsis*	The Latin genus name is capitalized, italicized, and frequently abbreviated as *Phal.* (or *P.*, as in this book)
Species	None	This hybrid has several different species in its parentage, so no single species is listed. When an orchid hybrid's parents are the same species, the Latin species name will also be shown, lowercase and italicized.
Grex or hybrid name	Sogo Cock	All the plants or progeny from this cross are given a name known as a *grex* or *hybrid*. The grex is always written in a language other than Latin, is capitalized, and is not italicized.
Cultivar (cultivated variety)	'Oriental Princess'	This selection from this grex or hybrid is deemed, in some way, superior to the other members of the progeny. The cultivar name is always in a language other than Latin, capitalized, not italicized, and in single quotation marks. Each grex often has several cultivars.
Award designation	HCC/AOS	*HCC* is the abbreviation for Highly Commended Certificate, and *AOS* is an abbreviation of the awarding organization, the American Orchid Society. Other awarding organizations add their respective abbreviations: OSSEA: Orchid Society of South East Asia RHS: Royal Horticultural Society RHT: Royal Horticultural Society of Thailand OSSA: Orchid Society of South Africa ODC: Orchid Digest Corporation JOS: Japan Orchid Society HOS: Honolulu Orchid Society DOG: Deutsche Orchideen-Gesellschaft JOGA: Japan Orchid Growers Association OSROC: Orchid Society of the Republic of China (Taiwan)

1
2
3
4
5
6

Chapter 2

Species *Phalaenopsis*

The genus *Phalaenopsis* was first named in 1825 by Carl Blume, who used *P. amabilis* as an example in describing the genus. All *Phalaenopsis* species are originally from the Old World Tropics including Malaysia, the Philippines, New Guinea, Borneo, and the northern part of Australia. A diversity of flower shapes, markings, and colors appear in the genus. The lips (modified petals) are usually the most flamboyant parts of the flower, and the distinctive differences found in the lips are used as a definitive way to identify and taxonomically separate one species from another.

Although this book focuses on "newer" *Phalaenopsis* hybrids, the genetic building blocks of all these hybrids—the nature-made species—are important to consider. Some of these *Phalaenopsis* species have played a much larger role than others as parents for the modern hybrids we enjoy today.

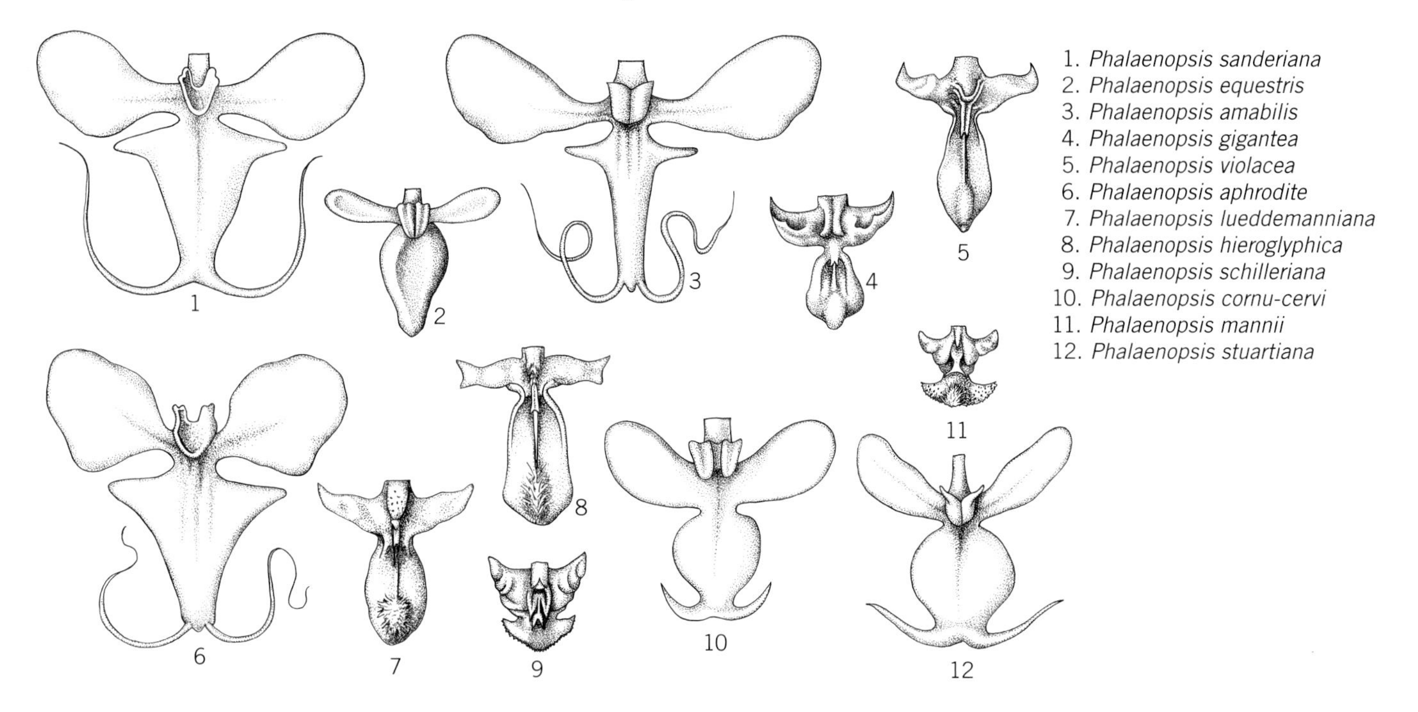

Lip structures of various *Phalaenopsis* species. Illustrations by Liena Dieck.

Opposite: Species *Phalaenopsis*: 1. *Phalaenopsis lobbii*; 2. *Phalaenopsis equestris*; 3. *Phalaenopsis sanderiana*; 4. *Phalaenopsis violacea* f. *coerulea*; 5. *Phalaenopsis reichenbachiana*; 6. *Phalaenopsis lindenii.* Paintings by Liena Dieck.

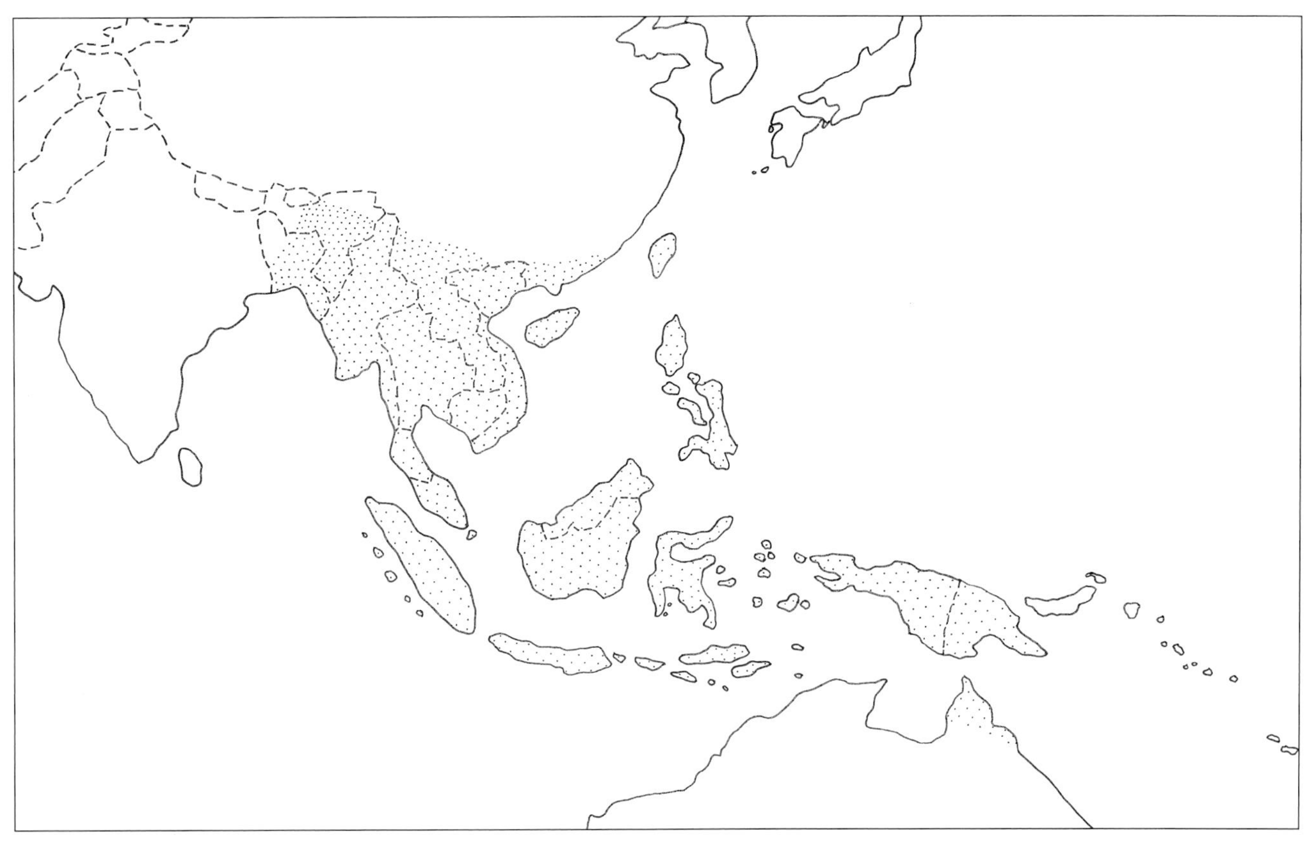

Distribution of *Phalaenopsis* species. Illustration by Liena Dieck.

Further reading

For detailed taxonomic treatment of all the *Phalaenopsis* species, the best reference is *Phalaenopsis: A Monograph*, by Eric A. Christenson (2001), which I have used as my guide for species nomenclature. Christenson's book provides detailed botanical descriptions and a more exhaustive treatment of *Phalaenopsis* species than provided in this book. For cultural guidelines on the *Phalaenopsis* species, Paul and Ann Tuskes's article "Culture of *Phalaenopsis* Species" (2002) provides detailed information and is well-illustrated. Other helpful articles on species culture are "The Species Challenge" by Charles Ufford (2005) and "Phalaenopsis Culture" by Tom Harper (2004a). Tom also authored the phalaenopsis section of *Complete Guide to Orchids* (McKinley 2005).

Phalaenopsis species interest and culture seem to be experiencing a revival. Specialist growers and hobbyists in the United States, Europe, and Asia have been selecting for fine forms of the various species, resulting in today's superior types, in terms of flower size, color, and quality available to the amateur grower at reasonable prices. These selections are much more vigorous and easy to grow than wild-collected orchids. They also allow conservation-minded orchid enthusiasts to buy nursery-grown plants instead of purchasing orchids that may have been inappropriately collected in their native habitats.

In terms of horticultural merit and contribution to the world of *Phalaenopsis* hybrids, two species stand well above the others: *P. amabilis* and *P. aphrodite*. These archetypical species define the ultimate phalaenopsis: round, white, elegant flowers borne in a graceful spray. They have some morphological differences and are found in slightly different native locales, so the

Phalaenopsis aphrodite. Photo by P. M. Tuskes.

Phalaenopsis amabilis. Photo by Peter Lin.

taxonomists say that justifies them being separate species; but to most of us they look very much alike.

Some general descriptions are included to cover horticulturally important species, with information about how each has contributed or has the potential to contribute to past, present, and future hybrids.

Phalaenopsis amabilis

Synonyms: *Phalaenopsis grandiflora, Phalaenopsis aphrodite*

This species was first described in 1753 by Linnaeus as *Epidendrum amabile*. Around this time, this orchid was sighted by Peter Osbeck in the west of Java, where only princesses were allowed to wear its revered flowers. In 1825, it was given the name it now assumes by C. C. Blume. Because he mistook the flowers for butterflies or moths when he viewed them through his field glasses, the common name for this genus, moth orchid, was born.

Phalaenopsis amabilis was first flowered in 1850 in England by J. H. Shroeder. This plant's merits were recognized early, as it received a Silver Banksian Medal from the Royal Horticultural Society.

A widely distributed native of Indonesia and its national flower, *P. amabilis* has the largest flower of the genus, 3 in. (7.5 cm) or more wide. A mature plant produces one or two branching inflorescences in the spring, 36 in. (90 cm) in height and displaying 75 or more lightly fragrant white flowers, each accentuated with a bright yellow lip. Different botanical varieties can vary slightly in flower color or form. Its four or more leaves are thick and glossy green, sometimes tinged in red underneath, and can be up to 18 in. (46 cm) long.

Found in shaded areas in trees throughout most of Indonesia and in Queensland, Australia, it is considered one of the easier species to grow in cultivation.

Contributions to hybrids: This species has been crucial to the development of modern white hybrids. With the largest and roundest flowers, this species's contribution cannot be overstated for passing on these highly desirable characteristics to white, pink, and other colored hybrids. It has also contributed to many novelty hybrids with rounder flower forms and increased floriferousness.

Phalaenopsis amboinensis

Synonyms: *Phalaenopsis hombronii, Phalaenopsis psilantha*

This phalaenopsis was first described by J. J. Smith in 1911 from Ambon, in Molucca Archipelago, close to New Guinea. It has stunning cream to yellow, flat, sometimes fragrant flowers, about 2½ in. (6 cm) across, with mahogany bars, which are borne simultaneously on a short stem of about 8 in. (20 cm). Because several flower spikes continue to produce sequential blooms, a large specimen plant can present a long-lasting and dramatic floral display. Several flower color forms show varying degrees of white, yellow, or green background colors. Its handsome, glossy light green leaves are about 10 in. (25 cm) long.

Contributions to hybrids: This species lends its flowers' waxy, thick substance to long-blooming hybrids. It will frequently produce offspring with three to five flowers, white to yellow, to shades of orange and red, on branched spikes up to 12 in. (30 cm). It is used frequently in novelty crosses and is considered a good grower and easy breeder. On the negative side, flowers tend to be star shaped rather than full and round. Also, the flower count can be reduced, and if solid flower colors are the breeding goal, the spotting and barring characteristics of this species are often dominant.

Phalaenopsis aphrodite

Synonym: *Phalaenopsis amabilis* var. *aphrodite*

This species was first recognized by Reichenbach in 1862, but it was actually discovered by a Jesuit brother, Georg Joseph Kamel, who had been assigned to Manila in the late 1600s. The range of this species is from the Philippines to Taiwan, and it is found in similar habitats, in the tops of trees, like closely related species *P. amabilis*. Both share many of the same characteristics.

Its round, usually white flowers with a green flush in the throat are slightly smaller than those of *P. amabilis*, about 3 in. (7.5 cm) across, with lips marked with red and yellow. They are borne on inflorescences of about 24 in. (60 cm) tall. Leaves up to 15 in. (38 cm) long are

Phalaenopsis amboinensis 'Queen' HCC/AOS

Phalaenopsis aphrodite subsp. *formosana*. Photo by P. M. Tuskes.

dark green, sometimes flushed with red on the undersides. It is considered to be easy to grow in cultivation.

Contributions to hybrids: Like *P. amabilis*, this species has contributed significantly to modern white *Phalaenopsis* hybrids. Some confusion once existed as to whether or not *P. amabilis* and *P. aphrodite* were synonyms or separate species; one cannot be separated from the other in terms of their use as parents for white hybrids. This species is said to be more cold tolerant than *P. amabilis* and is being used by breeders in Taiwan because of this. A smaller Taiwanese form of this species, sometimes referred to as *P. aphrodite* subsp. *formosana*, is used to produce miniature branched multifloras.

Phalaenopsis bellina

Synonyms: *Phalaenopsis violacea* 'Borneo', *Phalaenopsis violacea* var. *bellina*

This prized species was discovered in 1859 by Teijsman in Malaysia; its species name is derived from the Latin *bellus* (beautiful).

Two-inch (5 cm) flowers are cream, apple green, and pink, borne sequentially, three or four at a time, on short, 4 to 6 in. (10 to 15 cm) inflorescences. Flower spikes of this species as well as all other sequential bloomers should not be cut off after the flowers fade, as more will usually originate later on in this same inflorescence. Long-lasting flowers are thick and waxy, with a strong lemon fragrance that make it one of the sweetest smelling of all the *Phalaenopsis* species. Shiny green leaves of up to 10 in. (25 cm) long contribute to the handsomeness of this plant. Superior flower forms are being bred and sold; they are flatter and larger, with more substance and stronger colors than most of those that are wild-collected.

Phalaenopsis bellina

Contributions to hybrids: This species is very important in hybridizing, contributing thick substance and attractive flower color, compact growing habit, and sometimes fragrance to its offspring. It can contribute yellow, orange, and red colors to the flowers of its offspring. On the negative side, crosses of this species have reduced flower counts, and its difficult and slow-growing characteristics, especially in plants of less than 4 in. (10 cm) leaf spread, can be passed on to its offspring. It also tends to spread its spots and bars, creating a blended and sometimes solid color effect, which can be a negative or positive, depending on the breeder's objectives.

Phalaenopsis buyssoniana

Synonym: *Doritis pulcherrima* var. *buyssoniana*

The genus name of this species has gone back and forth between *Doritis* and *Phalaenopsis*. Today *Phalaenopsis* is the taxonomically preferred genus name, but it is sometimes listed in catalogs as a *Doritis*.

Unlike most other *Phalaenopsis* species with arching inflorescences, *P. buyssoniana* bears its dark pink flowers on an upright flower stem up to 36 in. (90 cm) tall. It is a terrestrial rather than an epiphyte (that is, it lives on the ground rather than in trees). Leaves are 10 in. (25 cm) long and are thick, stiff, and dark green, sometimes with purple stippling. The flat or sometimes reflexed flowers are about 2 in. (5 cm) across and vary in color intensity from light pink to dark rose-pink. This species is found only in northeastern Thailand and is usually a summer bloomer.

Contributions to hybrids: *Phalaenopsis buyssoni-*

ana is a tetraploid, which means that it has twice as many chromosomes as most *Doritis* species, which are usually diploids. The main benefit of this chromosome doubling is that its progeny often have larger flowers with more substance. It was influential in producing dark pink hybrids. During the time when hybridizing took place, this species was commonly referred to as *Doritis pulcherrima* var. *buyssoniana*, so when it was bred with phalaenopsis its hybrids took on the genus name *Doritaenopsis* (*Dorit* from *Doritis* and *aenopsis* from *Phalaenopsis*). It usually added substance and color intensity and produced more well-spaced flowers on the inflorescence. Earlier hybrids were generally smaller than other *Phalaenopsis* hybrids, but today's doritaenopsis are about the same size as any of the other modern *Phalaenopsis* hybrids.

Phalaenopsis buyssoniana

Phalaenopsis chibae

Synonym: *Kingidium chibae*

Named for Masaki Chiba of Japan, who discovered this Vietnamese native, the relatively new discovery is rare in cultivation. It has compact foliage, about 4 in. (10 cm) long, and bears about a dozen of its yellow to brownish, ½ in. (1 cm) flowers on an erect inflorescence.

Contributions to hybrids: In years past, when large flowers and plants were the goal, this species would probably not have gotten much attention, but the recent popularity of small orchids with many flowers is receiving plenty of interest from phalaenopsis breeders trying to produce miniatures.

Phalaenopsis cornu-cervi

Synonyms: *Phalaenopsis lamelligera, Phalaenopsis devriesiana*

First brought to England in 1864 by the famous orchid purveyors, Parish and Low, this species was initially described in 1827 as *Polychilos cornucervi*. An exotic-looking species from India, Java, and the island of Sumatra, it is valued for its ability to flower prolifically for most of the year. Individual, 2 in. (5 cm) star-shaped flowers appear along the inflorescences, usually starting in early summer; as the spikes elongate, more buds develop along their lengths. Since the flowers are born sequentially on new and old flower spikes, the spikes

Phalaenopsis cornu-cervi 'Rhegan'

Phalaenopsis cornu-cervi var. *alba* 'Jade'

should not be clipped off when the flowers fade, as they will produce still more in the weeks and months to come. The flower stem is flat, and yellow, glossy flowers are barred in maroon with two or three flowers open at one time. Light glossy green 10 in. (25 cm) leaves are an attractive feature. Various color forms include the attractive *P. cornu-cervi* var. *alba*, which is not white as the variety name would imply, but a lime green.

Contributions to hybrids: This species contributes yellow, greenish, or cream-colored pigments and sometimes barring to its offspring. When bred with whites it can yield various shades of green and rust-colored tones. On the negative side, it does not improve flower form if roundness is a breeding goal.

Phalaenopsis deliciosa

Synonyms: *Kingidium deliciosum, Phalaenopsis decumbens*

Found from the Philippines to Sri Lanka, this "mini" *Phalaenopsis* species has leaves up to 6 in. (15 cm) long. Its flowers of less than 1 in. (2.5 cm) across are waxy and white with pink or purple markings on an inflorescence of about 4 in. (10 cm) tall. The flowers are borne sequentially so the plant can be in bloom for many months. *Phalaenopsis deliciosa* subsp. *hookeriana* has yellowish flowers.

Phalaenopsis deliciosa. Photo by P. M. Tuskes.

Contributions to hybrids: The species has been used as a parent to decrease the size of plants and the length of the inflorescence, and to increase the duration of flowering. It has been bred with other genera including *Ascocentrum* and *Renanthera*.

Phalaenopsis equestris (peloric form)

Phalaenopsis equestris

Synonyms: *Phalaenopsis rosea, Stauroglottis equestris*

First collected in 1843 on the island of Luzon in the Philippines, this orchid is widely regarded as an outstanding, easy-to-grow dwarf. Flower color varies from light to dark pink (*P. equestris* var. *rosea*), to solid pink (*P. equestris*), to white (*P. equestris* var. *alba*), to white with yellow on the lip (*P. equestris* var. *aurea*). Individual flowers are 1 in. (2.5 cm) across and appear from winter to spring. Spikes will rebloom so should not be pruned. Keikis (plantlets) may also form along their lengths. The plant reaches to about 3 in. (7.5 cm), with leaves to 6 in. (15 cm). A mature plant can have many spikes and hundreds of flowers.

Contributions to hybrids: This species is often used to produce small, multi-branched, heavy flowering hybrids, sometimes with striping and colored lips. It can also pass its peloric flower characteristic to its hybrids. During 12 generations and for more than 150 years, it has been in the background of more than 14,000 hybrids, mostly miniatures and multiflora types.

Phalaenopsis fasciata

Synonym: *Polychilos fasciata*

Named by Heinrich G. Reichenbach in 1882, this Philippine native bears waxy, fragrant, intense yellow to orange-yellow 2 in. (5 cm) flowers, prominently marked with burgundy-red bars. The top of the lip is marked in bright pink. Its leaves are about 8 in. (20 cm) long.

Contributions to hybrids: *Phalaenopsis fasciata* lends its strong yellow color and waxy, fleshy flowers to its offspring. On the negative side, it can yield hybrids with recurving flower parts. This species has been used frequently in producing modern, non-fading yellow hybrids. Some veteran breeders believe that this is the ac-

Phalaenopsis fasciata. Photo by P. M. Tuskes.

Phalaenopsis fuscata. Photo by P. M. Tuskes.

tual parent of the famous old yellow hybrid, *P.* Golden Sands 'Canary' FCC/AOS, rather than *P. lueddemanniana*, which has been recorded as the parent. This species has been confused with *P. lueddemanniana* var. *ochracea*, which produces yellow flowers that tend to fade.

Phalaenopsis fuscata

Synonyms: *Polychilos fuscata, Phalaenopsis denisiana*

Found in the Philippines, Thailand, and Borneo, this large species has three or four leaves of 12 in. (30 cm) or more in length. Its 12 to 18 in. (10 to 46 cm) inflorescence bears a few to several star-shaped flowers about 1½ in. (3.5 cm) across. Waxy, pale to yellow-green flowers are stained in a burgundy-brown. The dark red lip points forward.

Contributions to hybrids: It can be used to produce hybrids with striped and/or spotted flowers of good substance and frequently with red lips. On the negative side, it can impart twisted petals and a reduced number of flowers, and it can be difficult to breed.

Phalaenopsis gigantea

Found in Sabah, Borneo, this species is rare or possibly extinct in its natural habitat. Its species name refers to the leaf size, which can reach 24 in. (60 cm) or more, making it an impressive plant and the largest in this genus. Because of its huge leaves, it is sometimes referred to as elephant ear orchid in its locale. Its sweetly scented flowers are waxy, variably colored white or yellow, with red or brown barring or spotting, and are about 2 in. (5 cm) across. A mature plant can display 30 or more flowers at once. One of the more difficult and slow species to grow and flower, a developed inflorescence can take months to bud up and flower. It will produce successive flowers on older flower spikes, so they should not be pruned until they wither and turn brown.

Phalaenopsis gigantea. Photo by Peter Lin.

Contributions to hybrids: *Phalaenopsis gigantea* contributes its round shaped and strongly barred, large flowers, borne on a pendant spike, that are well shaped and fragrant with a waxy substance. It also produces hybrids with handsome foliage, which is usually of normal size when this species is bred with tetraploid hybrid *Phalaenopsis*. It has been used frequently by the Taiwanese breeders of novelty phalaenopsis and is sometimes used to intensify reds and to produce spotted hybrids. On the negative side, it frequently passes on small lips and pendant flowers (especially on first-generation hybrids), and it can be a reluctant breeder. In addition, it bears its flowers 360 degrees on the inflorescence, which disrupts the "shingling" effect that most breeders prefer. H. P. Norton, noted phalaenopsis breeder, believes that this species still has much to impart to orchid breeding because of its dark red and yellow coloring and thick substance.

Phalaenopsis hieroglyphica

Synonym: *Phalaenopsis lueddemanniana* var. *hieroglyphica*

As its synonym suggests, this Philippine species was once believed be a botanical variety of *P. lueddemanniana*, and its flowers show a strong resemblance to those of this species, though they are generally more strongly barred. The sweetly scented flowers are about 2½ in. (6 cm) across and are creamy with prominent cinnamon-red barring that is said to resemble hieroglyphics, thus the variety name. It bears its flowers sequentially, in the same fashion as closely related species *P. lueddemanniana*, but it produces short spikes on mature plants.

Contributions to hybrids: Used in breeding to impart its strong barring and excellent flower substance to its offspring, this species's shape is a negative if round flowers are a breeding objective.

Phalaenopsis lindenii

Phalaenopsis lindenii was first described by Augustus Loher in 1895. Originating in the mountains of the Philippines, it has compact, dark green foliage with silver markings. It produces a flurry of small pink and sometimes striped and red-stippled, 1 in. (2.5 cm) flowers with teardrop-shaped lips on an 18 in. (46 cm) inflorescence that is multiple branched and successively blooming. It also has a white form. Because this species is found naturally in the mountains at higher altitudes, it can tolerate cooler growing conditions than most other *Phalaenopsis* species.

Contributions to hybrids: *Phalaenopsis lindenii* lends its stripes and sometimes red coloration, plus attractively marked lip, to the flowers of its offspring, which also feature generous quantities of flowers, extended flowering, and inflorescence branching. It has been used frequently to produce miniature multifloral hybrids with handsomely marked foliage. On the negative side, it is considered a reluctant breeder and, be-

Phalaenopsis hieroglyphica. Photo by Peter Lin.

Phalaenopsis lindenii. Photo by P. M. Tuskes.

cause of its cooler natural habitat, does not grow well in climates with hot summers.

Phalaenopsis lobbii

Synonym: *Phalaenopsis parishii* var. *lobbii*

From the eastern Himalayas, this handsome, small-flowered miniature bears up to six flowers at a time in the spring and summer. At only ½ in. (1 cm) across, they are charming—lightly reflexed and mostly white, with a lip of orange-red with yellow markings. Leaves are a mere 1½ in. (3.5 cm) across, and overall the plant spreads to 5 in. (13 cm) or so. This plant can be tough to grow and can be easily killed by overwatering. It can lose its leaves if the plant gets too dry, but it can recover and produce new foliage.

Contributions to hybrids: Although a reluctant breeder, this species has been used to produce charming miniature plants. Some of its well-known offspring are *P.* Partris, a result of crossing this species with dwarf species *P. equestris*, and *P.* Micro Nova, a result of crossing with *P. maculata*. A newer hybrid, *P.* Fantasy Musick (*P.* Micro Nova × *P. equestris*), is easier to grow.

Phalaenopsis lobbii

Phalaenopsis lueddemanniana

Phalaenopsis lueddemanniana

French horticulturist Lueddemann was reportedly the first to flower this Philippine native. The species is highly variable in its flower form but commonly bears 2½ in. (6 cm) wide, waxy-textured, and vanilla-white or light yellow flowers with purple-red barring. Flowers emanate a soft, sweet scent. Starting in the spring, 12 in. (30 cm) inflorescences bear three to five elegant flowers. On a mature, well-grown plant, 50 or more flowers can appear on a single inflorescence. Later on, after the flowers pass, keikis (plantlets) may appear and can be potted up separately. The leaves are glossy green and up to 9 in. (22 cm) long.

Contributions to hybrids: It has been used with varying degrees of success to add its substance, color, barring, and spotting by crossing it primarily to complex white hybrids. 'Woodlawn' is the cultivar of this species with the reddest flower so is the one most frequently used for adding this color to hybrids. This species has been important in the early development of red *Phalaenopsis* hybrids.

Phalaenopsis maculata

Synonym: *Polychilos maculata*

From Borneo, this miniature species's leaves are about 4 in. (10 cm) long, with an inflorescence of 6 in. (15 cm) tall, bearing 3/4 in. (2 cm) creamy to pure white flowers strikingly marked with bright red bars. It has a reputation of being difficult to grow and seems particularly susceptible to bacterial rot.

Contributions to hybrids: This species is used to reduce plant size and to introduce red barring on the flowers. On the negative side, it can reduce flower size, may reduce plant vigor, and can cause the flower petals and sepals of its offspring to be narrow. Its characteristics of being a poor grower and breeder have minimized its use as a parent.

Phalaenopsis mannii

Synonyms: *Polychilos mannii, Phalaenopsis boxallii*

Native to China, India, Nepal, and Vietnam, this species was discovered in 1868 in Sikkim, India, by Gustav Mann. In midspring, the inflorescences begin to branch and display 1 to 2 in. (2.5 to 5.0 cm) narrow, glossy yellow flowers, with cinnamon-brown accent marks and a white and purple lip. A typical inflorescence on a well-established plant may have as many as 70 individual flowers that can last up to three months. They emit the scent of fresh-cut oranges. The plant itself is only about 2 in. (5 cm) tall and has glossy green leaves that spread outward 6 to 18 in. (15 to 46 cm). It is considered easy to grow.

Contributions to hybrids: This species is not favored by breeders because it tends to pass its revolute (convex) and twisting flower parts to its offspring. It was used in the 1950s to add its yellow color when bred with white hybrids, but the color reputedly frequently faded and resulting hybrids were sterile triploids. Selections of this species have been used by some Taiwanese breeders to produce greens.

Phalaenopsis maculata. Photo by P. M. Tuskes.

Phalaenopsis mannii

Phalaenopsis mariae

Frederick Burbridge named this species after his wife when it was discovered in the Philippines, and it was first published as a species in 1883. The species flowers in various color forms. The star-shaped, mildly fragrant flower is marked with heavy bars of mahogany and red and is so glossy it looks shellacked. Multiple short flower spikes appear in the spring and summer.

Contributions to hybrids: *Phalaenopsis mariae* has not contributed a great deal to hybrids. The flowers of

Phalaenopsis mariae. Photo by P. M. Tuskes.

its hybrids are usually not well shaped. It has been used to a limited degree for breeding red flowers (its color is not as steadfast as hybrids of some other species), and it appears to add floriferousness to its offspring.

Phalaenopsis micholitzii

Synonym: *Polychilos micholitzii*

This Philippine species has yellow or pale white, star-shaped, fleshy flowers, borne two or three at once, about 2 in. (5 cm) across, and displayed on short 2 in. (5 cm) but frequently multiple inflorescences. It was named in honor of Wilhelm Micholitz by Robert Rolfe in 1890. It is considered slow growing and somewhat difficult to cultivate.

Contributions to hybrids: This reluctant breeder is starting to be used in mini phalaenopsis breeding to produce free-flowering plants with shorter, but multiple, flower spikes with green and "no-fade" yellow flowers. On the negative side, it sometimes passes on its poor (twisted) flower shape.

Phalaenopsis philippinensis

A lesser known species from the Philippines, *P. philippinensis* was described in 1984. Flowers of this handsome orchid are displayed gracefully on the inflorescence, and it has attractively marked leaves. Three-inch (7.5 cm) glistening white flowers are accentuated by bright, clear yellow to orange lip lobes.

Contributions to hybrids: This species passes on its high-quality flowers that all open at once on the inflorescence, its distinct flower form, and its yellow lip. This results in an impressive display.

Phalaenopsis pulcherrima

Synonyms: *Doritis pulcherrima, Phalaenopsis esmeralda*

This important species was first described as *P. esmeralda* in 1874 and was later called *Doritis pulcherrima*, which is still used. Similar in flower and plant charac-

Phalaenopsis philippinensis. Photo by P. M. Tuskes.

Phalaenopsis micholitzii. Photo by P. M. Tuskes.

Phalaenopsis pulcherrima var. *champornensis* (peloric form)

teristics to *P. buyssoniana*, its flowers are generally smaller, about 1 in. (2.5 cm) across, and vary in color from light to intense cerise pink, bluish pink, or white. Several flower spikes can appear on a single mature plant. The leaf spread is about 6 in. (15 cm). *Phalaenopsis pulcherrima* var. *champorensis* is a peloric form, *P. pulcherrima* f. *alba* is white-flowering, and *P. pulcherrima* var. *coerulea* has blue flowers.

Contributions to hybrids: Like its close relative *P. buyssoniana*, this species has been important in contributing its brilliant flower color, upright flower spike, and compact plant size to its offspring. The blue form is used to add bluish flowers to doritaenopsis hybrids.

Phalaenopsis pulcherrima f. *alba*

Phalaenopsis sanderiana

Synonym: *Phalaenopsis amabilis* var. *aphrodite*

In 1882, this Philippine species was named after the famous British orchid nursery, Sander & Sons, by Heinrich G. Reichenbach. It looks similar to *P. amabilis* and *P. aphrodite*. In fact, at one time it was thought to be a variety of *P. aphrodite* or a hybrid between *P. amabilis* and *P. schilleriana*. Fragrant flowers are white with an overlay of pink or purple and approximately 3 in. (7.5 cm) across. They are borne on an arching inflorescence about 36 in. (90 cm) tall and are set off by attractive and succulent leaves of about 10 in. (25 cm) long, dark green

Phalaenopsis sanderiana. Photo by P. M. Tuskes.

Phalaenopsis sanderiana var. *alba*. Photo by P. M. Tuskes.

with silver-gray undersides. *Phalaenopsis sanderiana* var. *alba* is a pure white form.

Contributions to hybrids: *Phalaenopsis sanderiana* is important as a parent in producing modern pink, red, and lavender flowers with excellent shapes on graceful inflorescences. This species is summer flowering, unlike *P. amabilis* and *P. aphrodite*, which are early spring bloomers. Using this species in a phalaenopsis breeding program can extend the blooming season of hybrids in the genus. Hybrids bred with this species are more heat-tolerant, so their flowers do not blast (dry up and fall off) in the summer like many hybrids from *P. amabilis* or *P. aphrodite*.

Phalaenopsis schilleriana

Synonyms: *Phalaenopsis schillerana, Phalaenopsis curnowiana*

A Philippine beauty, this species was named in 1860 by Heinrich G. Reichenbach for the first person to have bloomed it in Europe, Consul Schiller. A mature plant can produce 100 or more pretty and fragrant pastel flowers, displayed from the dangling, branched inflorescences of up to 36 in. (90 cm) long every winter to spring. Measuring from 2½ to 3½ in. (6 to 9 cm) across, flowers are soft rosy pink, creamy white, or a hue somewhere in between; the scent is soft and sweet, like roses.

The large plant is notable for it attractive leaves, which are dark green, marbled with silver, and brushed with magenta below; these reach up to 12 in. (30 cm) in height and up to 5 in. (13 cm) wide. The flat roots ramble and cling to surfaces, and keikis can appear on the roots. It can require a cooler temperature than other phalaenopsis to trigger flower spike production.

Phalaenopsis schilleriana

Contributions to hybrids: An important and often used parent for pink hybrids, *P. schilleriana* contributes branching spikes, flower substance and form, and many large flowers. Its lovely marbled foliage is sometimes inherited by its offspring and has been a major contributor to spotted pink hybrids.

Phalaenopsis stuartiana

Reputedly closely related to *P. schilleriana*, this species also shows strikingly handsome, silvery patterned foliage that can reach about 18 in. (46 cm). A mature plant can have up to 100 white, slightly fragrant, long-lasting flowers with purple-maroon markings on branched spikes. The inflorescence can reach about 24 in. (60 cm) tall.

Phalaenopsis stuartiana

Contributions to hybrids: This species contributes its floriferousness, branching, spotting, flower form and spacing, strikingly patterned lip, and long inflorescences and has been a popular parent in the production of multifloral phalaenopsis.

Phalaenopsis venosa

Synonym: *Phalaenopsis psilantha*

A native of Indonesia, *P. venosa* was introduced into cultivation in 1979. It bears 2 in. (5 cm) wide, thick, waxy, slightly cupped, star-shaped floral segments that vary quite a bit in their coloration from bright yellow to orange-brown, barred in red to mahogany with a white center. They are borne sporadically, one or two at a time, on a short, 8 in. (20 cm) inflorescence. Foliage is light green.

Phalaenopsis venosa. Photo by Peter Lin.

Contributions to hybrids: This species is important in the production of strongly colored yellow hybrids that tend to have non-fading flowers. It has also produced oranges and reds. When crossed with white hybrids, its yellow floral segments and white center usually prevail. Hybrids can show reduced flower count but increased spike production. Sixty hybrids were registered with *P. venosa* as a parent from 1986 to 1990.

Phalaenopsis violacea

Hauntingly beautiful, highly aromatic flowers adorn this orchid from Malaysia, Sumatra, and Borneo. Measuring about 2 in. (5 cm) across, its flowers are star-shaped, usually a rose-purple, supported by stout 5 in. (13 cm) stems, and emanate a rich, spicy-sweet fragrance that has been compared to that of freesias. The

Phalaenopsis violacea

Phalaenopsis violacea 'Purity'

plant reaches about 4 in. (10 cm) tall. Though it is never loaded with flowers, it generates up to seven blooms at a time over a long period from early spring through the summer months. Rich green foliage is shiny and about 10 in. (25 cm) long. Blue-flowered forms are being developed that are quite dramatic; pure white selections are also available.

Contributions to hybrids: *Phalaenopsis violacea* is important for breeding compact-growing fragrant hybrids whose flowers are long-lasting with excellent substance. It frequently contributes its bright lip and excellent fragrance to its hybrids. A drawback is that most of its earlier hybrids had few flowers and a short inflorescence. This species was used along with *P. amabilis* to produce the first phalaenopsis hybrid, *P.* Harriettiae, registered by Veitch in 1887. This hybrid won the FCC from the Royal Horticultural Society in England in 1887 and was still a winner in 1974 when it won an AM from the American Orchid Society. When *P. bellina* and *P. violacea* were both considered violaceas, the two species were interbred, resulting in a superior *violacea* flower form.

These species, as well as several minor species, have been the genetic raw material used to create many marvelous hybrids. Species are continuing to be selected and hybridized to produce better forms and are still used frequently to produce novelty, miniature, and multiflora phalaenopsis.

2
1
3
4
5

Chapter 3

Standard Whites and Pink Base Colors

Round, pristine-white flowers epitomize the elegance and look of the genus *Phalaenopsis*. The white species, *P. amabilis* was the first in the genus to be described. Some of the earliest white types that were grown and displayed were *P. amabilis*, *P. aphrodite*, *P. sanderiana*, and *P. stuartiana*.

Though these species are beautiful, breeders sought to improve their natural form. They wanted larger, flatter, and rounder overlapping petals and sepals with heavier substance; flowers that were displayed and spaced better on the inflorescence; and plants that were vigorous and more floriferous. Although breeding efforts with white *Phalaenopsis* hybrids undoubtedly started, in a limited way, shortly after the species was discovered, they began in earnest in the early to mid-1900s in the United States and Europe.

One of the first notable white hybrids was *P.* Elisabethae, then considered a primary hybrid between *P. amabilis* and *P. rimestadiana* (now thought to be a Australian tetraploid form of *P. amabilis*). It was bred by the famous French orchid firm, Vacherot & Lecoufle, and named by the firm in 1927.

Although gradual improvements were made in the flower form, shape, and size for decades, one of the biggest breakthroughs for the large whites was *P.* Doris, registered in 1940. Hugo Freed, noted American phalaenopsis breeder, writes glowingly about this hybrid in *New Horizons in Orchid Breeding* (1979) and refers to it as the "Champion of Champions and the Queen of Queens." The result of crossing two fine parents, *P.* Elisabethae and *P.* Katherine Siegwart (bred and introduced by J. W. Slotter in 1932), *P.* Doris was introduced by Duke Farms, named after Doris Duke, and bred by T. W. Carr. Interestingly, this gorgeous hybrid was not that far removed from its species parents, as shown in the genealogy chart. The predominant contribution of the species *P. amabilis* in this hybrid's background is apparent.

Phalaenopsis Doris is a beauty, with 3¼ in. (8 cm) snow white flowers, but its real claim to fame is the role it played as a super parent. It is a tetraploid, with the usual advantages of double chromosomes, larger flower

Opposite: White and pink phalaenopsis: 1. *Phalaenopsis* Hakalau Queen (*P.* Hakalau Wonder × *P.* Danny Lee), a white hybrid; 2. *Doritaenopsis* Dark Victory (*D.* Esperanto × *P.* Abendrot), a pink hybrid; 3. French spotted hybrid; 4. striped hybrid; 5. *Phalaenopsis* Spanish Dance (*P.* Lippeschmuck × *P.* Su's Red Lip), a picotee. Paintings by Liena Dieck.

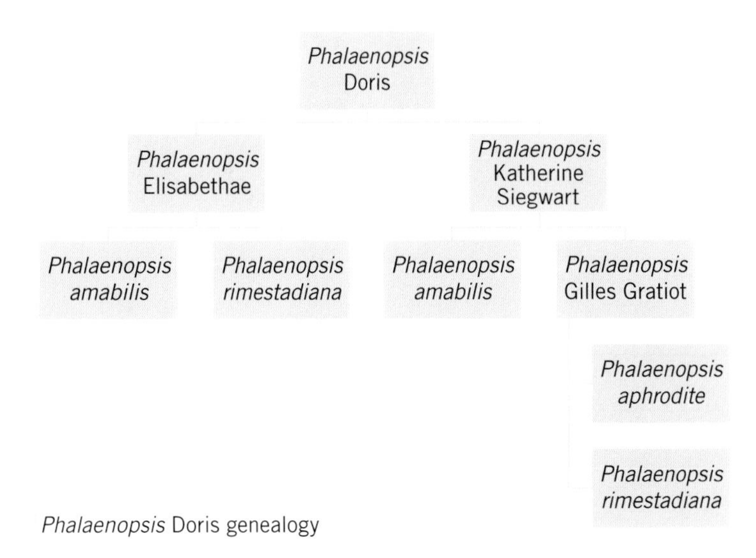

Phalaenopsis Doris genealogy

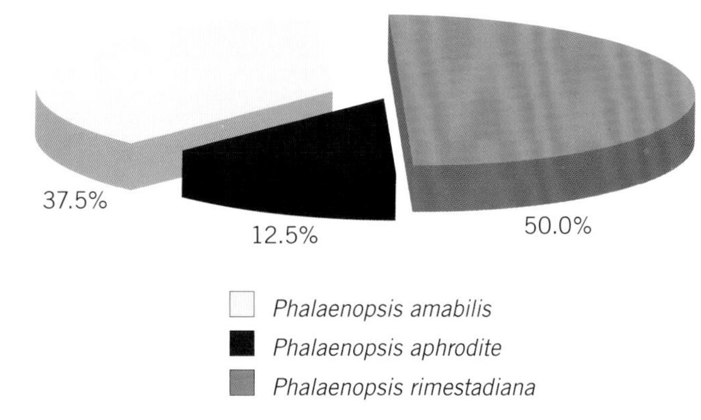

Species composition of *Phalaenopsis* Doris

size, and greater substance, all of which were frequently passed on to its offspring. Its better flower substance also proved to extend the staying power of the flowers and their resistance to air pollution. As of 2007, this grex has earned 29 awards, produced more than 260 F1 offsprings, and is in the breeding background of almost 24,000 hybrids!

The various grexes that further contributed to the development of modern white *Phalaenopsis* hybrids include *P.* Alice Gloria, *P.* Cast Iron Monarch, *P.* Dos Pueblos, *P.* Elinor Shaffer, *P.* Gladys Read, *P.* Grace Palm, *P.* Joseph Hampton, *P.* Juanita, *P.* Palm Beach, *P.* Ramona, *P.* Richard Shaffer, and *P.* Sonja. All these were registered in the 1950s to 1960s. Improvements continued with flatter, rounded, larger flowers of greater substance.

One of the most prolific and successful breeders of white phalaenopsis was Keith Shaffer of Shaffer's Tropical Gardens in Capitola, California. His company was responsible for more than 400 awards for superior white hybrids. Shaffer's white hybrids also served as important parents for future hybrid development.

In recent years, Taiwanese breeders have contributed their talents to creating award-winning whites, including those produced by W. H. Chen of Taiwan Sugar Company (Taisuco) such as *P.* Taisuco Bright, *P.* Taisuco Crane, *P.* Taisuco Kochdian, *P.* Taisuco Snow, *P.* Taisuco Swan, and *P.* Taisuco Windian. All these hybrids have used the grex hybrids as stepping stones and are not far removed from the old standby, *P.* Doris.

Phalaenopsis Cygnus 'Renaissance' (*P.* Tokyo Bridal × *P.* Silky Moon)

The standard whites have now reached such perfection in size, shape, substance, and texture that it is difficult to imagine how they could be improved significantly. One of the more modern whites, *P.* Cygnus (*P.* Tokyo Bridal × *P.* Silky Moon), bred and introduced by Kokubunji in 1997, offers clones bearing perfectly round flowers that are almost 6 in. (15 cm) across! It seems that many breeders also believe the whites have reached their zenith, since relatively little breeding work is being carried on with large whites. Instead, the emphasis seems to be on breeding and producing smaller flowering (1½ to 3 in., or 3.5 to 7.5 cm) multiflora whites (20 to 40 flowers) on compact-growing plants, by combining the multiflowering characteristics of white forms of *P. equestris* and *P. stuartiana* with classic whites such as *P.* Doris and newer hybrid whites. Some of the stars in this group are *P.* Be Glad, *P.* Brother Amar, *P.* Cassandra, *P.* Ho's Amaglad, and *P.* Timothy Christopher.

Semi-alba Hybrids

Semi-alba phalaenopsis, which are white with a colored lip, followed a development time frame similar to that of standard whites. Unfortunately for breeders, not many white species with darker colored lips were available to to use as parents. Some of the earliest breeding efforts used *P. equestris* var. *rosea* and a natural hybrid with this species, *P.* Intermedia (*P. aphrodite* × *P. equestris*).

Hawaiians played an important role as some of the first serious phalaenopsis breeders in the United States in the 1950s and 1960s. They selected some forms of species with darker lips, such as *P. equestris* var. *rosea*, forms of *P.* Intermedia, and *P. lueddemanniana*. One of the early results, registered in 1942 by F. C. Atherton, was *P.* Roselle (*P.* Elisabethae × *P. equestris*). More crosses were made by using the best white species and hybrids of the day, including the omnipresent and revered *P.* Doris. One such successful result was *P.* Ruby Lips (*P.* Roselle × *P.* Doris) that was registered in 1955 by Hazel McCoy. This hybrid was a great leap forward for semi-albas, and it was also a very prolific and a high-quality parent. A year earlier, another noted Hawaiian orchid breeder, Oscar M. Kirsch, introduced *P.* Sally Lowry (*P. equestris* × *P.* Pua Kea), which proved to be an important parent in the pursuit of fine whites. McCoy continued her contributions by registering *P.* Queen Emma (*P.* Doris × *P.* Ruby Lips) in 1960.

During the same time breeding was underway in Hawaii, various breeders on the US West Coast were working on producing semi-albas. In 1957, Philip Karleen produced *P.* Judy Karleen (*P.* Chieftain × *P.* Sally Lowrey) and *P.* Sharon Karleen (*P.* Sally Lowrey × *P.* Thomas Tucker). Legendary phalaenopsis breeder Herb Hager created a wealth of new hybrids: *P.* Mildred Karleen (1960), *P.* Sparkle (1960), *P.* Karleen's Wendy (1964), *P.* Bandleader (1967), *P.* Bright Lights (1974), and *P.* Devon Michele (1985).

The Rod McLellan Company, another well-known West Coast orchid breeder, produced *P.* Spitfire (1960), *P.* Mad Hatter (1965), and *P.* Rodco's Lady (1975). Hugo Freed, in Malibu, California, was also very active in breeding these types and in 1959 registered *P.* Lipstick, which was bred by Ralph Kiesewetter; *P.* Arthur Freed; *P.* Career Girl; and *P.* Show Girl. The noteworthy firm of Zuma Canyon Orchids, also located in Malibu, pro-

Judging white phalaenopsis

Several standards are used by orchid judges for discerning the "perfect" white phalaenopsis flower. These guidelines hold true for most of the other "standard" or large-flowered hybrids.

Form: Flowers of full, round shape with smooth edges. Dorsal sepal should be broader than the lateral sepals, and the space between the sepals should be filled with the petals.

Size: The hybrid should have flowers at least as large as its parents. It is interesting to note that flower size used to mean everything to the judges, but as the flowers got larger, in general, the orchid's flower count got lower. Today, flower count has become at least as important as flower size.

Substance: As with size, the substance (the thickness of the petals and dorsals) should be at least as good as its parents. Thicker substance usually translates to longer flower life and is a desirable quality.

Texture: Smooth, crystalline texture of the surface of the flowers is most desirable.

Habit of inflorescence: The inflorescence (flower spike) should be vertical and then gracefully arch forward and downward.

Number of flowers and buds: The hybrid should have a flower count equal to or greater than what could be expected from its parents. In general, the more flowers the better. A relationship exists between the number and size of flowers. Usually, a smaller flowering hybrid is expected to be more floriferous than a hybrid with very large flowers. For a standard white to be judged a winner, it usually needs to have a spread of about 5 in. (13 cm) with about a dozen flowers on the inflorescence.

Arrangement: Judges look for flowers to be spaced well on the inflorescence with no hidden blooms.

duced *P.* Firefly (1962) and *P.* Zuma Red Eye (1985). The highly regarded *P.* Zuma Urchin (*P.* Shu King × *P.* Debbie Wallace) was registered by this same company in 1984.

Florida orchid breeders were not left out of the action. Charles Beard, a very productive phalaenopsis breeder, produced *P.* Suemid in 1965 and *P.* Eva Lou in 1971.

Orchids by Hausermann in Chicago was and still is one of the largest orchid growers in the United States. This orchid firm produced *P.* Andrew Hausermann, registered in 1977, and *P.* Prairie du Sac, registered in 1980.

Vacherot & Lecoufle, a venerable orchid establishment in France, first started breeding semi-albas, using *P. stuartiana* as one of the parents. Some of this breeder's notable hybrids were *P.* Morzine (1970), *P.* Minouche (1971), *P.* Fifi (1974), *P.* Vivaldi (1975), and *P.* Alida (1976). One of its most influential hybrids was *P.* Line Renaud (*P.* Regine Debris × *P.* Redfan) in 1978.

Throughout the United States and Europe, semi-alba phalaenopsis have received much attention from orchid breeders. Many orchidophiles would agree that by the 1980s, large-flowering semi-albas has just about reached their zenith. Although somewhat newer and superior hybrids continue to be produced, the leaps in improvement are very incremental. An example of one of the newer hybrids is *P.* Formosa Best Girl 'Ching Ruey' (*P.* China Best Girl × *P.* New Glad), bred and introduced by Formosa Orchid Nursery in 1996. Interestingly, like the solid whites, many breeders of semi-albas are now working on producing multifloras with smaller but more flowers on compact-growing plants instead of larger flowered hybrids on standard-sized plants.

Striped Hybrids

Striped phalaenopsis are sometimes referred to as peppermint or candy-striped phalaenopsis. Their flowers are white with stripes of dark pink or red that vary in the intensity, number, and thickness of the stripes. Most are descended from *P. lindenii*, since it is one of the few species with striped flowers. One of the early

Phalaenopsis Samba (*P.* Star of Rio × *P. amboinensis*)

hybrids, registered by J. H. Miller in 1960, was *P.* Robert W. Miller. Parent *P. lindenii* added striping, and parent *P. sanderiana* contributed its large flower size. A few later hybrids using *P. lindenii* were *P.* Baguio (*P. sanderiana* × *P. lindenii*), bred and registered by Goodale Moir in 1966, and *P.* Peppermint (*P. lindenii* × *P.* Pink Profusion), bred and registered by Arthur Freed in 1964.

Phalaenopsis lueddemanniana was added to the genetic mix to produce *P.* Star of Rio (*P.* Bataan × *P. lueddemanniana*) that was bred by Burgeff and registered by Morgenstern in 1956. A later popular hybrid with more bars than stripes that used *P. amboinensis* as one of its parents was *P.* Samba (*P.* Star of Rio × *P. amboinensis*). *Phalaenopsis equestris* is in the background of some of the earlier hybrids that eventually produced *P.* Ruby Lips, bred and registered by McCoy in 1955. Other species playing more minor roles in flower striping are *P. fuscata* and *P. javanica*.

Some of the hybrids registered in the late 1960s to mid-1970s that have served as important stepping stones in the development of striped or peppermint varieties include *P.* Barbara Freed Saltzman, *P.* Career Girl, *P.* Chorus Girl, *P.* Ella Freed, and *P.* Pin Up Girl. These older hybrids, considered high breeding accomplishments in their time, have be far surpassed by today's hybrids, with larger flowers that are far more prominently striped. Taiwanese breeders have introduced some superior striped hybrids. Compare *P.* Seventh

Phalaenopsis Seventh Heaven (*P.* Ministripes × *P.* Alice Gloria)

Phalaenopsis Jackie Debonis (*P.* Ruey Lih Stripes × *P.* Chih Shang's Stripes)

Phalaenopsis Chih Shang's Stripes 'Marginata'

Heaven (*P.* Ministripes × *P.* Alice Gloria), bred and registered in 1974 by Jones and Scully, with *P.* Jackie Debonis (*P.* Ruey Lih Stripes × *P.* Chih Shang's Stripes), bred and registered in 1996 by Norman's Orchids.

Some striped varieties feature beautifully variegated leaves, such as *P.* Chih Shang's Stripes 'Marginata', which is a variant in this grex that was originally bred and registered by M. Lin in 1989.

The judging standards for these hybrids are similar to those used for the standard whites, but judges also consider distinct and sharp markings. Some prefer hybrids that display up to 20 flowers with shapes, substance, and textures similar to the favored whites.

Spotted White Hybrids

Although spotted white phalaenopsis have been bred for a long time, French breeders, specifically the firm of Vacherot & Lecoufle, made a commitment to breed high-quality spotted hybrids. As a result, fine spotted hybrids are sometimes called "French spots." Some of the outstanding hybrids produced by Vacherot & Lecoufle include *P.* Elise de Valec (*P.* Raptigny × *P.* Mouchette) in 1980, and *P.* Rouserrole (*P.* Cataracte × *P.* Frisson) and *P.* Dame de Coeur (*P.* Elise de Valec × *P.* Frisson), both registered in 1984.

Phalaenopsis Elise de Valec features white flowers

with an even distribution of maroon spots, except for the margins, which are white. The flower markings reveal the predominant species in its background—strong doses of *P. stuartiana* for markings, and *P. amabilis* and *P. aphrodite* for larger flower size. This hybrid proved to be a prolific parent, producing 66 F1 offspring as of 2007, including *P.* Dame de Coeur (*P.* Elise de Valec × *P.* Frisson), which received four awards. *Phalaenopsis* Rousserole was a standout and created quite a stir when it was introduced in the 1980s. The red spotting of its flowers are intense and dramatic and its flowers show superior form. This grex produced six awards and 93 F1 hybrids.

Contributions from the United States include *P.* Snow Leopard (*P.* Alida × *P.* Francine), developed by C. Hoover and registered by Southwood in 1982. Krull-Smith introduced *P.* Mary Krull (*P.* Alida × *P.* Red-Hot Chili), registered in 1985, and *P.* Ann Krull (*P.* Alida × *P.* Royal Satin), registered the following year. Of these two hybrids *P.* Mary Krull has the strongest markings, but both exhibit excellent substance.

Doritaenopsis Leopard Prince 'KHM430', a clone, was awarded first place at the 2006 Taiwan International Orchid Show. Photo by Marshall Ku.

Spotting was also introduced to white flowers via *P. lueddemanniana*. The markings on some of the earlier hybrids were often not as strong as those produced with *P. stuartiana* in their background, but the flower substance was superb. One of the earlier hybrids in this group was *P.* Cabrillo Star (*P.* Ramona × *P. lueddemanniana*), registered by Santa Cruz Orchids in 1961. A later breakthrough cross with this species in its background was *P.* Paifang's Queen (*P.* Mount Kaala × *P. lueddemanniana*), which was produced and registered in 1977 by Taiwanese breeder and grower Paifang's Orchid Garden. During this same time period, the American firm Orchids by Hausermann was producing fine spotted phalaenopsis using parents such as *P.* Carnival Queen (*P.* Carnival × *P. amboinensis*).

Recently, Taiwanese breeders have so dominated the breeding and introductions in this group that they are now frequently referred to as "Taiwanese spots." Taiwanese spots hybrids differ from French spots in that the Taiwanese flowers are generally smaller, with heavier substance and denser spotting, and breeders have used *P. gigantea* instead of relying on *P. stuartiana* to provide the spotting patterns. One of the newer and best known and loved hybrids, *Doritaenopsis* Leopard Prince (*D.* Sun Prince × *P.* Ho's French Fantasia), with dramatically marked and well-shaped flowers, was bred and registered by Sogo in 1997.

Interestingly, the spotted species and hybrids were important as forerunners to the wildly popular harlequin hybrids. The species *P. amboinensis*, *P. fasciata*, *P. gigantea*, and *P. lueddemanniana* all played important roles. Some of the key spotted hybrids that contributed were *P.* Samba (*P.* Star of Rio × *P. amboinensis*) and *P.* Spica (*P. fasciata* × *P. lueddemanniana*).

Pink Hybrids

Most early pink *Phalaenopsis* hybrids started off using as parents the species *P. schilleriana* and *P. sanderiana* for their desirable flower color. One of the first pink hybrids of note was *P.* Grand Conde (*P. sanderiana* × *P. schilleriana*), registered in 1929 by Vacherot & Lecoufle. These pink species were crossed with whites, such as *P. aphrodite* or *P. amabilis* hybrids, to add increased flower size and shape. A couple of the early hybrids were *P.* Versailles (*P. rimestadiana* × *P. sanderiana*), registered by Vacherot & Lecoufle in 1929, and *P.* Alger (*P. aphrodite* × *P. sanderiana*), bred and registered by the same firm in 1930. Later, *P. schilleriana* became the preferred parent, since its offspring produced a stronger pink color. When *P.* Alger was crossed to *P. schilleriana*, the hybrid *P.* Rêve Rose resulted and was registered by Vacherot & Lecoufle in 1932. *Phalaenopsis* Clara I. Knight (*P.* Marmouset × *P.* Doris), registered in 1951, was an important step toward larger pink flowers.

Pink hybrids started reaching the flower size of whites with better shape and color distribution with the introduction of hybrids such as *P.* Zada (*P.* San Songer × *P.* Doris), registered in 1958 by Fields Orchids; *P.* Barbara Beard (*P.* Virginia × *P.* Zada), bred and registered by C. Beard in 1962; and *P.* Ann Marie Beard (*P.* Palm Beach Rouge × *P.* Rozada), bred and registered by Beard in 1966.

The next important advances were made by German phalaenopsis breeder Fritz Hark with several of his most notable introductions, including *P.* Lipperose (*P.* Ruby Wells × *P.* Zada), registered in 1968; *P.* Zauberrose (*P.* Lipperose × *P.* Lippezauber) in 1972; *P.* Abendrot

Phalaenopsis Lipperose

Hilo Lip *Phalaenopsis*

Phalaenopsis flowers in various shades of pink with white lips are a strain called Hilo Lip *Phalaenopsis*, named after the Hawaiian city on the Big Island. The hybrid, *P.* Hilo Lip (*P.* Hilo Beauty × *P.* Elaine Mishima), was bred by Gregory Kobayashi and registered by Hayato Tanaka in 1985. Most of the plants within this grex were solid pink, but one special plant displayed a sparkling white lip, and this cultivar was called 'Lightfoot'. Soon other cultivars appeared from this cross, also showing a light lip; these were named 'White Lip'. The characteristics of a pink flower with a contrasting white lip is thought to have come primarily from one of its species parents, a tetraploid form of *P. schilleriana*. In today's parlance, any pink phalaenopsis with a white lip is commonly referred to as a Hilo Lip *Phalaenopsis*—*P.* Hilo Lip 'Winter Frost' is a fine example of this type.

Phalaenopsis Hilo Lip 'Winter Frost'

(*P.* Lippezauber × *P.* Lippstadt) in 1974; *P.* Lippeglut (*P.* Lippstadt × *P.* Zauberrose) in 1975; and *P.* Lippegruss (*P.* Abendrot × *P.* Lippstadt) in 1983. Of these, *P.* Lipperose, although never garnering any flower award from the American Orchid Society and only one Award of Merit from the Royal Horticultural Society, has been a huge influence in producing newer pink hybrids, with more than 5000 progeny! This hybrid was the first in the line of pinks produced by Hark that were commonly referred to as "German Pinks" (although its parents were both American hybrids). In a similar timeframe, Vacherot & Lecoufle registered *P.* Danse (*P.* Romance × *P.* Abondance) in 1976. In 1988, some nice pinks were registered, including one with a darker pink lip, *P.* Ida Fukumura (*P.* Rose Heart × *P.* Mi Cha), bred and introduced by G. Fukumura.

Gallery of White and Pink Hybrids

Hybrids are listed by the year in which they were registered to demonstrate changes and evolution over time.

1963

Phalaenopsis Samba
Origin: *Phalaenopsis* Star of *Rio* × *Phalaenopsis amboinensis*
Originator: Bracey's
Registered by W. Sanders

1965

Doritaenopsis Memoria Clarence Schubert
Origin: *Doritis buyssoniana* × *Phalaenopsis* Zada
Originator: Clarelen
Registered by Fields Orchids

1983

Doritaenopsis Happy Valentine 'Fangtastic'
Origin: *Phalaenopsis* Otohime × *Doritaenopsis* Odriko
Originator: Dogashima
Registered by Morita Inc.

Phalaenopsis Samba

Doritaenopsis Memoria Clarence Schubert

Doritaenopsis Happy Valentine 'Fangtastic'

Phalaenopsis Bonnie Vasquez 'Zuma Creek' HCC/AOS
Origin: *Phalaenopsis* Memoria Natalie Wood × *Phalaenopsis venosa*
Originator: Zuma Canyon
Registered by Zuma Canyon

Phalaenopsis Fortune Saltzman 'Maple Bridge' AM/TCA
Origin: *Phalaenopsis* Liu Tuen-Shen × *Phalaenopsis* Barbara Freed Saltzman
Originator: Brother Orchid Nursery
Registered by Brother Orchid Nursery

1988

Phalaenopsis Flight of Birds
Origin: *Phalaenopsis* Misty Green × *Phalaenopsis* Pine Hill
Originator: Carter and Holmes
Registered by Carter and Holmes

1990

Phalaenopsis Ever-Spring Spot 'Montclair'
Origin: *Phalaenopsis* Paifang's Auckland × *Phalaenopsis* George Seurat
Originator: Ever Spring
Registered by Ever Spring

1991

Doritaenopsis Hybridizer's Dream
Origin: *Doritaenopsis* Pretty Nice × *Phalaenopsis* Classic Carmela
Originator: Carmela
Registered by Carmela

1992

Phalaenopsis Brother Mirage
Origin: *Phalaenopsis* Paiho Rose × *Phalaenopsis* Frisson
Originator: Brother Orchid Nursery
Registered by Brother Orchid Nursery

Phalaenopsis Bonnie Vasquez 'Zuma Creek' HCC/AOS

Phalaenopsis Flight of Birds. Photo by Allen Black.

Doritaenopsis Hybridizer's Dream. Photo by Charlie Kovac.

Phalaenopsis Fortune Saltzman 'Maple Bridge' AM/TCA

Phalaenopsis Ever-Spring Spot 'Montclair'

Phalaenopsis Brother Mirage

1993

Phalaenopsis Taisuco Chinfang
Origin: *Phalaenopsis* Paiho Lucky Stripe × *Phalaenopsis* Chih Shang's Stripes
Originator: Jean Chin-Shang
Registered by Taiwan Sugar Company

1996

Doritaenopsis Minho Princess
Origin: *Doritaenopsis* Sun Prince × *Phalaenopsis* Ta Lin Freeds
Originator: Sogo Team Co.
Registered by Sogo Team Co.

Doritaenopsis Minho Princess 'Watercolor Princess' HCC/AOS
Origin: *Doritaenopsis* Sun Prince × *Phalaenopsis* Ta Lin Freeds
Originator: Sogo Team Co.
Registered by Sogo Team Co.

1997

Doritaenopsis Leopard Prince 'Brennan's Orchids' HCC/AOS
Origin: *Doritaenopsis* Sun Prince × *Phalaenopsis* Ho's French Fantasia
Originator: Sogo Team Co.
Registered by Sogo Team Co.

Doritaenopsis Leopard Prince 'KH4338'
Origin: *Doritaenopsis* Sun Prince × *Phalaenopsis* Ho's French Fantasia
Originator: Sogo Team Co.
Registered by Sogo Team Co.

1998

Doritaenopsis Brother Little Hatter
Origin: *Phalaenopsis* BeTris × *Doritaenopsis* City Girl
Originator: Brother Orchid Nursery
Registered by Brother Orchid Nursery

Phalaenopsis Taisuco Chinfang

Doritaenopsis Minho Princess 'Watercolor Princess' HCC/AOS

Doritaenopsis Leopard Prince 'KH4338'

Doritaenopsis Minho Princess. Photo by Allen Black.

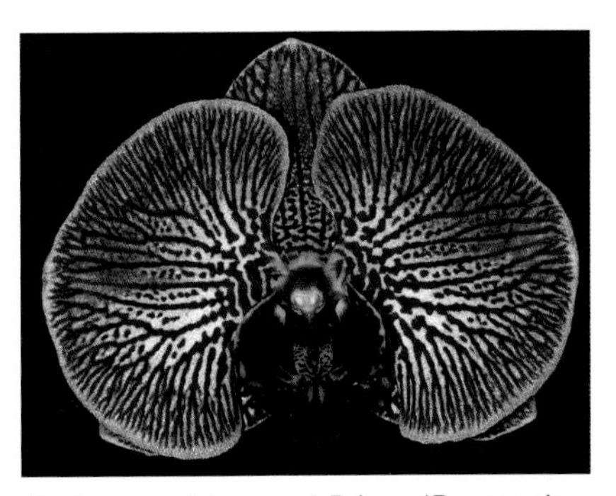

Doritaenopsis Leopard Prince 'Brennan's Orchids' HCC/AOS

Doritaenopsis Brother Little Hatter

Phalaenopsis Brother Oconee 'Maria Teresa'
Origin: *Phalaenopsis* Carmela's Pixie × *Phalaenopsis* Brother Purple
Originator: Brother Orchid Nursery
Registered by Brother Orchid Nursery

1999

Doritaenopsis Chian-Huey Red Rose
Origin: *Doritaenopsis* Taisuco Firebird × *Phalaenopsis* Cinderella
Originator: J. S. Wu
Registered by J. S. Wu

Doritaenopsis Montclair Valentine 'Picotee'
Origin: *Phalaenopsis* Taisuco Lien-hung × *Doritaenopsis* Happy Valentine
Originator: Norman's Orchids
Registered by Norman's Orchids

Doritaenopsis Scarlet in Snow
Origin: *Doritaenopsis* Tinny Sweetgirl × *Doritaenopsis* Mount Lip
Originator: Ming-Rong Tsay
Registered by Ming-Rong Tsay

Doritaenopsis Sinica Sunday 'KHM364'
Origin: *Phalaenopsis* Tinny Roseheart × *Doritaenopsis* Taisuco Firebird
Originator: I-Hsin Orchids
Registered by Shen Nung Agr.

Phalaenopsis Brecko Dawnphil
Origin: *Phalaenopsis philippinensis* × *Phalaenopsis* Dawn Treader
Originator: Breckenridge
Registered by Breckenridge

Phalaenopsis Brother Oconee 'Maria Teresa'

Doritaenopsis Chian-Huey Red Rose

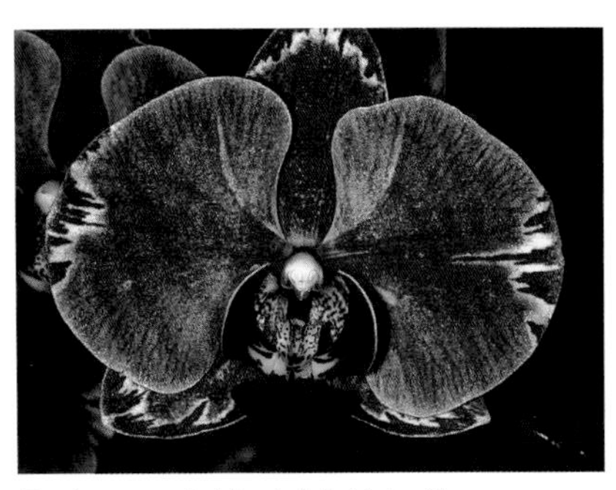

Doritaenopsis Montclair Valentine 'Picotee'

Doritaenopsis Scarlet in Snow

Doritaenopsis Sinica Sunday 'KHM364'. Photo by Marshall Ku.

Phalaenopsis Brecko Dawnphil

2000

Doritaenopsis Brother Success
Origin: *Doritaenopsis* Rose Valentine × *Phalaenopsis* Strawberry Sugar
Originator: Brother Orchid Nursery
Registered by Brother Orchid Nursery

Doritaenopsis Hsinying Mount 'Ching Ruey'
Origin: *Doritaenopsis* Mount Lip × *Doritaenopsis* Tinny Ace
Originator: Ching Hua
Registered by Ching Hua

Phalaenopsis Brother John
Origin: *Phalaenopsis* Brother Delight × *Phalaenopsis* Brother Brungor
Originator: Brother Orchid Nursery
Registered by D. Diehm

2001

Phalaenopsis Taida Lovely 'M'
Origin: *Phalaenopsis* Love × *Phalaenopsis* Bonbori
Originator: Pen-Chih Lai
Registered by Taida

2002

Doritaenopsis Happy King
Origin: *Doritaenopsis* Happy Smile × *Doritaenopsis* King Shiang's Rose
Originator: Unknown
Registered by H. P. Norton

Doritaenopsis Yu Pin Lover
Origin: *Doritaenopsis* Minho Princess × *Doritaenopsis* Minho Kingbeauty
Originator: N. I. Chang
Registered by N. I. Chang

Doritaenopsis Brother Success

Phalaenopsis Brother John

Phalaenopsis Taida Lovely 'M'. Photo by Marshall Ku.

Doritaenopsis Happy King. Photo by Allen Black.

Doritaenopsis Yu Pin Lover

2003

Doritaenopsis Ruey Lih Beauty 'Formosa'
Origin: *Phalaenopsis* Hsinying Lady × *Doritaenopsis* Formosa Rose
Originator: Cheng-S. Chen
Registered by Ching Ann

2005

Doritaenopsis Brother Sheridan
Origin: *Doritaenopsis* Brother Isable × *Doritaenopsis* Brother Comet
Originator: Brother Orchid Nursery
Registered by Wickford Orchids

Doritaenopsis Happy Ending
Origin: *Doritaenopsis* Minho Princess × *Doritaenopsis* Happy King
Originator: Allen Black
Registered by Allen Black

2006

Phalaenopsis Frog Hollow Fantasia 'Montclair'
Origin: *Phalaenopsis* Ho's French Fantasia × *Phalaenopsis* Salu Peoker
Originator: Frog Hollow Orchids
Registered by Frog Hollow Orchids

Unregistered

Phalaenopsis Raymond Burr 'Tahiti Sunset'
Origin: *Phalaenopsis* Salu Spot 'Sunkist' × *Phalaenopsis* Ho's French Fantasia 'Fangtastic'
Originator: Unknown
Registered by Norman's Orchids

Doritaenopsis Ruey Lih Beauty 'Formosa'

Doritaenopsis Happy Ending. Photo by Allen Black.

Phalaenopsis Raymond Burr 'Tahiti Sunset'

Doritaenopsis Brother Sheridan

Phalaenopsis Frog Hollow Fantasia 'Montclair'

1
2
3
4
5

Chapter 4

Standard Yellows and Oranges

In 2002, Doug Conkin wrote an interesting and informative article for *Orchid Digest* entitled "Pilgrimage to the Holy Grail: The Development of Modern Yellow *Phalaenopsis* Hybrids in America." He provides a short history of the development of yellow *Phalaenopsis* hybrids in the United States, including a synopsis of the important hybrids and species that have contributed to breeding yellows. Some of the information presented here is drawn, with his permission, from this article.

At the outset of the search for high-quality yellow phalaenopsis, the path was fraught with seemingly insurmountable obstacles. Originally, the goal was to produce hybrids in the "standard" form—that is, plants with large flowers of round, full shape, and a high flower count of eight to twelve flowers per inflorescence borne on a gracefully arching stem. Ideally, the plants would be easy to grow, quick to flower from seed, and free of any deformities. In addition, the plants would produce seed easily and plentifully, and the seed would be highly viable.

From the viewpoint of the first hybridizers, the goals certainly looked easy to achieve. After all, the breeding qualities of classic white-flowered phalaenopsis were well understood, and high-quality pinks and semi-alba forms were well along in their development. The leap to yellows seemed to be a foregone conclusion: simply cross a high-quality, proven white such as *Phalaenopsis* Doris with a yellow species, and, voilà, instant yellows! Unfortunately, it was not so simple.

Opposite: Yellow and orange phalaenopsis: 1. yellow-spotted hybrid; 2. yellow-green hybrid; 3. yellow hybrid with red lip; 4. *Doritaenopsis* Kelsie Takasaki (*D.* Autumn Leaves × *Phalaenopsis* Bonnie Vasquez), an orange hybrid; 5. red-orange hybrid. Paintings by Liena Dieck.

The Quest for the Perfect Yellow Hybrid

The quest begins with *P.* Golden Chief 'Candace Mary' AM/AOS (*P.* Chieftain × *P. manii*) and *P.* Gold Coast 'Vaughn's' AM/AOS (*P.* Hymen × *P.* Doris), registered by the Vaughns in 1958 and 1959, respectively. Although plants from both grexes were awarded by the American Orchid Society (AOS), with sixteen awards to *P.* Golden Chief and two to *P.* Gold Coast, both were something of a disappointment. Both hybrids yielded the requisite cream to yellow flowers, but the colors produced were pale and faded within a week. With *P. mannii* in the mix to impart the yellow coloration, this trait might be expected, since the flower colors of this species fade rapidly. *Phalaenopsis mannii* produces many flowers per inflorescence, so the hybrids' flower count was quite high; plants of these early hybrids often made excellent display plants with up to 100 open flowers. The form, though, was atrocious. The fine form of the white-flowered parents was lost to the starry and leggy form of the yellow/brown-flowered species. These two early hybrids proved that the quest for yellow was to be neither quick nor easy. They were, however, a step in the right direction.

Phalaenopsis Gold Coast apparently was not a successful parent, as its use resulted in only one further cross, *P.* Sandalwood (*P.* Gold Coast × *P. sanderiana*), registered by the Vaughns in 1965. *Phalaenopsis* Sandalwood has no registered progeny and was a dead end. *Phalaenopsis* Golden Chief fared somewhat better, producing ten hybrids in the first generation and two second-generation offspring. However, none of these progeny was used in further breeding.

These first hybrids gave rise to a new set of problems and few hints at a solution. A significant shortcoming was, and still may be, the tendency for the yellow color to fade. A partial solution was found by looking back into the history of white phalaenopsis breeding. Many of the white-flowered species show a pink flush on the back of the flowers. Although it is a natural occurrence and often quite pleasing, it was not a desirable trait for those looking for pure white flowers. Early hybridizers sought a solution by breeding first for color, and then for form. Only those plants that produced clear white flowers from each cross were retained and used to breed further. By continuing along this line, pure white blooms were achieved. Once the desired color was in place, form could be improved relatively easily.

Following this historical example, breeders began to establish and build on the gene pool for colorfast yellows. Three *Phalaenopsis* species rose to the forefront as parents of yellow breeding: *P. fasciata* (often identified in those early days as *P. lueddemanniana* var. *ochracea*), *P. amboinensis*, and, much later, *P. venosa*. The 1960s produced a number of landmark yellow *Phalaenopsis* hybrids. While each had its own faults, each also contributed strongly to the overall development of the class.

In addition to developing the color gene pool, work was begun on the defects of form. Several breeders noticed that form was significantly improved when diploid parents, hybrid or species, were used instead of tetraploids. Current hybridizers have a much greater understanding of the actual workings of genetics, so this may seem a simple deduction. However, in the early 1960s, the science of genetics was still in its relative infancy. James Watson and Francis Crick had first described the structure of DNA in 1953, and the influence of their work had just begun to be realized. Hybridizers of the 1960s were still working primarily with the Mendelian laws of inheritance. Further, the full force of the effects of ploidy was not completely understood. Many of these hybridizers, however, had an enormous understanding of the breeding characteristics of the plants with which they were working. They knew which plants functioned best as pod parents and which should provide the pollen, which traits a given plant would transmit to its progeny, and which traits it would suppress. Experience is the best teacher, and these pioneers had it in abundance. They set several essential stepping stones on the path to yellow *Phalaenopsis* hybrids.

Three of the most important developments in the 1960s were *P.* Inspiration, *P.* Mambo, and *P.* Golden Sands. Each provided solutions to earlier problems; when taken together, they formed the key that unlocked the door to some of the mysteries of yellow phalaenopsis. Inspiration was the first of the three to be registered, in 1961. Registered as a cross between *P.* Juanita and *P. lueddemanniana*, the species parent was definitely *P. fasciata*. This hybrid was a repeat and far more successful attempt at breeding a standard white by a yellow-flowered species. *Phalaenopsis* Inspiration received a total of 15 AOS awards, the most recent being an AM of 80 points in 1987, some 26 years after its initial registration. It has a total of 75 registered progeny through five generations, many of which have become famous in their own right.

Phalaenopsis Mambo, registered in 1965, was one of the first offspring of a yellow form of *P. amboinensis*, introduced in the early 1960s. With its slightly larger flower size and much flatter, rounder proportions, *P. amboinensis* was a godsend. *Phalaenopsis* Mambo (*P. amboinensis* × *P. mannii*) proved to play an important role in fixing the color of the flowers. Breeders noticed almost immediately that the flower of *P. amboinensis* did not fade over time. This trait was inherited by its offspring and to greater and lesser degrees throughout subsequent generations of hybrids. The overall form of *P.* Mambo was greatly improved, being much flatter and fuller in all flower segments, and the influence of *P. mannii* appeared in the higher flower count. *Phalaenopsis* Mambo has garnered 11 awards, the most recent of which was in 1999, an HCC of 78 points. Not bad for a hybrid that is more than 40 years old! It has produced 134 registered progeny through three generations, including the Apollo series, *P.* Golden Emperor, and *P.* Mambo Maid. It is still being actively used as a parent today.

Phalaenopsis Golden Sands (*P.* Fenton Davis Avant × *P. lueddemanniana*) was registered by the great Roy Fields in 1964 and produced a sensation. Beyond a doubt, Fields used *P. fasciata* as the species parent in this grex, yet that parent continues to be listed as *P. lueddemanniana* var. *ochracea*. Even in light of the current trend to follow the "splitter" taxonomic mindset, the entrenched notion that the original species and genus registrations are inviolate continues to cause much confusion for hobbyist and hybridizer alike. In any event, nothing can take away from this hybrid's enormous influence over the years. With fifteen awards—eight AMs, five HCCs, one FCC, and one CCM—this hybrid stands head and shoulders above its contemporaries.

The use of *P. fasciata* was a milestone as well, though it does have some shortcomings: it bears fewer flowers per inflorescence, petals and sepals often have wavy margins, the form is frequently very open, and in some clones the flower segments are nearly tubular. However, at this stage hybridizers were trying to establish a strong color gene pool with the intention of fixing the form problems at a later date. On the plus side, *P. fasciata* contributes non-fading qualities to its progeny. The clone *P. fasciata* 'Canary' FCC/AOS had extremely flat, full-formed flowers with amazingly rich color. It refused to breed for many years, leading Fields and many others to believe that it was sterile. Eventually, some breeding was accomplished with the clone, but by this time other clones of the grex had proven to be very satisfactory parents and the breeders came another step nearer to their goal.

To date, *P.* Golden Sands has produced more than 1700 progeny through seven generations. Its important progeny are a veritable who's who of high-quality yellows. The orchid world would owe Fields an incredible debt if this were the only hybrid to be born from his incredibly fecund mind. But this is only one among many he created.

The decade of the 1970s saw some remarkable steps in the journey toward quality yellow phalaenopsis. *Phalaenopsis amboinensis* shook the orchid world much in the same way an 8.0 magnitude quake might shake the state of California. With 10 generations and more than 6000 progeny to date, *P. amboinensis* has shaped the world of phalaenopsis breeding to an extraordinary degree. California breeder Irene Dobkin began working with *P. amboinensis* in the early 1970s and produced several important crosses, including *P.* Gold Coin, *P.* Gold Medal, and *P.* Golden Pride. Perhaps the most significant breakthrough came in 1976 with *P.* Golden Amboin, registered by Jones and Scully. In the hands of American hybridizers, this happy marriage of *P.* Golden Sands × *P. amboinensis* has produced some of the most influential progeny in the history of phalaenopsis breeding. *Doritaenopsis* Autumn Sun, *P.* Ambo Harvest, *P.* Goldberry, and *P.* Prospector's Dream were all bred in California from *P.* Golden Amboin and have revealed an incredibly rich vein of phalaenopsis ore that has been mined extensively by orchid hybridizers around the world.

Although not a *P.* Golden Amboin hybrid, *P.* Golden Buddha (*P.* Cher Ann × *P.* Spica) cannot be ignored. Registered by Pete Lista in 1977, this hybrid continues the sometimes successful strategy of using line-bred whites with primary hybrids. Self-pollination and sibling crosses of selected *P.* Golden Buddha clones have resulted in extremely consistent progeny without many of the negative traits of *P.* Spica, while further integrating the positive qualities that *P.* Golden Buddha transmits to its progeny. These clones have increased fullness in the floral segments, strengthened colors, and improved flower count, resulting in some wonderful lines of breeding.

Progress can be made slowly, step by step, or it can come in great intuitive leaps, springing up from the source like a torrent. Phalaenopsis breeding during the early 1980s was a time of great leaps. Two hybrids and one species forever changed the landscape of yellow phalaenopsis breeding and, oddly enough, led to a slowdown in the American efforts to produce the plants.

Originally made by W. van Deventer in 1927, *P.*

Deventeriana (*P. amabilis* × *P. amboinensis*) came to the spotlight in the early 1980s. Using diploid forms of the two species, Frederick Thornton remade the hybrid in the late 1970s or early 1980s, with spectacular results. The three awarded clones, 'Goldie' HCC/AOS, 'Treva' HCC/AOS, and 'Sky Island' HCC/AOS, have contributed enormously to the success of modern yellow hybrids. *Phalaenopsis* Deventeriana transmits good form, colorfastness, and heightened flower count to its progeny. The ability to pass on desirable traits while suppressing negative traits has made it the super parent of the genus. Although the grex itself has garnered only three awards, the number of awards granted to its 619 registered progeny in four generations of breeding is mind-boggling. *Phalaenopsis* Deventeriana's usefulness as a parent has not yet ended; almost every new RHS registration report contains new hybrids with this plant as one of the parents.

Phalaenopsis Orchid World (*P.* Malibu Imp × *P.* Deventeriana) may be the pinnacle of the hybridizer's art in the genus. Perhaps the single most awarded phalaenopsis in the history of the various judging systems, it has received a whopping 93 quality awards from the AOS alone. This happy combination of four lovely species, *P. amabilis*, *P. amboinensis*, *P. lueddemanniana*, and *P. violacea*, has produced a flower that has everything: brilliant, long-lasting color; outstanding substance; and superb form. Its fragrance is also one of the strongest and sweetest to be found in *Phalaenopsis* hybrids. Each species seems to have contributed only its finest genes to the pool. Its only drawback is lowered flower count, but the propensity for well-established adult plants to produce bloom after bloom on the same stem makes up for this minor flaw. Although *P.* Orchid World has only 19 registered progeny through 2001, we can expect that at least one of its future offspring will reach the heights of its progenitor.

Phalaenopsis Orchid World 'Bonnie Vasquez'

The final stop on our journey to yellows is the introduction of *P. venosa* into cultivation in 1982. This species produces flat, full flowers with wider petals and deeper coloration than *P. amboinensis*. The dark yellow is dominant in its hybrids and, unlike almost every other yellow *Phalaenopsis* species, the flowers of *P. venosa* actually darken with age. The substance of the flowers is extremely heavy. On the negative side, its flowers tend to bunch at the end of the stem and presentation is less than ideal. A white "halo" at the center of the flower is almost invariably inherited by the progeny and, depending on the extent of the halo, can be distracting to the overall color balance of the flowers. Fertility may also be low, and problems have been encountered in second-generation hybrids. However, many hybridizers believe that the use of a diploid *P. venosa* mated with a tetraploid parent may be the root of the problem, as most of the resulting offspring would be triploids, and thus sterile. Clearly, this is not consistently a problem since we are now working on the fifth generation of hybrids. *Phalaenopsis venosa* has produced 697 registered progeny in five generations since its introduction in 1982, and it has received 18 quality awards during the more than two decades in which it has been in cultivation. American hybridizers found the answers to many of their most difficult challenges in *P. venosa*.

Other important contributions to the development of yellow phalaenopsis by American breeders include *P.* Hausermann's Goldcup (*P.* Acker's Beauty × *P.* Just Me) by Orchids of Hausermann. Much breeding work done by H. P. Norton at Orchidview resulted in *P.* Golden Bells (*P.* Golden Sands × *P. venosa*), *P.* Wappaoola (*P.* Dos Pueblos × *P.* Golden Pride), *P.* Golden

Daybreak (*P.* Wappaoola × *P.* Hausermann's Goldcup), and *P.* King's Ransom (*P.* Wappaoola × *P.* Deventeriana). Some of the newer hybrids registered in the 1990s include *P.* Melodious Bells (*P.* Golden Bells × *P.* Golden Buddha), *P.* Orchidview Bellringer (*P.* Deventeriana × *P.* Golden Bells), and *P.* Orchidview Gold (*P.* Hausermann's Goldcup × *P. amboinensis*) by Norton; and *P.* Golden Circles (*P.* Misty Green × *P.* Golden Bells) by Carter and Holmes.

Despite successes of the 1970s and exciting new developments of the early 1980s, American hybridizers found that yellow hybrids were not always a commercially profitable and rewarding venture, and by the mid-1980s, most of the larger phalaenopsis nurseries in the United States had severely curtailed their breeding efforts. A casual perusal of catalogs from the major firms reveals an interesting phenomenon. During the 1970s, it was not unusual to see 10 or 20 new yellow crosses introduced or reoffered each year. However, beginning in the very late 1970s and through the mid-1980s, the number of crosses dropped precipitously, down to 5 to 10.

Problems with sterility and genetic imbalances have always plagued the breeding lines, resulting in extremely low germination rates and deformity of the flowers or the plants. While a hobbyist might be happy with 100 seedlings from a seed capsule, most commercial producers would consider this rate commercially sterile, since it would produce few seedlings for eventual sale. The plants themselves were slow to mature, costing more per pot to grow to adult size. This led to a great deal of frustration on the part of the purchaser of small seedlings. In general, most phalaenopsis are quick to mature and the hobbyist can expect to bring a seedling to first flower within 18 months, certainly within two years. However, many yellow hybrids take considerably longer to flower, and flower production may take up to four years to reach its full potential. The market itself always controls commercial production, and at that time the American market was more interested in classic white or pink phalaenopsis. Spotted and striped hybrids reached a new height of development in the United States during the same period, as the American market showed more interest in these hybrids than yellows.

Consequently, much of the hybridizing activity moved eastward to Asia, especially Taiwan. The Taiwanese market has always appreciated vibrant color contrasts, and the dramatic yellow and red markings of the hybrids ensured they were tailor-made for that market. Asian cultures also place a high value on the symbolic meanings of colors. White phalaenopsis were a difficult sale in much of Asia because white flowers symbolize mourning and death. Yellow, on the other hand, symbolizes wealth, and red represents happiness and well being. Consequently, yellow flowers with red markings were certain to be in high demand in Asia. Although sterility was still a factor, with the advent of better techniques of meristematic propagation for monopodial genera, this was no longer a bottleneck. The ability to meristem a particularly good plant ad infinitum made the mass marketing of recalcitrant hybrids possible, though there is still room for improvement.

The yellow "stars and bars" type of breeding as typified by *P.* Orchid World and the various Taiwanese lines has been firmly established, yet a true "standard" yellow phalaenopsis has not been produced consistently. The search for the yellow equivalent of *P.* Doris is still underway.

Many of the yellow hybrids being produced in Taiwan may be considered novelties, since they have smaller and less flowers than the standard large whites; however, these hybrids are showing progress toward the targeted flower size and number. The yellow pigmentation in the flower is also getting stronger and more colorfast. Some of the newer clones and hybrids are finally starting to reach their glory. Outstanding parents such as *Doritaenopsis* Sogo Manager, *P.* Brother Lawrence, *P.* Brother Oxford, *P.* Brother Passat, *P.* Brother Stage, *P.* Golden Gift, *P.* Goldiana, *P.* I-Hsin Sunflower, *P.* Liu Tuen-shen, *P.* Misty Green, *P.* Sogo Lisa, *P.* Taida Lawrence, and *P.* Taipei Gold are beginning to produce some brilliant and impressive yellow hybrids.

Doritaenopsis Sogo Manager 'Nina'

Phalaenopsis Brother Passat

Phalaenopsis Brother Lawrence 'Montclair'

Phalaenopsis I-Hsin Sunflower 'KHM-95-1'

Hot Orange Hybrids

Eric Goo of Phoenix Orchids contributes his viewpoint on the development orange *Phalaenopsis* hybrids in this section.

Recent years have seen tremendous advancement in breeding consistent orange phalaenopsis. Until recently, "art shades" of orange phalaenopsis merely hinted at the color and were generally created by combining a large pink with a yellow. Breeders today, however, are creating some vibrant oranges. Though no one has yet cracked the code to breeding consistent bright oranges, much progress toward that goal has been made.

Despite the improvements in breeding, clear orange flowers are still a rarity. As a breeder, I am trying to understand how to breed good oranges and can merely observe and hypothesize. My simple hypothesis at this point is that orange can be obtained by breeding a yellow with either a red or purple to create flower colors from burnt orange to orange-red.

Breeders must overcome a few potential obstacles to get a hybrid with a good orange color. First, the yellow pigment needs to be passed to the progeny in a manner that does not fade. If the yellow fades noticeably, hybrids display weakly colored flowers in the rusty-pink and rusty-lavender range. Also, noticeable fading will likely be the kiss of death if a breeder has hopes of obtaining any awards from the AOS. Second, the red or purple pigment needs to be spread more or less evenly across the flower. If this fails to happen, a yellow flower results with red to purple spots or blotches, but this is not orange. Third, the blending of the yellow and red or purple must be pleasing. Sometimes the blending takes place but produces muddy colors. If brown is your favorite color, you might like this effect, but most breeders are looking for bright, clear, pleasing colors. Finally, the goal is good form as well as decent size, floriferousness, and presentation.

So, while my hypothesis of how to produce oranges is simple enough, actually producing a good orange is no easy task. Russ Vernon, phalaenopsis breeder and owner of New Visions Orchids, says that red colors are produced by crossing a yellow parent with a bright magenta-purple. Oranges are a bit more tricky because the yellow intensity must be reduced just enough to favor the magenta. Russ has produced various orange crosses as well as shades of tan, brown, cinnamon, and red.

Several orchids that are available today will hopefully provide some insights in breeding the oranges of tomorrow.

Phalaenopsis Mary Lilian Taylor

My first success with breeding an orange hybrid was *P.* Mary Lilian Taylor 'Desert Orange' AM/AOS (*P. venosa* 'Frank Smith' HCC/AOS × *P.* Red Devil 'Mona' AM/AOS). I bloomed only about a dozen plants from this cross, and 'Desert Orange' was by far the best. The *P. venosa* parent contributed non-fading yellow and the *P.* Red Devil parent contributed a purple-red color. Through other crosses I had made with *P.* Red Devil 'Mona', I noticed that it could spread its red color evenly, at least to a portion of its progeny.

Phalaenopsis Mary Lilian Taylor 'Desert Orange' AM/AOS. Photo by Eric Goo.

The flowers of *P.* Mary Lilian Taylor 'Desert Orange' open red and fade to orange. The orange does not fade and the flowers last a very long time, so after all the flowers have opened and faded, they are all the same orange color. The fading is more rapid and more pronounced in warm weather. When it was presented for judging in June 1998, with 20 orange flowers on two branched inflorescences, it received an AM/AOS.

After this orchid matures, it is virtually always in bloom or in spike. It tends to send up a spike each time it grows a new leaf, and because the flowers last so long, its mildly fragrant flowers appear throughout the year. This orchid is fertile as a pod parent and appears to pass its color, lasting flowers, and tendency to bloom throughout the year to its progeny.

Phalaenopsis Bev Tall

The first cross I made with *P.* Mary Lilian Taylor 'Desert Orange' was with one of my favorite breeders, *P.* Zuma Garnet 'Plantation' HCC/AOS. This was kind of

Phalaenopsis Bev Tall 'Carnelian Queen' AM/AOS. Photo by Eric Goo.

Phalaenopsis Phoenix Flame 'Orange Glow' AM/AOS. Photo by Eric Goo.

a test cross to see what 'Desert Orange' might do as a parent. From previous experience, I knew that *P.* Zuma Garnet 'Plantation' was capable of passing its good red color to its progeny. My thought was that perhaps I could get non-fading solid reds from this cross.

While I bloomed only about a dozen plants from the cross, two have received AMs from the AOS. I named the cross after my good friend. The color of the flowers of *P.* Bev Tall 'Desert Rose' were described by the judges as "smooth rich reddish brown." The flowers of *P.* Bev Tall 'Carnelian Queen' AM/AOS are slightly more orange than those of its sibling. (By the way, 'Carnelian Queen' is named after a type of brown-red agate, not as has been speculated, after *Star Wars* Princess Leia's evil nemesis from Carnelia.) I recognize that neither of these *P.* Bev Tall cultivars are orange, but their color lies somewhere near the midpoint of the orange to red spectrum. In addition, they provide some indication of the breeding qualities of *P.* Mary Lilian Taylor 'Desert Orange'.

Phalaenopsis Phoenix Flame

Phalaenopsis Phoenix Flame 'Orange Glow' AM/AOS was produced by crossing *P.* Summer Joy 'Majestic' AM/AOS with *P.* Hausermann's Goldcup 'Everlasting Lenette #1'. *Phalaenopsis* Summer Joy is a *P.* George Vasquez hybrid and has both a pattern of purple concentric bars and a lighter magenta suffusion over the face of the flower. *Phalaenopsis violacea* seems to contribute its magenta color spread evenly across the flowers of its progeny. Since *P.* George Vasquez has quite a bit of *P. violacea* in its background, I speculated that *P.* Summer Joy might be able to share its purple color spread more or less evenly across the flowers of its progeny. The other parent, *P.* Hausermann's Goldcup 'Everlasting Lenette #1' is a variant of the 'Everlasting' cultivar that occurred in mericloning and has proven to be a very good breeder of yellows.

We bloomed only about 15 plants from this cross, and overall the plants were very nice, but the flowers tended to fade. They were great plants and sold quickly, but only 'Orange Glow' AM/CCE/AOS had minimal fading. As indicated by the CCE, and because this plant tends to form keikis at its base, it can be grown to an impressive specimen with many flowers. At the time of award it displayed 36 flowers and nine buds on seven branched inflorescences. The judges described the flower color as "light mustard yellow with magenta spots coalesced to concentric circles apically, giving an orange cast overall." Unfortunately, we have not yet been able to get this plant to breed.

Doritaenopsis Sau Goo 'Orange Beauty' HCC/AOS. Photo by Eric Goo.

Phalaenopsis Sherri Pantano 'Tangelo'. Photo by Eric Goo.

Doritaenopsis Sau Goo

Doritaenopsis Sau Goo 'Orange Beauty' HCC/AOS was our most recent awarded orange. The parents of this plant are *D.* Red Elf 'Lenette #4' HCC/AOS and *P.* Hausermann's Goldcup 'Everlasting Lenette #1'. *Doritaenopsis* Red Elf 'Lenette #4' HCC/AOS is purple-red and has created quite a line of red multifloras. My experience with *P. pulcherrima* (formerly *Doritis pulcherrima*) suggests that it has a strong tendency to spread its purple color evenly across the flowers of its progeny. Since *D.* Red Elf is a primary *P. pulcherrima* hybrid, I was hoping that it would also contribute its color evenly spread across the flowers of its progeny.

I bloomed only about a dozen plants from this cross. The only orange, *P.* 'Orange Beauty' HCC/AOS, has quite a few soft orange flowers that do not fade. When it was awarded it carried 22 flowers and 17 buds on three spikes, two of which were branched. The judges described the color as "soft coral orange" and gave it 79 points. Unfortunately, we have not yet been able to get this plant to breed, but it puts out a spectacular display.

Phalaenopsis Sherri Pantano

This hybrid was made by crossing *P.* Spirit House 'Redwine' AM/AOS with *P.* Venimp 'Sedona #11' CCE/AOS. *Phalaenopsis* Spirit House 'Redwine' has fantastic red color and, unlike most reds, the color is the same on the back of the flowers as the front. It was speculation on my part that this parent would contribute its red color spread evenly on the flowers of its progeny. I was also interested in using *P.* Spirit House because of the yellow species in its background (namely *P. fasciata* and *P. mariae*). *Phalaenopsis* Venimp also has both red and yellow flowers in its parentage.

While I do bloom more than a dozen plants from a few crosses, I bloomed only about a dozen from this cross. The flowers ranged from dark red to orange, with cultivar 'Tangelo' showing the most orange. Interestingly enough, it opens red and then fades to an orange that does not fade. Even though flowers open red on their fronts, their backs are more orange. As we have not tried to breed with this cultivar, I cannot comment on its fertility.

Doritaenopsis Firepower

Doritaenopsis Firepower was made by crossing *P.* Spirit House 'Redwine' AM/AOS with *D.* Inferno 'Champ'. The *P.* Spirit House parent was mentioned previously, so I will not address it again here. *Doritaenopsis* Inferno 'Champ' is from the *D.* Red Elf breeding line. In fact, *D.* Inferno 'Champ' has been the most successful breeder in the line of breeding from *D.* Red Elf. It tends to be dominant in breeding, passing an even red color, floriferousness, and small flowers to its progeny. Both par-

Doritaenopsis Firepower 'Cinnamon Glow'. Photo by Eric Goo.

Doritaenopsis Flash Point 'Orange Glow'. Photo by Eric Goo.

ents in this case are red, but they have yellows in their backgrounds.

We have bloomed about a dozen plants from the cross, and most have been red. 'Cinnamon Glow' is the most orange, with a non-fading cinnamon-orange highlighted by a bright magenta lip. It is floriferous and all the flowers tend to face the same direction. We have not yet tried to breed with this plant.

Doritaenopsis Flash Point

Doritaenopsis Flash Point (*P.* Franz Liszt 'Dotty' HCC/AOS × *D.* Inferno 'Champ') is similar to *D.* Firepower. *Phalaenopsis* Franz Liszt is the product of *P.* Malibu Imp × *P.* Spirit House. The *P.* Malibu Imp parent has contributed both red and yellow from its background. Of our dozen or so blooming plants, their colors range from red to brown-orange. As with *D.* Firepower, they are floriferous and non-fading with lips that tend to accent the color of the petals and sepals. Our favorite from this cross is the cultivar 'Orange Glow', which has red-orange flowers. In fact, the color of its flowers lies close to the midpoint between orange and red. We have not attempted to breed with this plant.

The future of orange breeding

Producing high-quality oranges today is as much art as science (and also requires a bit of luck). The same situation existed with the development of reds in the 1980s. In fact, "reds" at that time were more purple or magenta than red. It took some latitude then to discuss red breeding because true reds did not exist. Perhaps it is the same today with oranges. In any case, with the increasing variety of *Phalaenopsis* hybrids available, the hybridizer has more genetic material at his or her disposal than ever before. In the years ahead, as better oranges develop, we shall see 3 in. (7.5 cm), full-formed, floriferous oranges.

In addition to the work at Phoenix Orchids, Taiwanese breeders continue to introduce more rich orange phalaenopsis. One standout from Brother Orchids is *P.* Brother Sara Gold (*P.* Sara Lee × *P.* Taipei Gold).

Many yellows also display orange casts, and some yellows have red stripes that provide an "orange look." One example is the extremely popular hybrid, *P.* Baldan's Kaleidoscope (*P.* Hausermann's Candy × *P.* Daryl Lockhart), bred and registered by Baldan Orchids in 1990. Another classic with a similar look that shows the importance of *P. venosa* for adding deep yellow to novelty hybrids is *P.* Bonnie Vasquez (*P.* Memoria Natalie Wood × *P. venosa*), developed and introduced by Zuma Canyon Orchids in 1985. A newer hybrid, *P.* Dragon's Dazzler (*P.* Taipei Gold × *P. venosa*) was bred and introduced by Dragon Fire Orchids in 1991.

Phalaenopsis Brother Sara Gold 'Peach'

Phalaenopsis Bonnie Vasquez 'Zuma Creek' FCC/AOS.
Photo by Allen Black.

Phalaenopsis Baldan's Kaleidoscope

Gallery of Yellow and Orange Hybrids

Hybrids are listed by the year in which they were registered to demonstrate changes and evolution over time.

1969

Phalaenopsis Spotted Moon 'Jo Ann' HCC/AOS
Origin: *Phalaenopsis* Gertrude Beard × *Phalaenopsis lueddemanniana*
Originator: Charles Beard
Registered by Charles Beard

1988

Phalaenopsis Brother Girl
Origin: *Phalaenopsis* Brother Canary × *Phalaenopsis* Cindy Danseuse
Originator: Brother Orchid Nursery
Registered by Brother Orchid Nursery

1994

Phalaenopsis Chromium Emperor 'Rising Sun' AM/AOS
Origin: *Phalaenopsis* Chromium Flame × *Phalaenopsis* Motorhead
Originator: A. Klehm
Registered by A. Klehm

1995

Phalaenopsis Brother Lawrence 'Montclair'
Origin: *Phalaenopsis* Taipei Gold × *Phalaenopsis* Deventeriana
Originator: Brother Orchid Nursery
Registered by Brother Orchid Nursery

Phalaenopsis Brother Passat
Origin: *Phalaenopsis* Taipei Gold × *Phalaenopsis* Brother Knight
Originator: Brother Orchid Nursery
Registered by Brother Orchid Nursery

Phalaenopsis Katie Morris 'Burnished Copper' HCC/AOS
Origin: *Phalaenopsis* Donald Rigg × *Phalaenopsis* Harford's Jewel
Originator: H. P. Norton
Registered by H. P. Norton

Phalaenopsis Spotted Moon 'Jo Ann' HCC/AOS

Phalaenopsis Chromium Emperor 'Rising Sun' AM/AOS

Phalaenopsis Brother Passat

Phalaenopsis Brother Girl

Phalaenopsis Brother Lawrence 'Montclair'

Phalaenopsis Katie Morris 'Burnished Copper' HCC/AOS. Photo by Allen Black.

1997

Doritaenopsis Sogo Manager 'Neo' HCC/AOS
Origin: *Phalaenopsis* Brother Lawrence × *Doritaenopsis* Autumn Sun
Originator: Sogo Team Co.
Registered by Sogo Team Co.

Doritaenopsis Sogo Manager 'Nina'
Origin: *Phalaenopsis* Brother Lawrence × *Doritaenopsis* Autumn Sun
Originator: Sogo Team Co.
Registered by Sogo Team Co.

Phalaenopsis Brother Sara Gold 'Sogo F-623'
Origin: *Phalaenopsis* Sara Lee × *Phalaenopsis* Taipei Gold
Originator: Brother Orchid Nursery
Registered by Brother Orchid Nursery

1998

Phalaenopsis Lawless Red Peppers
Origin: *Phalaenopsis* Carmela's Brite Lights × *Phalaenopsis* Brother Pirate King
Originator: Carmela
Registered by Brother Orchid Nursery

Phalaenopsis Phoenix Flame 'Orange Glow' AM/AOS
Origin: *Phalaenopsis* Summer Joy × *Phalaenopsis* Hausermann's Goldcup
Originator: Eric Goo
Registered by Phoenix Orchids, Eric Goo

1999

Phalaenopsis Black Ball
Origin: *Phalaenopsis* Ever-Spring King × *Phalaenopsis* Salu Princess
Originator: Sogo Team Co.
Registered by Sogo Team Co.

Doritaenopsis Sogo Manager 'Neo' HCC/AOS. Photo by Eric Goo.

Phalaenopsis Brother Sara Gold 'Sogo F-623'. Photo by Eric Goo.

Phalaenopsis Phoenix Flame 'Orange Glow' AM/AOS. Photo by Eric Goo.

Doritaenopsis Sogo Manager 'Nina'

Phalaenopsis Lawless Red Peppers

Phalaenopsis Black Ball

Phalaenopsis Perfection Is 'Chen' FCC/AOS
Origin: *Phalaenopsis* Golden Peoker × *Phalaenopsis* Black Eagle
Originator: Unknown
Registered by Howard Ginsberg

Phalaenopsis Shenandoah Fire 'Ember'
Origin: *Phalaenopsis* Golden Music × *Phalaenopsis* Penang Girl
Originator: Brennan's
Registered by Brennan's

Phalaenopsis Sogo David 'Peachy'
Origin: *Phalaenopsis* Brother Sara Gold × *Phalaenopsis* Fireberry
Originator: Sogo Team Co.
Registered by Sogo Team Co.

2000

Phalaenopsis Brother Dendi 'Mary' HCC/AOS
Origin: *Phalaenopsis* Brother Lawrence × *Phalaenopsis* Sara Lee
Originator: Diehm
Registered by Brother Orchid Nursery

Phalaenopsis Sogo Lion 'Amber'
Origin: *Phalaenopsis* Brother Lawrence × *Phalaenopsis* Sogo Lisa
Originator: Sogo Team Co.
Registered by Sogo Team Co.

2001

Phalaenopsis I-Hsin Sunflower 'KHM-95-1'
Origin: *Phalaenopsis* Taipei Gold × *Phalaenopsis* Brother Nugget
Originator: W. T. Chien
Registered by W. T. Chien

Phalaenopsis Perfection Is 'Chen' FCC/AOS

Phalaenopsis Shenandoah Fire 'Ember'

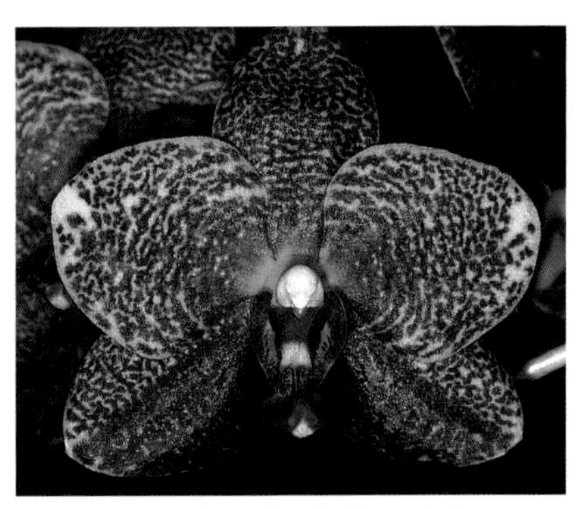

Phalaenopsis Sogo David 'Peachy'

Phalaenopsis Brother Dendi 'Mary' HCC/AOS. Photo by Eric Goo.

Phalaenopsis Sogo Lion 'Amber'

Phalaenopsis I-Hsin Sunflower 'KHM-95-1'

Phalaenopsis I-Hsin Sunflower 'M' AM/AOS
Origin: *Phalaenopsis* Taipei Gold × *Phalaenopsis* Brother Nugget
Originator: W. T. Chien
Registered by W. T. Chien

Phalaenopsis Taisuco Date 'F. L.'
Origin: *Phalaenopsis* Brother Lawrence × *Phalaenopsis* Taisuco Glory
Originator: Ming-I Chuang
Registered by Taisuco/Taiwan Sugar Company

Phalaenopsis Taisuco Rosemary
Origin: *Phalaenopsis* Taisuco Kaaladian × *Phalaenopsis* Taisuco Gold
Originator: Taisuco/Taiwan Sugar Company
Registered by Taisuco/Taiwan Sugar Company

2002

Doritaenopsis Taisuco Sunset
Origin: *Doritaenopsis* Taisuco Happy × *Phalaenopsis* Golden Amboin
Originator: Taisuco/Taiwan Sugar Company
Registered by Taisuco/Taiwan Sugar

Phalaenopsis Canyon Sun
Origin: *Phalaenopsis* Brother Lawrence × *Phalaenopsis* Leucadia Sun
Originator: A. D. Stock
Registered by A. D. Stock

2003

Doritaenopsis I-Hsin Balloon 'KHM1316'
Origin: *Phalaenopsis* Sogo Lisa × *Doritaenopsis* I-Hsin Gem
Originator: Chien
Registered by Chien

Phalaenopsis I-Hsin Sunflower 'M' AM/AOS. Photo by Eric Goo.

Phalaenopsis Taisuco Rosemary

Phalaenopsis Canyon Sun

Phalaenopsis Taisuco Date 'F. L.' Photo by Marshall Ku.

Doritaenopsis Taisuco Sunset

Doritaenopsis I-Hsin Balloon 'KHM 1316'. Photo by Marshall Ku.

Phalaenopsis I-Hsin Gold Dust 'Neo' AM/AOS
Origin: *Phalaenopsis* Salu Spot × *Phalaenopsis* Salu Peoker
Originator: W. T. Chien
Registered by W. T. Chen

Phalaenopsis Memoria Flora Ho 'Gold Emerald' HCC/AOS
Origin: *Phalaenopsis* Mok Choi Yew × *Phalaenopsis* Brother Golden Potential
Originator: Eric Goo
Registered by Eric Goo

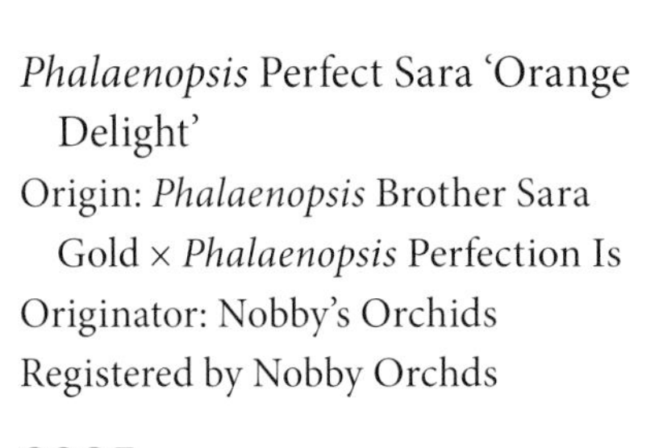

Phalaenopsis Perfect Sara 'Orange Delight'
Origin: *Phalaenopsis* Brother Sara Gold × *Phalaenopsis* Perfection Is
Originator: Nobby's Orchids
Registered by Nobby Orchds

2005

Doritaenopsis Taida Fortune 'Taida Golden Girl'
Origin: *Doritaenopsis* Guan Ames × *Phalaenopsis* Brother Fortune Green
Originator: Pen-Chih Lai
Registered by Taida

Phalaenopsis Hilo Gold 'Mary' HCC/AOS
Origin: *Phalaenopsis* Kenneth Wong × *Phalaenopsis* Brother Lawrence
Originator: Hawaiian Hybrids
Registered by Eric Goo

Phalaenopsis Memoria Phoebe Kwock 'Bold Beauty' HCC/AOS
Origin: *Phalaenopsis* Golden Imp × *Phalaenopsis* Rainbow's End
Originator: Eric Goo
Registered by Eric Goo

Phalaenopsis I-Hsin Gold Dust 'Neo' AM/AOS. Photo by Eric Goo.

Phalaenopsis Perfect Sara 'Orange Delight'

Phalaenopsis Hilo Gold 'Mary' HCC/AOS. Photo by Eric Goo.

Phalaenopsis Memoria Flora Ho 'Gold Emerald' HCC/AOS. Photo by Eric Goo.

Doritaenopsis Taida Fortune 'Taida Golden Girl'. Photo by Marshall Ku.

Phalaenopsis Memoria Phoebe Kwock 'Bold Beauty' HCC/AOS. Photo by Eric Goo.

Phalaenopsis Yellow Brite Lites 'Neo' HCC/AOS
Origin: *Phalaenopsis* Taida Lawrence × *Phalaenopsis* Carmela's Brite Lites
Originator: Carmela
Registered by Coqui (Carmela)

Unregistered

Phalaenopsis Raymond Burr 'Montclair'
Origin: *Phalaenopsis* Salu Spot × *Phalaenopsis* Ho's French Fantasia
Originator: Norman's Orchids

Phalaenopsis Yellow Brite Lights 'Neo' HCC/AOS. Photo by Eric Goo.

Phalaenopsis Raymond Burr 'Montclair'

1
2
3
4

Chapter 5

Reds and Purples

Obtaining a pure red phalaenopsis is the Holy Grail for some phalaenopsis breeders. This quest for red is complex and convoluted, and dissension among breeders concerns what constitutes a "good" red. Hybrids have reached a standard of strong and lasting color, good form, attractive flower presentation on the inflorescence, and excellent substance. In general, the flowers are not as large as the whites and pinks, and fewer flowers appear on the inflorescence, but they are rapidly being improved on both fronts. Although the biggest commercial market will probably always drive most breeders toward phalaenopsis with bigger and more flowers, some phalaenopsis hobbyists are content with the sometimes fragrant, smaller flowered, compact plants that are ideal for smaller growing spaces.

One of the challenges with red *Phalaenopsis* hybrids is defining what the color *red* actually means. In a 1985 article in the *American Orchid Society Bulletin* entitled "In Search of Red Phalaenopsis," breeder John G. Martin defined *red* as follows: "Let's say that red is any variation between reddish purple and carmine, with pigmentation distributed solidly or in stripes or spots." This is a broad definition that some would say still holds today, although most red phalaenopsis breeders now seem to have as their goal solid red flowers with less purple. Martin states that the primary pigment responsible for red coloration in phalaenopsis is a group of compounds called *anthocyanins*, and that the expression of these pigments are influenced by various genetic and environmental factors. The factors that encourage more production of red pigments include low pH (high acidity) and the combination of more light and lower temperature. He writes that some parent species tend to pass on stronger, more colorfast reds than others. Yellow coloration is another important contributor. A warm red flower requires the pigments of both purple-red and the strong, non-fading, non-spotted, bright yellows.

Opposite: Red and purple phalaenopsis: 1. true red hybrid; 2. *Phalaenopsis* Red Hot Imp (*P.* Red-Hot Chili × *P.* Malibu Imp), a red hybrid; 3. *Phalaenopsis* Sogo Cock 'Joy' (*P.* Sogo Peak × *P.* Sogo Kaiulani), a purple-red hybrid; 4. *Phalaenopsis* Chingruey's Fancy (*P.* Sogo John × *P.* Brother Fancy), a clear red hybrid. Paintings by Liena Dieck.

History and Development of Reds

Eric Goo, owner of Phoenix Orchids and a breeder and grower of phalaenopsis, specializes in producing red, yellow, and novelty hybrids. His creations have won an array of awards from the American Orchid Society. Much of this information was collected (with permission) from articles Eric wrote regarding his experiences to provide some perspective on the history and development of reds.

Recent years have shown notable advancement in red phalaenopsis breeding with some breakthroughs in producing reliable, larger, more floriferous reds. Precious few truly red phalaenopsis have been bred thus far; most "red" phalaenopsis have strong secondary pigmentations of purple or yellow. Consequently, when we refer to *red*, we are actually referring to a broad spectrum of colors ranging from purple to red-orange to garnet red.

Another important consideration in terms of breeding is *quality*. One measure of quality of a cross is based on the American Orchid Society awards that it receives. The AOS awards system, while not perfect, is an important system in judging an orchid's quality and is widely used today. Many breeders and collectors rely on the decisions of the AOS judges to obtain some objective evidence of quality. Certain phalaenopsis parents have contributed significantly to breeding quality reds, and several star contributors have produced important progeny as measured by the AOS judging system.

One of the basic genetic building blocks of red breeding is the species *Phalaenopsis bellina* (formerly *P. violacea*, Borneo type). Another closely related species, *P. violacea* (formerly *P. violacea*, Malayan type), has red flowers, while *P. bellina* is a light yellow-green flower with vibrant red-purple on the inner portions of the lateral sepals. It is intriguing that *P. bellina* has contributed more to red breeding than its red cousin from the Malayan peninsula.

Near the end of the nineteenth century, *P. violacea* (and *P. bellina*) and *P. lueddemanniana* were cross bred, and the resultant hybrid was registered as *P.* Luedde-violacea. This cross has been remade a number of times and has produced some good red clones with 19 AOS awards to its credit. *Phalaenopsis* Luedde-violacea has proven to be a fine parent of reds and has provided a firm foundation for many of the best red breeding lines.

Two hybrids of *P.* Luedde-violacea have left a legacy of awarded red progeny. When crossed with *P. amboinensis*, *P.* Luedde-violacea produced *P.* Malibu Imp. Backcrossing *P.* Luedde-violacea to *P. violacea* produced *P.* George Vasquez, which was registered by Arthur

Phalaenopsis bellina has been an important contributor to red flower breeding.

Phalaenopsis Luedde-violacea 'Anna Red' HCC/AOS. Photo by Peter Lin.

Phalaenopsis George Vasquez 'An Lin'. Photo by Peter Lin.

Freed Orchids in 1974. As of the end of 2006, *P.* George Vasquez has received nine AOS awards and has produced many fine red progeny.

One particularly fine cultivar that has been used successfully as a parent of reds, *P.* George Vasquez 'Eureka', received an Award of Merit in 1978 and was upgraded to a First Class Certificate (the coveted highest AOS award) in 1981 with 92 points. Of its many outstanding characteristics, its rich dark purple coloration is perhaps its most important attribute as far as red breeding is concerned.

Phalaenopsis Zuma Garnet 'Plantation' HCC/AOS. Photo by Eric Goo.

Phalaenopsis Tabasco Tex 'Garnet Glow' AM/AOS. Photo by Peter Lin.

The accompanying table demonstrates that *P.* George Vasquez has been a fine parent of reds such as *P.* Zuma Garnet 'Plantation' HCC/AOS and *P.* Tabasco Tex 'Garnet Glow' AM/AOS. What the table does not show is that some of the progeny of *P.* George Vasquez have also been used to produce fine reds. It is difficult to imagine where red phalaenopsis breeding would be today without this superior grex.

Another outstanding contributor to red phalaenopsis breeding is *P.* Malibu Imp (*P. amboinensis* × *P.* Luedde-violacea), registered in 1977 by Arthur Freed Orchids. To date, *P.* Malibu Imp has received 15 awards from the AOS, which attests to the quality of the cross. Some plants from the cross are yellow with varying degrees of red markings, while others are solid red. The good solid red selections have been the most useful in red breeding.

The table on the next page shows the successes obtained in breeding reds using *P.* Malibu Imp as a parent. What is not shown in the table is that most of the

Awarded red progeny of *P.* George Vasquez
(as of December 2006)

PARENTAGE AND PROGENY	HCC	AM
× Bonita Roja = Fire-Engine Red	2	
× Carnival Queen = Cardinal	1	2
× Cebu = Zuma Firebird		1
× Eye-Catcher = Kuangfeng's Queen		3
× Eye Dee = Frank Hughes	2	1
× Malibu Imp = Zuma Garnet	2	2
× Manitoba = Jackie Friedman	1	2
× Mayaimi = Estrella Rojo	1	1
× Princess Kaiulani = Tabasco Tex	3	2
× Samba = Summer Joy	3	2
× Stellar Beauty = Glenmore	6	8
× Summer Wine = Jo Vernon	2	1
× *venosa* = John Ewing	2	2
× *violacea* = Grosbeak		1
× Violet Charm = Radiant Ember	1	
× Zada = Malibu Mademoiselle	4	2

listed hybrids are relatively recent developments, with half of them being registered by John Martin since the 1990s. Two fine examples of the results of breeding with this parent are *P.* Venimp 'Sedona #11' and *P.* Wes Addison 'Ruby Glow' HCC/AOS.

Deserving of special mention is *P.* Zuma Garnet (*P.* Malibu Imp × *P.* George Vasquez). This thoughtful cross was registered in 1984 by Zuma Canyon and has proved to be a useful breeder of reds. Another important hybrid, *P.* Red Hot Imp, registered in 1992 by John Martin, is the most successful of the red Malibu Imp hybrids to date. In the parent, *P.* Red-Hot Chili, we again find *P.* George Vasquez at work. *Phalaenopsis* Red Hot Chili (*P.* Carnival × *P.* Tabasco Tex) was registered in 1982 by John Ewing Orchids. Not surprisingly, *P.* Tabasco Tex (*P.* Princess Kaiulani × *P.* George Vasquez) shows a familiar parent.

The point of singling out these hybrids is twofold: It continues to emphasize the value of *P.* George Vasquez

Phalaenopsis Malibu Imp 'Evergreen Hill' AM/AOS. Photo by Eric Goo.

Awarded red progeny of *P.* Malibu Imp
(as of December 2006)

PARENTAGE AND PROGENY	HCC	AM
× *Doritaenopsis* Jim = *D.* Ruby Imp	1	
× Fire-Engine Red = Red Galaxy		1
× Fire-Water = Liberty Hill	4	
× George Vasquez = Zuma Garnet	2	2
× Golden Pride = Imp's Pride	1	2
× Heart's Desire = Brecko Impheart	1	
× Imp's Pride = Gottabe Red	1	1
× Malibu Girl = Laura's Valentine		2
× Red-Hot Chili = Red Hot Imp	3	10
× Spirit House = Franz Liszt	2	1
× Summer Morn = Wes Addison	1	
× *venosa* = Venimp	3	4
× Zauberrot = Julia Wilson		1
× Zuma Garnet = Straits Garnet	1	

Phalaenopsis Venimp 'Sedona #11'. Photo by Eric Goo.

Phalaenopsis Wes Addison 'Ruby Glow HCC/AOS. Photo by Eric Goo.

in breeding reds and demonstrates the difficulty of categorizing red breeding lines. For example, should *P.* Zuma Garnet and its progeny be primarily attributed to the George Vasquez breeding line or to that of Malibu Imp? In either case, it is very difficult to escape a *P.* Luedde-violacea background when discussing good modern red phalaenopsis.

Moving away from the *P.* Luedde-violacea line, another important contributor to red breeding is *P* Golden Buddha. Registered by Peter Lista in 1977, *P.* Golden Buddha results from the combination of the semi-alba *P.* Cher Ann and the primary hybrid, *P.* Spica. Unlike the best clones of *P.* George Vasquez and *P.* Malibu Imp, the best clones of *P.* Golden Buddha have larger flowers that are less star shaped. In addition, *P.* Golden Buddha generally has higher flower counts and longer flower spikes that those from the *P.* Luedde-violacea line. *Phalaenopsis* Golden Buddha was recognized early as an important hybrid with great breeding potential. Between 1981 and 1983, 20 grexes were registered with this hybrid as one of its parents.

Most of the plants from the original *P.* Golden Buddha cross featured star-shaped yellow flowers with red markings. Through selective breeding of siblings and chance genetic variation, several *P.* Golden Buddha clones have bloomed mostly red with a hint of yellow in the background. One of the nicest of these is *P.* Golden Buddha 'Raspberry Delight', which is a nearly solid, deep red-purple and received an 80-point Award of Merit in 1987. Another highly regarded clone is *P.* Golden Buddha 'Ken Peterson'.

The red pigmentation in *P.* Golden Buddha is almost certainly attributable to the *P.* Spica parent. *Phalaenopsis* Spica's parentage consists of *P. fasciata* × *P. lueddemanniana*. Without knowing which form of *P. lueddemanniana* was used, it is difficult to assess the degree of its contribution to the red pigmentation in *P.* Spica. It is safe to assume, however, that both *P. fasciata* and *P. lueddemanniana* contributed to the red pigmentation that manifests itself in both *P.* Spica and *P.* Golden Buddha.

Phalaenopsis Golden Buddha hybrids, by their nature, are quite variable. Unfortunately, many of them exhibit poor flower form and colors that fade significantly with age. Consequently, it is often not easy to bloom a good *P.* Golden Buddha hybrid, but the good ones are so incredibly stunning that breeding attempts are worth the effort. One brief glimpse at a better cultivar of *P.* Cordova will make any skeptic a true believer. Another winning grex for warm reds is *P.* Spirit House.

The table on page 80 tells the story of *P.* Golden Buddha's legacy. It will be interesting to see if the progeny of *P.* Golden Buddha will continue to breed improvement in reds.

Phalaenopsis Penang (*P.* Rosy Charm × *P. amboinensis*), registered in 1972 by Herb Hager, is perhaps the most interesting of the red parents. As of December 2006, five AOS awards have been granted to *P.* Penang.

Phalaenopsis Golden Buddha. Photo by H. P. Norton.

Phalaenopsis Spirit House 'D & B' AM/AOS. Photo by Eric Goo.

Awarded red progeny of *P.* Golden Buddha
(as of December 2006)

PARENTAGE AND PROGENY	HCC	AM
× Bonita Roja = Spirit House	3	3
× Candle Glow = Summer Morn	1	3
× Dora = Cathy Fogarty	2	1
× Kathleen Ai = Ai Gold	1	1
× Single Shot = Red Buddha	1	1
× Waxwing = Phil-n-Jill	1	
× Zuma Garnet = Cordova	8	6

Most of these awarded clones have pink flowers with red spotting. *Phalaenopsis* Penang 'Lacquer', which is a solid red-purple clone, has also received an Award of Merit.

Of all the red phalaenopsis discussed in Eric's series of articles, only *P.* Penang has distinguished itself by producing progeny that received a First Class Certificate. *Phalaenopsis* Mahalo 'Carmela Orchids' garnered an 82-point AM in 1986. In 1990 this was upgraded to a 90-point FCC. At the time this plant received the FCC, its flowers were described by judges as "intense vibrant red-purple." The floriferousness of this clone is also remarkable. When it received its FCC, it displayed 67 flowers and 30 buds, and it also received a 90-point Certificate of Cultural Merit. As the accompanying table shows, *P.* Penang has offered fertile ground for breeders interested in pursuing reds.

While *P.* Penang has produced some outstanding red progeny, it has also served as the grandparent of outstanding red hybrids. In fact, *P.* Penang can be found as the grandparent of some of the best recent red hybrids shown in the table. Two such offspring are *P.* Ben Goo and *P.* Ember.

Awarded red progeny of *P.* Penang
(as of December 2006)

PARENTAGE AND PROGENY	HCC	AM	FCC
× Malibu Heir = Mahalo	3	3	1
× *mariae* = Sophie Hausermann	1	1	
× Mayaimi = Midnight Rose	1		
× Princess Kaiulani = Sarah Rose	1		
× Redwine = Tapestry		1	
× *sumatrana* = Molokai Prince	1	1	

Phalaenopsis Mahalo is emerging as a worthwhile breeder of reds. The *P.* Penang breeding line produced a second FCC in the cross *P.* Strawberry Sundae (*P.* Sara Rose × *P.* Malibu Heir), as *P.* Penang makes its appearance here in *P.* Sarah Rose (*P.* Princess Kaiulani × *P.* Penang). *Phalaenopsis* Strawberry Sundae 'Red Vengeance' received a 90-point FCC in 1990 and was described by judges as having "vibrant magenta flowers with very fine arrangement." While the goal of a 4 in.

Phalaenopsis Ben Goo 'Radiant Ruby' HCC/AOS. Photo by Eric Goo.

Phalaenopsis Ember 'Blumen Insel' AM/AOS

Notable second-generation red progeny of *P.* Penang
(as of December 2006)

PARENTAGE AND PROGENY	HCC	AM	FCC	AQ
Mahalo × Cherokee Chief = Donna Goo	1	1		
Mahalo × George Vasquez = Ember	6	7		
Mahalo × Tabasco Tex = Clara Schuman		1		
Mahalo × Zauberrot = Hawaiian Classic		1		
Mahalo × Zuma Garnet = Ben Goo	2	2		1
Paifang's Penangeorge × Heart's Desire = Flaming Desire	1	1		
Red Sail × amboinensis = Red Devil		1		
Sarah Rose × Malibu Heir = Strawberry Sundae	1		1	

(10 cm), floriferous, full-formed, solid red phalaenopsis has not yet been obtained, red breeding lines are making definite progress.

Contributions of *Phalaenopsis pulcherrima*

Recent literature on red breeding has addressed breeding lines stemming primarily from the species *P. violacea*, *P. lueddemanniana*, and *P. amboinensis*. Another contributor to red breeding is *P. pulcherrima* (formerly *Doritis pulcherrima*). To see some of its contributions to red breeding, we can examine this line that has produced important progeny as measured by the AOS judging system.

Some of the best results to date can be traced to *Doritaenopsis* Red Elf (*D. pulcherrima* × *P. fasciata*), which was created by Oak Hill and registered by Lenette in 1982. While the color of *P. pulcherrima* flowers are basically a bright, deep purple, crossing it with *P. fasciata* has produced progeny appearing less purple and more red. One cultivar from this cross, 'Lenette #4' received a 78-point HCC from the AOS in 1991. At the time of the award, the color of its flowers were described by judges as "brilliant fuchsia."

In addition to the flower color, the attribute of floriferousness seems to be dominant in *P. pulcherrima* hybrids. First-generation progeny of this species tend to have upright spikes with good flower counts. This attribute is especially desirable in breeding reds, which frequently have relatively few flowers on short inflorescences. Given its *Phalaenopsis* (*Doritis*) parent, one should not be surprised that *Doritaenopsis* Red Elf 'Lenette #4' received an 83-point Certificate of Cultural Merit in 1984 for a specimen bearing a spectacular 82 flowers and 101 buds on 13 branched inflorescences.

Frequently, the hybridizer of reds must contend with the issue of fertility—or, more accurately, the lack thereof. Red phalaenopsis are often reported to be completely sterile or fertile to a limited degree. This is especially true with the triploid hybrids. Some will produce seed only when used as the pod parent, and very few produce large quantities of seed. This is probably one reason that large commercial growers do not offer a variety of red *Phalaenopsis* hybrids. Fortunately, *D.* Red Elf does breed. The record of orchid hybrids shows that *D.* Red Elf has produced a total of 10 first-generation hybrids through 2006. The progeny of *D.* Red Elf have been successfully used as parents as well.

The hybrid *D.* Tony (*D.* Red Elf × *P. venosa*) was registered in 1986 by H. P. Norton (who is regarded as one of the most astute red phalaenopsis breeders in the United States). This cross shows improved form and color. The size of the flowers remains small at about 1⅝ in. (4.2 cm), as could be expected due to the small size of both parents. The cultivar *D.* Tony 'H. P.' received a 78-point HCC in 1991. At the time of award, the plant bore 14 flowers and 7 buds on 3 inflorescences with a flower color that was described by judges as "cinnabar with a light blue cast." In 2001, this cultivar's award was upgraded to an AM.

Crossing *D.* Red Elf with *P. amboinensis* produces *D.* Inferno, registered by Norton in 1984. *Doritaenopsis* Inferno is about the same size as the *D.* Red Elf parent, with 1⅝ in. (4.2 cm) flowers. The color, however, is improved, having more red and less purple than its *D.* Red

Elf parent. In 1993, cultivar 'H. P. Norton' received a 78-point HCC. At the time of the award, this cultivar had 23 flowers and 15 buds on 3 branched inflorescences, with the flower color described by judges as "wine red."

Continuing this line of breeding is a cross with *D.* Inferno listed as the pollen parent. This is noteworthy, because having a plant that functions as both a pod and pollen parent increases a breeder's options and aids in advancing the breeding line. *Doritaenopsis* Rebel (*P.* Fire-Water × *D.* Inferno) was registered by Norton in 1991. The flowers of this cross are larger and have better form than the *D.* Inferno parent. In this cross, although the flower size has been increased, the doritaenopsis parent is dominant in flower size, causing the flowers to be smaller than the average of the parents. This cross also shows the continued improvement in flower color as it approaches a true red pigmentation. As of December 2006, four cultivars from this cross had received HCCs from the AOS. A good example of this hybrid is the cultivar 'Durham', which received a 79-point HCC in 1995. At the time of award, this plant bore 31 flowers and 14 buds on 3 branched inflorescences. Its 2 in. (5 cm) flowers were described by judges as "ruby red."

No discussion of the *D.* Red Elf breeding line would be complete without the mention of *D.* Abed-nego (*D.* Inferno × *P.* Malibu Imp), which was registered by Norton in 1996. Arguably the best cross in this fine line, *D.* Abed-nego has distinguished itself by receiving three HCCs as well as the prestigious Award of Quality, all in 1996. The AQ grouping consisted of 15 plants, the majority of which were first-bloom seedlings. These plants carried approximately a dozen flowers and buds on each branched inflorescence. The 1½ in. (3.5 cm) blossoms were flat and well formed, red, red-purple, and rusty red in color. This grex went on to garner six more HCCs and four more AMs by the end of 2006.

Similar to *D.* Red Elf is *D.* Jim (*Doritis pulcherrima* × *P. venosa*), registered by Norton in 1984. The cultivar 'Burgundy Smile' received a 77-point HCC in 1991. At the time of award, it displayed 17 flowers and 12 buds on 1 inflorescence, and the 1¾ in. (4.5 cm) flowers were described by judges as "reddish lavender." The flowers of this hybrid are slightly larger than *D.* Red Elf.

Crossing *D.* Jim with the well-known yellow breeder *P.* Hausermann's Goldcup produces *D.* Lonnie Morris. One cultivar of this cross, 'Nationwide', received a 79-point HCC in 1996. At the time of award, the plant bore seven flowers and one bud on one branched inflorescence. The flowers of this cultivar were 2¼ in. (5.5 cm) across, larger than any other awarded cultivar from this breeding line, and were described by judges as "brilliant garnet." This clone was upgraded to an AM in 1997. Plants from this grex also received an HCC and an AM.

In the family tree shown in the accompanying illustration, one attribute of each phalaenopsis parent is especially interesting: it contains genetic material that manifests itself in yellow flower pigmentation. The *P. fasciata* parent of *D.* Red Elf is a yellow species with red-brown bars. *Phalaenopsis venosa*, a well known yellow breeder and parent of both *D.* Jim and *D.* Tony, has a yellow flower that is overlain with brown blotches. *Phalaenopsis amboinensis*, parent of *D.* Inferno, has yellow flowers with brown bars. *Phalaenopsis* Hausermann's Goldcup, parent of *D.* Lonnie Morris, is a well-known breeder of yellows. *Phalaenopsis* Malibu Imp, parent of *D.* Abed-nego, is the product of the yellow species *P. amboinensis* and *P.* Luedde-violacea. Finally, *P.* Fire-Water (*P.* Goldiana × *P.* Hugo Freed) is parent of the very successful *D.* Rebel and is a product of the yellow *P.* Golden Sands breeding line.

Doritaenopsis Inferno seems to be emerging as the premier breeder in this line. Its grexes *D.* Rebel and *D.* Abed-nego have received many AOS awards. In addi-

Doritaenopsis Lonnie Morris 'Nationwide'. Photo by Allen Black.

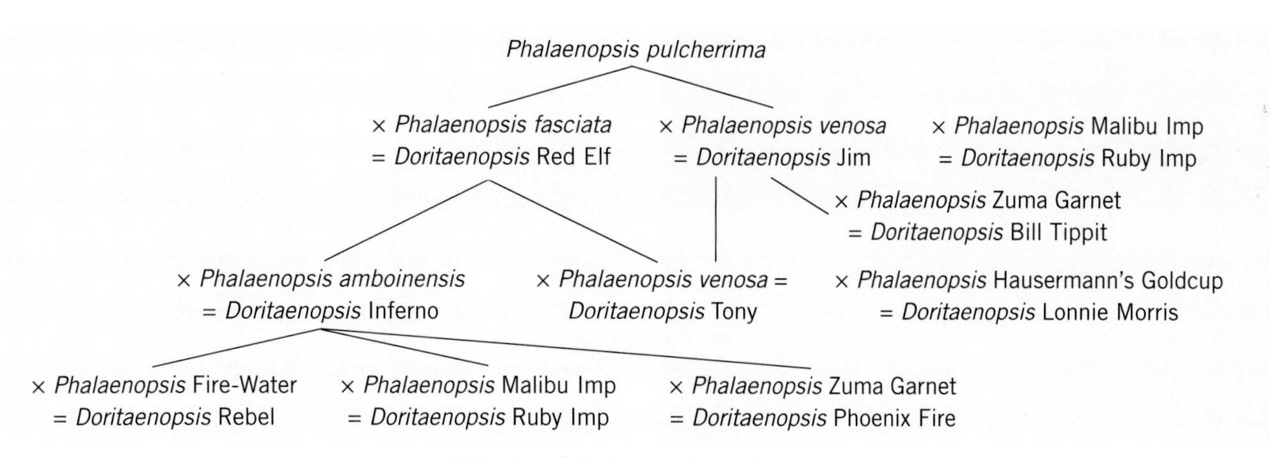

Offspring of *Phalaenopsis pulcherrima*

tion, *D.* Abed-nego is perhaps the first cross within the *Phalaenopsis* alliance to receive an AQ with flowers approaching a true red color.

Overall, this breeding line has produced brilliant, saturated colors with very good flower counts. In fact, it would not be inaccurate to describe these hybrids as red multifloras. Given the success of this line of breeding, it seems as though continued improvements in red breeding could be made by extending the use of *P. pulcherrima* and its hybrids. The task for the hybridizer will be to maintain the intense flower color of this line while increasing flower size.

Many contributions to red breeding were made by parent plants *P.* George Vasquez, *P.* Golden Buddha, *P.* Malibu Imp, and *P.* Penang. These breeding lines and their progeny have performed well.

Alberta Welcome
  Award: HCC
  Breedling lines: Penang
Ben Goo
  Awards: AQ, AM (2), HCC (2)
  Breedling lines: George Vasquez, Malibu Imp, Penang
Cathy Fogarty
  Awards: AM, HCC (2)
  Breedling lines: Golden Buddha
Franz Liszt
  Awards: AM (2), HCC
  Breedling lines: Malibu Imp, Golden Buddha
Mary Lilian Taylor
  Award: AM
  Breedling lines: Penang
Mary Tauscher-Goo
  Awards: AQ, HCC (4)
  Breedling lines: George Vasquez, Malibu Imp
Neon Magenta
  Awards: HCC
  Breedling lines: Penang
Red Thrill
  Awards: AM, HCC
  Breedling lines: Golden Buddha, Penang
Rubylight
  Award: AM
  Breeding lines: George Vasquez, Penang
Ruth Tauscher
  Awards: AQ, AM (4), HCC (3)
  Breedling lines: George Vasquez, Malibu Imp, Golden Buddha
Straits Garnet
  Award: HCC
  Breedling lines: George Vasquez, Malibu Imp

One of the grexes with *P.* George Vasquez as a parent is *P.* Mary Tauscher-Goo 'The Queen' HCC/AOS.

Several other important hybrids have led the way in the quest for red. Tom Harper, phalaenopsis breeder and owner of an orchid nursery specializing in phalaenopsis, states (2002) that some of the "benchmark" varieties in the development of red phalaenopsis include *P.*

Phalaenopsis Mary Tauscher-Goo 'The Queen' HCC/AOS. Photo by Eric Goo.

Super Stupid (*P.* Brother Yew × *P.* Brother Peacock), *P.* Ruby Blaze (*P.* Corning's Violet × *P.* Malibu Heir), *P.* Pago Pago (*P. venosa* × *P.* Lippeglut), *P.* Summer Wine (*P.* Bettylee Burke × *P. amboinensis*), *P.* Sweet Revenge (*P.* Sara Lee × *P.* Deventeriana), and *P.* Princess Dee (*P.* Eye Dee × *P.* Princess Kaiulani).

Important Efforts in Breeding Reds

Most of the red breeding efforts described so far have been made by breeders in the United States. The pioneers include Hugo Freed, the Shaffers, Stewart Orchids, Bill Livingston, Herb Hager, Norito Hasagawa, Howard Koopowitz, Westcott Orchids, Peter Lista, John Ewing, George Vasquez, Zuma Canyon Orchids, Crestwood Orchids, John Miller, and Jones and Scully. Other notable contributors today include Tom Harper, H. P. Norton, Meir Moses, A. Dean Stock, Howard S. Ginsburg, Frank Smith, Eric Goo, and Bill Mitchell.

Homer P. Norton of Moncks Corner, South Carolina, is generally regarded as one of the most astute red phalaenopsis breeders in the United States. Most of the important work done in breeding *P. pulcherrima* was accomplished by him at Orchidview. From a hybridizing perspective, he has boldly gone where no one has gone before. He seems to have the uncanny ability to choose parents that will produce the best quality offspring. He has contributed many new hybrids.

Phalaenopsis Katie Morris (*P.* Donald Rigg × *P.* Harford's Jewel), registered by Norton in 1995, won an AQ/AOS for the grex and has produced four awarded clones. In 2006, Norton registered *P.* Orchidview Tabasco (*P.* Krull's Red Hot × *P.* Green Sun). So far, the largest flowers from this tetraploid grex have measured 3¼ in. (8 cm) across. Breeders are excited about the possibilities of this parent of some of the many super Taiwanese hybrids.

Phalaenopsis Katie Morris 'Caroline'. Photo by H. P. Norton.

Phalaenopsis Orchidview Tabasco. Photo by H. P. Norton.

Frank Smith of Krull-Smith Orchids produced *P.* Florida Heat (*P.* Golden Buddha × *P.* Cordova). He also produced *P.* Krull's Red Hot (*P.* Katie Morris × *P.* Florida Heat), which was registered in 2001 and has since racked up nine AOS awards. Krull's Red Hot has proven to be a productive breeder that adds a touch of yellow to its offspring, which make the reds clearer without much purple tint. Using it as a stepping stone to finer reds, Smith produced probably his most famous and praised grex, *P.* H. P. Norton (*P.* Brother Pirate King × *P.* Krull's Red Hot), which was and named after his esteemed colleague and registered in 2003. This grex is a beauty that has produced plenty of prize-winning clones—by December 2006, this amounted to six AMs and five HCCs. *Phalaenopsis* H. P. Norton 'Kathy' was awarded an AM/AOS in 2004 for a plant with five flowers with an overall spread of almost 3 in. (7.5 cm). The cross was also awarded an AQ. As a parent, it is considered one of the prime tetraploid candidates for red breeding.

Phalaenopsis Florida Heat 'Gemma' HCC/AOS. Photo by H. P. Norton.

Rows of phalaenopsis flasks await their turns at a Taiwanese phalaenopsis nursery. Photo by Yin-Tung Wang.

During the 1960s and 1970s, breeders in the United States, in addition to some European orchid houses, were the prime movers and shakers in the phalaenopsis breeding arena. Since the 1980s, however, Taiwan has taken the lead in producing the vast majority of *Phalaenopsis* hybrids on the world market today. Taiwanese breeders are especially fond of red and yellow phalaenopsis, since in their culture these colors represent happiness and prosperity, and they have made great strides in breeding superior flowers in these colors. Also, the Taiwanese government has encouraged the orchid industry by subsidizing phalaenopsis research and growing facilities. This island's low cost of labor, phalaenopsis growing environment, and large, modern production greenhouses and laboratories make it ideal for phalaenopsis production. These breeders are producing seemingly countless flasks of *Phalaenopsis* hybrids and clones.

Taiwan is now dubbed the "Land of Phalaenopsis" and has 50 or more large commercial growers cranking out millions of plants for the mass market. Thanks to Taiwanese growers, prizewinning phalaenopsis are being produced so quickly and in such quantity that they are now available in nearly every marketing channel, from supermarkets to home and garden centers, at modest prices.

One of the earliest Taiwanese hybrids to catch the attention of red phalaenopsis lovers was *P.* Brother Purple (*P.* Golden Peoker × *P.* Brother Glamour), registered by Brother Orchid Nursery in 1995. This waxy, purple-red flower is a standout and has proven to be an excellent, highly fertile, parent that passes on its high flower count, compact growth habit, and large (for a red), flat, round flowers to its offspring. *Phalaenopsis* Brother Purple has been responsible for more than 40 prize-winning offspring, including such stars as *P.* Brother Supersonic (× *P.* Sara Lee), registered in 1997; the highly acclaimed *P.* Brother Purple; *P.* Brother Precious Stones (× *P.* Brother Fancy); *P.* Brother Pirate King (× *P.* Fortune Buddha), of which 22 plants have received awards as of December 2006; and *P.* Brother Sally Taylor (× *P.* Super Stupid), all registered in 1998. Another winner registered in 1998 spawned from *P.* Brother Purple is *P.* Brother Oconee (× *P.* Carmela's Pixie). This floriferous multiflora type has so far garnered seven AOS awards. In 1999 *Doritaenopsis* Brother Tom Walsh (× *D.* Brother Julius) was registered to add yet another distinguished grex to *P.* Brother Purple's family. Much of this red-flower breeding work at the famous Brother Orchid Nursery in Taiwan was accomplished by hybridizer Yung-Yu Lin.

Phalaenopsis Brother Purple is a complex hybrid,

Phalaenopsis seedlings in a Taiwanese grower's greenhouse. Photo by Erik S. Runkle.

Phalaenopsis Brother Pirate King. Photo by H. P. Norton.

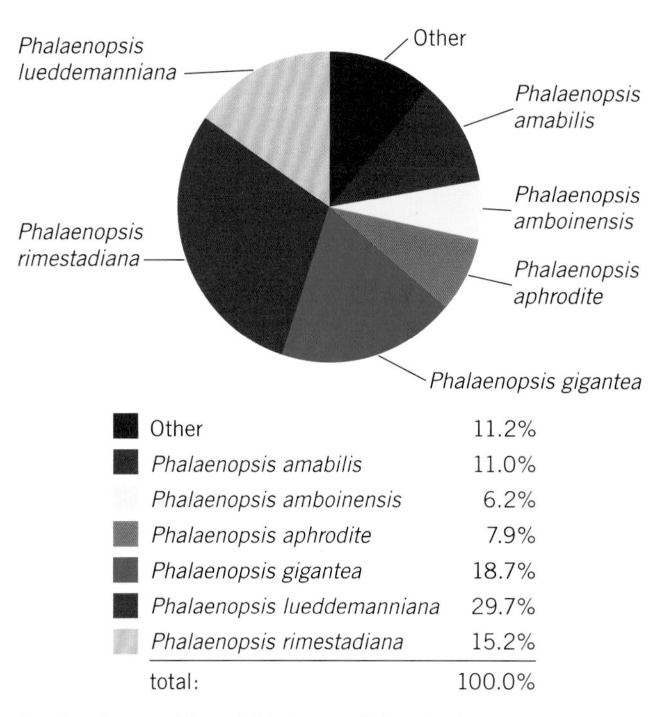

Species Composition of *Phalaenopsis* Brother Purple. Used with permission from *OrchidWiz Encyclopedia*.

the result of blending various *Phalaenopsis* species. The species composition of this hybrid is shown in the accompanying graphic.

Phalaenopsis Sogo John (*P.* Auckland Buddha × *P.* Golden Sun) was registered by Sogo Team in 1997. This grex also served a parent of another impressively large-flowering grex, *P.* Green Sun (*P.* Ching Her's Light × *P.* Sogo John), which was registered by Ching Her in 2000. The largest flower so far reported in this grex is almost 3½ in. (9 cm) across.

To produce flowers of a "truer red" with less of a purple hue, hybrids containing yellow pigmentations were added to the genetic mix. One super result was *P.* Chingruey's Blood-Red Sun (*P.* Golden Sun × *P.* Ching Her Goddess), registered by Ching Ruey Orchids in 2000.

To improve flower count and add more orange to the flowers and to make the inflorescence shorter and branched, Sogo Team Co. started using selections of *P.* Sogo Kaiulani (*P.* Princess Kaiulani × *P.* Yungho Princess Gelb) in its breeding program. One of the superior results of this effort was *P.* Sogo Cock. This outstanding grex, registered in 1999 by Sogo Team Co., had received

Phalaenopsis Sogo Cock 'Oriental Beauty' AM/AOS

Phalaenopsis Sogo Cock 'Joy'. Photo by Marshall Ku.

Phalaenopsis Sogo Rose 'Joy'. Photo by Peter Lin.

nine HCCs and two AMs by the end of 1996, and a clone, 'Joy', was honored with a Gold Medal at the 2005 World Orchid Congress in France.

Phalaenopsis Sogo Rose (*P.* Golden Sun × *P.* Sogo Kaiulani), registered by Sogo in 2000, has received much attention and admiration, with six cultivars receiving AOSs. This grex produces a half dozen or so purple to garnet-red flowers approaching 3 in. (7.5 cm) wide that are attractively presented on the inflorescence.

The Future of Reds

Red *Phalaenopsis* hybrids still have a ways to go to reach the flower size, round shape, and higher flower count that have become the standard with whites, pinks, and stripes. What path must be taken to get there? That is the charge of many phalaenopsis breeders today.

Most red hybrids are *diploids* or *triploids*. A. Dean Stock, retired cytogeneticist and present-day phalaenopsis breeder, believes that the future of reds with large and many flowers rests with tetraploid hybrids. He states (2005) that breeding with large, dark tetraploid pinks and yellows will lead to the coveted red 4 in. (10 cm) flower size. He envisions many existing tetraploids as future breeding material, and these grexes are worth searching out and enjoying as they are.

Auckland Buddha
Black Rose
Brother Delight
Brother Fancy
Brother Glamour
Brother Jungle Cat
Brother Kaiser
Brother Passion
Brother Peacock
Brother Pirate King
Brother Precious Stones
Brother Purple
Brother Sally Taylor
Brother Spots Way
Brother Supersonic
Brother Utopia
Brother Yew 'La Flora'
Chimei Buddha
Ching Her Goddess
Chingruey's Blood-Red Sun
Chingruey's Goddess
Chingruey's Sika Deer
Dou-dii Golden Princess
Fortune Buddha 'Tinny'
Golden Amboin
Golden Bells
Golden Peoker
Golden Sun
Goldiana
Liu Tuen-Shen

Paifang's Auckland
Paifang's Queen 'Brother'
Queen Spot
Salu Peoker
Salu Spot
Salu Sun
Sara Lee 'Eye Dee'
Sentra
Sogo Champion
Sogo Yew
Strawberry Wine
Super Stupid
Taipei Gold 'Gold Star'

Several parents lead in the march to larger, more floriferous reds. One that has already proven itself is a tetraploid, *Doritaenopsis* Brother Cortez Red (*D.* Sinica Knight × *P.* Brother Purple), which was registered in 2000 by Brother Orchids. By December 2006, five plants within the first generation of this grex have been awarded. The cultivar 'Steinfurt' received an AM/AOS in 2004 with a flower 3¼ in. (8 cm) wide.

Phalaenopsis Chingruey's Fancy (*P.* Sogo John × *P.* Brother Fancy) is another winning grex, registered in 2000 by Ching Ruey Orchids. This fuchsia-red–flowered grex earned a 2005 AM/AOS for 'Kimo', whose flowers spread a little more than 3 in. (7.5 cm). It already has superior progeny, such as the cultivar 'Haur Jih Fancy' (*P.* Chingruey's Blood-Red Sun × *P.* Chingruey's Fancy), registered in 2003.

Strides are being made to produce larger flowers by using natural tetraploids as parents and by working on species improvements—bigger and more flowers with thicker substance—by treating these plants with colchicine to convert them from their natural diploid (2n) state to tetraploid (4n). In due time, some in this beautiful group of phalaenopsis will graduate from novelties to standards. Of course, some phalaenopsis collectors will still prefer the novelty reds. Even though they may not have the 4 in. (10 cm) flowers on large inflorescences, these reds are colorful, frequently fragrant, and compact—ideal for light gardens or windowsills.

Phalaenopsis Chingruey's Blood-Red Sun (*P.* Golden Sun × *P.* Ching Her Goddess). Photo by A. Dean Stock.

Gallery of Red and Purple Hybrids

Hybrids are listed by the year in which they were registered to demonstrate changes and evolution over time.

1967

Phalaenopsis Coral Isles 'Lung Ching' AM/AOS
Origin: *Phalaenopsis* Princess Kaiulani × *Phalaenopsis lueddemanniana*
Originator: Frederick Thornton
Registered by Frederick Thornton

1991

Phalaenopsis Dotty Woodson 'Orchidland'
Origin: *Phalaenopsis* Tabasco Tex × *Phalaenopsis* George Vasquez
Originator: Woodson
Registered by Woodson

1992

Phalaenopsis Carolina Red Magic 'Lenette' AM/AOS
Origin: *Phalaenopsis* Bettylee Burke × *Phalaenopsis* Arthur Zeller
Originator: Tom Harper
Registered by Lenette

1993

Phalaenopsis Jungle Cat 'Bloody Mary'
Origin: *Phalaenopsis* Hawaiian Pinstripes × *Phalaenopsis* Golden Spice
Originator: Norman's Orchids
Registered by Norman's Orchids

1995

Phalaenopsis George Leather 'Peter Lin'
Origin: *Phalaenopsis* George Vasquez × *Phalaenopsis* Leather
Originator: Unknown
Registered by Orchid Hatchery

Phalaenopsis Katie Morris 'Dixie Sunset'
Origin: *Phalaenopsis* Donald Rigg × *Phalaenopsis* Harford's Jewel
Originator: H. P. Norton
Registered by H. P. Norton

Phalaenopsis Coral Isles 'Lung Ching' AM/AOS. Photo by Eric Goo.

Phalaenopsis Dotty Woodson 'Orchidland'. Photo by Eric Goo.

Phalaenopsis Min-Chao Yeo-Man 'Hwa Yuan'
Origin: *Phalaenopsis* Brother Yew × *Phalaenopsis* Yungho Princess Gelb
Originator: C. N. Wan
Registered by C. N. Wan

Phalaenopsis Carolina Red Magic 'Lenette' AM/AOS. Photo by Peter Lin.

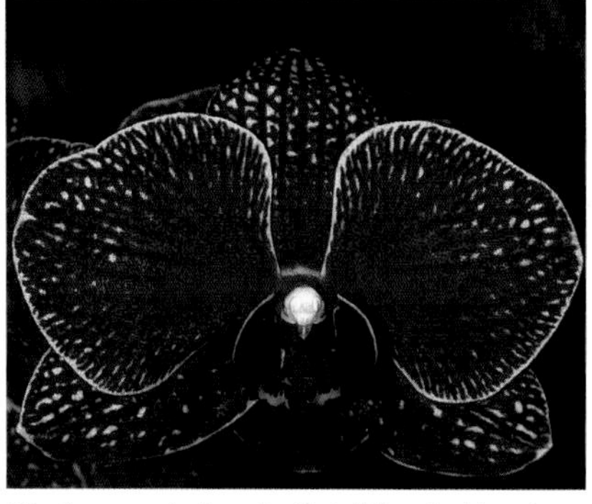

Phalaenopsis Jungle Cat 'Bloody Mary'

Phalaenopsis George Leather 'Peter Lin'. Photo by Peter Lin.

Phalaenopsis Summer Garnet 'Neo' HCC/AOS
Origin: *Phalaenopsis* Summer Morn × *Phalaenopsis* Zuma Garnet
Originator: Orchid Plantation
Registered by Orchid Plantation

Phalaenopsis Katie Morris 'Dixie Sunset'. Photo by H. P. Norton.

Phalaenopsis Min-Chao Yeo-Man 'Hwa Yuan'. Photo by Peter Lin.

Phalaenopsis Summer Garnet 'Neo' HCC/AOS. Photo by Eric Goo.

1996

Phalaenopsis Sogo Grape
Origin: *Phalaenopsis* Super Stupid × *Phalaenopsis* Princess Kaiulani
Originator: Sogo Team Co.
Registered by Sogo Team Co.

1997

Doritaenopsis Taida Salu
Origin: *Phalaenopsis* Salu Spot × *Doritaenopsis* Happy Beauty
Originator: Taida
Registered by Taida

Phalaenopsis Sogo Grape

Doritaenopsis Taida Salu

1999

Doritaenopsis Jack Beckwith
Origin: *Phalaenopsis* Katie Morris × *Doritaenopsis* Regal Velvet
Originator: H. P. Norton
Registered by H. P. Norton

Doritaenopsis Mepkin Bells 'Katherine'
Origin: *Doritaenopsis* Neopolis × *Phalaenopsis* Golden Bells
Originator: H. P. Norton
Registered by H. P. Norton

Doritaenopsis Jack Beckwith. Photo by H. P. Norton.

Doritaenopsis Mepkin Bells 'Katherine'. Photo by H. P. Norton.

Doritaenopsis Taisuco Bloody Mary
Origin: *Doritaenopsis* Taisuco Firebird × *Phalaenopsis* Taisuco Spidra
Originator: Taiwan Sugar Company/Taisuco
Registered by Taiwan Sugar Company/Taisuco

Phalaenopsis Arizona Gem 'Ruby Glow' HCC/AOS
Origin: *Phalaenopsis* Mahalo × *Phalaenopsis* Olatt
Originator: Eric Goo
Registered by Phoenix Orchids: Eric Goo

Doritaenopsis Taisuco Bloody Mary

Phalaenopsis Arizona Gem 'Ruby Glow' HCC/AOS. Photo by Eric Goo.

Phalaenopsis Purple Majesty 'Burgundy Beauty' AM/AOS. Photo by Eric Goo.

Phalaenopsis Arizona Princess 'Purple Gem' HCC/AOS. Photo by Eric Goo.

Doritaenopsis Kiss Me Kate 'Carol'. Photo by H. P. Norton.

Phalaenopsis Ruth Tauscher 'Garnet Beauty' HCC/AOS. Photo by Eric Goo.

Phalaenopsis Arizona Princess 'Spotted Beauty' AM/AOS. Photo by Eric Goo.

Phalaenopsis Wes Addison 'Ruby Glow' HCC/AOS. Photo by Eric Goo.

Phalaenopsis Purple Majesty 'Burgundy Beauty' AM/AOS
Origin: *Phalaenopsis* Andalusia × *Phalaenopsis* Malibu Imp
Originator: Eric Goo
Registered by Eric Goo

Phalaenopsis Ruth Tauscher 'Garnet Beauty' HCC/AOS
Origin: *Phalaenopsis* Spirit House × *Phalaenopsis* Zuma Garnet
Originator: Eric Goo
Registered by Eric Goo

2000

Phalaenopsis Arizona Princess 'Purple Gem' HCC/AOS
Origin: *Phalaenopsis* Andalusia × *Phalaenopsis* Princess Kaiulani
Originator: Eric Goo
Registered by Phoenix Orchids, Eric Goo

Phalaenopsis Arizona Princess 'Spotted Beauty' AM/AOS
Origin: *Phalaenopsis* Andalusia × *Phalaenopsis* Kaiulani
Originator: Eric Goo
Registered by Phoenix Orchids

2001

Doritaenopsis Kiss Me Kate 'Carol'
Origin: *Phalaenopsis* Katie Morris × *Doritaenopsis* Neopolis
Originator: H. P. Norton
Registered by H. P. Norton

Phalaenopsis Wes Addison 'Ruby Glow' HCC/AOS
Origin: *Phalaenopsis* Summer Morn × *Phalaenopsis* Malibu Imp
Originator: Eric Goo
Registered by Eric Goo

2002

Phalaenopsis Gene Wentz
Origin: *Phalaenopsis* Brother Sally Taylor × *Phalaenopsis* Brother Pirate King
Originator: K & D Emig
Registered by K & D Emig

2003

Doritaenopsis Bill Tippit 'Purple Glow' HCC/AOS
Origin: *Doritaenopsis* Jim × *Phalaenopsis* Zuma Garnet
Originator: Eric Goo
Registered by Eric Goo

Phalaenopsis Gene Wentz

Doritaenopsis Bill Tippit 'Purple Glow' HCC/AOS. Photo by Eric Goo.

Doritaenopsis Jiuhbao Red Rose 'Brilliant'
Origin: *Doritaenopsis* Taisuco Firebird × *Doritaenopsis* King Shiang's Rose
Originator: JiuhBao Orchids
Registered by JiuhBao Orchids

Doritaenopsis Memorial Bud Terrell 'Red Beauty' HCC/AOS
Origin: *Phalaenopsis* Summer Morn × *Doritaenopsis* Inferno
Originator: Eric Goo
Registered by Eric Goo

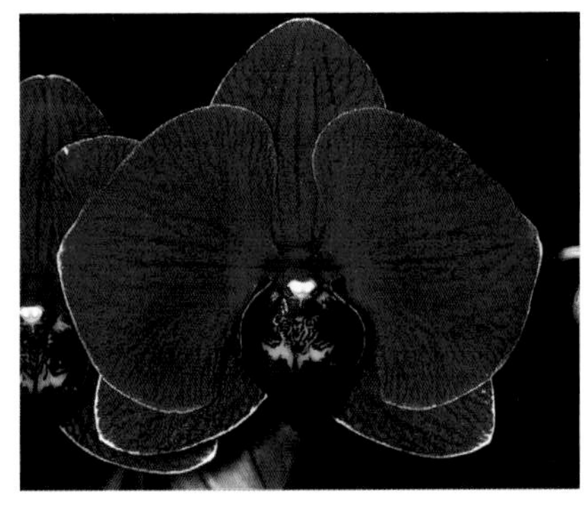

Doritaenopsis Jiuhbao Red Rose 'Brillant'

Doritaenopsis Memorial Bud Terrell 'Red Beauty' HCC/AOS. Photo by Eric Goo.

Phalaenopsis Cris Lee 'Red Beauty'
Origin: *Phalaenopsis* Cordova × *Phalaenopsis* Malibu Imp
Originator: Eric Goo
Registered by Eric Goo

Phalaenopsis Sherri Pantano 'Red Beauty'
Origin: *Phalaenopsis* Spirit House × *Phalaenopsis* Venimp
Originator: Eric Goo
Registered by Eric Goo

Phalaenopsis Cris Lee 'Red Beauty'. Photo by Eric Goo.

Phalaenopsis Sherri Pantano 'Red Beauty'. Photo by Eric Goo.

2004

Phalaenopsis Bev Tall 'Carnelian Queen' AM/AOS
Origin: *Phalaenopsis* Mary Lilian Taylor × *Phalaenopsis* Zuma Garnet
Originator: Eric Goo
Registered by Eric Goo

Phalaenopsis Bev Tall 'Carnelian Queen' AM/AOS. Photo by Eric Goo.

2005

Phalaenopsis Memoria Don Tauscher 'Purple Beauty' AM/AOS
Origin: *Phalaenopsis* Andalusia × *Phalaenopsis* Crimson Cape
Originator: Eric Goo
Registered by Phoenix Orchids: Eric Goo

Phalaenopsis Memoria Don Tauscher 'Purple Beauty' AM/AOS. Photo by Eric Goo.

1
2
3
4
5

Chapter 6

Harlequins

Send in the clowns! Harlequin *Phalaenopsis* hybrids have some of the wildest and most unpredictable flower color patterns in the entire orchid world. In fact, flowers on the same inflorescence can each have slightly different markings. Some of these variations from flower to flower are caused by environmental conditions, while others are attributed to complex genetics.

Environmental factors include temperature and light levels in which the orchids are grown, especially during flowering. When temperatures are warm—above 80° F (26° C) or so—as the flowers are forming, the pigmentation of the spotting and overall flower color is usually fainter; when the light is bright, the spots tend to be smaller. From a genetics viewpoint, significant variability can be seen within a single grex. An image from Allen Black shows this variability well, with flowers from the progeny of the hybrid *Phalaenopsis* Sunrise Red Peoker.

As with all modern hybrids, the harlequins include several species in their genetic makeup. Some of the prime players are the same orchids that had a role in the development of striped and spotted *Phalaenopsis* hybrids—*P. amboinensis*, *P. fasciata*, *P. gigantea*, and *P. lueddemanniana*. Spotted hybrids were also forerunners to the harlequins.

Opposite: Harlequin phalaenopsis: 1. white hybrid with burgundy overlay; 2. yellow hybrid with burgundy overlay; 3. *Doritaenopsis* Chain Xen Pearl (*D.* Ching Hua Spring × *D.* Nobby's Pink Lady), a white hybrid with red spots; 4. yellow hybrid with red spots; 5. *Phalaenopsis* Ever Spring Gentle 'Hwa Yuan' (*P.* Maki Watanabe × *P.* Golden Peoker), a white hybrid with red spots. Paintings by Liena Dieck.

Meir Moses, phalaenopsis breeder and grower and owner of Orchid Konnection, has a special fondness for these hybrids and is familiar with their development. He shares his knowledge about harlequins.

In the mid-1980s, Ever Spring Orchids in Taiwan purchased mericlone plants of *P.* Golden Peoker 'Brother' (*P.* Misty Green × *P.* Lui Tuen-Shen). By all appearances, it was a fairly routine purchase. However, when these orchids started blooming, one showed a pattern that differed from the rest. Some of the fine spots of the 'Brother' clone were solid, with heavier markings on the lateral sepals. Even the flower's overall shape was different from the others.

The owner of Ever Spring Orchids realized he had bloomed something unique and named it *P.* Golden Peoker 'Ever-Spring'. He did not realize at the time,

Flowers from various offspring in the grex *Phalaenopsis* Sunrise Red Peoker. Photo by Allen Black.

however, that he and his nursery were about to make history in the orchid world, and that this orchid was destined to change every aspect of novelty breeding.

In 1996 at the Taiwan International Orchid Show, three AOS awards were granted to this new line of moth orchid: *P.* Golden Peoker 'Ever-Spring' was awarded a JC/AOS, *P.* Golden Peoker 'Nan-Cho' received an AM/AOS, and *P.* Golden Peoker 'S. J.' was awarded an HCC/AOS. The 'Nan-Chou'and 'S. J.' clones were a further mutation of *P.* Golden Peoker 'ES' mericloning. Paul Bechtel, one of the AOS judges who traveled to Taiwan to judge this show, used the term *harlequin* to describe the bold pattern, wild colors, and different shapes of *P.* Golden Peoker 'Ever-Spring'. The name stuck, not only for *P.* Golden Peoker 'ES' JC/AOS as the original harlequin pattern, but as a term to describe this entire line of hybrids. Subsequent to these three plants, another mutant of *P.* Golden Peoker 'ES' was awarded in 1998 in Canada—the 'BL' clone received an HCC/AOS.

The first two hybrids using *P.* Golden Peoker 'ES' JC/AOS as a parent were *P.* Ever-Spring King (*P.* Chih Shang's Stripes × *P.* Golden Peoker) and *P.* Ever-Spring Light (*P.* Ever-Spring Star × *P.* Golden Peoker), both registered in 1992. The flowers of *P.* Chih Shang's Stripes sported dark pink candy stripes, while those of *P.* Ever-Spring Star were spotted pink. Both new hybrids caused an immediate sensation in Taiwan when they started to bloom in the early 1990s. Local nurseries were paying top dollar to own selected plants from these new crosses. This never-before-seen pattern was known as the "Black Spots type" among Taiwanese nurserymen.

Phalaenopsis Ever-Spring King Hybrids

Since the appearance of the first hybrid of *P.* Ever-Spring King, five AOS awards have been granted for the quality of the flowers. Ironically, the 'Lee' clone, which received a JC/AOS, is the orchid that is most available today. Due to an early mericloning that produced thousands of plants, this clone is available for a fraction of the price paid for the first plants of the clone. Although other selected clones of *P.* Ever-Spring King, such as 'Ching Ruey' and 'Sun Jye', have a better shape than the 'Lee' clone and have their own unique patterns, 'Lee' is a better breeder and is widely available.

Another hybrid from this group, *P.* Ever-Spring King 'Panda' JC/AOS, is now believed to be a hybrid of *P.* Ever-Spring Light. This conclusion is based on the flower size and the plant's blooming habit. Apparently, two groups of seedlings of *P.* Ever-Spring King and *P.* Ever-Spring Light were grown side-by-side in a nursery in Taiwan. Some of the seedlings of *P.* Ever-Spring

Phalaenopsis Golden Peoker 'BL' HCC/AOS

Phalaenopsis Ever-Spring King 'Lee' JC/AOS. Photo by Allen Black.

Light had been mixed with the group of *P.* Ever-Spring King and supposedly were labeled incorrectly. When the new orchid bloomed, it was labeled *P.* Ever-Spring King 'Panda' and was registered and awarded as such. Since it was better than most seedlings and had superior color, it was selected for further mericloning.

Phalaenopsis Ever-Spring Light Hybrids

The second hybrid of *P.* Golden Peoker 'Ever-Spring' JC/AOS was *P.* Ever-Spring Light (*P.* Ever-Spring Star × *P.* Golden Peoker). *Phalaenopsis* Ever-Spring King and *P.* Ever-Spring Light were created at the same time, but the flowers are quite different from clone to clone. Although other selected cultivars of *P.* Ever-Spring Light have been bred in Taiwan, they have never been propagated in large quantities and were therefore sold only locally.

Doritaenopsis Ever-Spring Pearl (*P.* Golden Peoker × *D.* King Shiang's Beauty) was registered in 1995 and produces very dark spotted flowers. One award has been issued to this group—*D.* Ever-Spring Pearl 'Montclair' HCC/AOS has nearly solid colored blooms and can produce many flowers on branched inflorescences.

Doritaenopsis Ever Spring Prince Hybrids

The most intriguing hybrid so far, which also produces the most variations within its own group, is *Doritaenopsis* Ever Spring Prince. This hybrid was created from a *P.* Golden Peoker 'Nan-Cho'/'BL' type orchid, and the pollen parent was an extremely dark pink *D.* Taisuco

Phalaenopsis Ever-Spring Light

Doritaenopsis Ever Spring Prince 'Plum Flower'

Doritaenopsis Ever Spring Prince 'Harlequin.' Photo by Allen Black.

Beauty. Registered in 1997, its first award was granted the following year at the Taiwan International Orchid show in Kaohsiung.

The flowers of awarded clone *Doritaenopsis* Ever Spring Prince 'YN' HCC/AOS were described by judges as "deep maroon, highlighted with white." Most of the selected clones in this group of *D.* Ever Spring Prince, such as 'FD' HCC/AOS, '5K' HCC/AOS, and 'Orchis-02', are very similar, and many have the same characteristics, with a triangular flower shape and white tips on the margins. This shape is inherited from the pollen parent, *D.* Taisuco Beauty. Some selected clones, however, have a better shape and larger flowers. A good example is *D.* Ever Spring Prince 'Alisun', which received an AM/AOS and was grown by Irma and José Sellés in Puerto Rico. New mericlone plants are now available in many North American shows, with prices that will not cause sticker shock.

Another excellent plant in this group is *D.* Ever Spring Prince 'H. J.', which was being sold by a Taiwanese company under the clonal name 'Pretty Cat'. It was also shown under the clonal name 'Harlequin' when it was awarded an HCC/AOS. Unfortunately, this particular clone appears under five different clonal names.

Taiwanese hybridizers realized the potential buried in this line of breeding and the endless possibilities and patterns that *P.* Golden Peoker (mutated form) could provide. They were fast to breed and bloom out large populations of seedlings, knowing that very few would have superior shape and spotting, despite many admirers and great demand. Breeders typically bloom as many plants as possible so that they can choose the few stand-outs for the market. Since hybridizers are dealing with plants that have unstable genes and chromosomes, it is difficult to predict the outcome of a certain cross. After about 10 years of breeding, hybridizers can track a pattern of a line to determine certain colors or patterns in a new hybrid, with an increased use of second- and third-generation harlequin types.

Breeders need to make careful selections of the pod parent versus the pollen parent, which dictates the outcome of a new hybrid. A good example is *D.* Black Prince (*P.* Ever-Spring Light × *P.* Ever-Spring Pearl). Careful line breeding of this grex has produced orchids with better shape, crisper colors, and a higher percentage of seedlings that will possess superior qualities.

Market demands can also dictate the directions hybridizers follow, as many nurseries pay heed to those demands. For example, one nursery that was specializing in line breeding yellows with red spots incorporated *P.* Golden Peoker 'BL' HCC/AOS into its breeding program. The result was *P.* Haur Jin Diamond (*P.* Golden Peoker × *P.* Ching Her Buddha). Another excellent hybrid in this line of breeding is *P.* Bright Peacock (*P.* Golden Peoker × *P.* Yungho Princess Gelb).

Names such as *D.* I-Hsin Black Jack (*P.* Golden Peoker × *D.* Leopard Prince), *P.* I-Hsin Black Panther (*P.* Ever-Spring King × *P.* I-Hsin Leopard), *D.* Black Butterfly (*P.* Golden Peoker × *D.*Taisuco Sweet), and *P.* Black Dense (*P.* Golden Peoker × *P.* Brother Danseuse) are becoming familiar names to many orchid collectors.

Harlequins Rise in Popularity

With the cross *P.* Ever Spring Fairy (*P.* Taisuco Kochdian × *P.* Golden Peoker 'Ever-Spring') in the late 1990s, attention was focused on harlequins. One particular clone, *P.* Ever Spring Fairy 'Shang Pin', was so commanding that it received a 90-point FCC/AOS. The impressive awarded plant was quickly purchased by a Japanese nursery, which offered a large sum of money

Phalaenopsis Ever Spring Fairy. Photo by Charlie Kovac.

to the original owner, Shang-Pin Orchids. After buying the orchid, the nursery changed the clonal name to 'Tokai Silky Star' FCC/AOS.

The year 2001 yielded another FCC/AOS for harlequin breeding using *P.* Golden Peoker. *Doritaenopsis* Chain Xen Diamond 'Celebration' (*P.* Golden Peoker × *D.* Judy Valentine) proved another superb example of the novelty breeding underway in Taiwan, with a large white flower overlaid with pink spots and blotches.

At the 1999 Taiwan International Orchid Show, of the seven awarded phalaenopsis, two were hybrids of *P.* Ever-Spring King and *P.* Golden Peoker. At the 2002 show, eighteen phalaenopsis awards included one FCC/AOS to a hybrid of *P.* Golden Peoker 'Brother' AM/AOS and *P.* Perfection Is 'Chen' FCC/AOS, exhibited by Chen. It seems that more awards are given to plants using the harlequin type breeding every year. Perhaps the number of awards for harlequin orchids will surpass the number granted to the standard type of phalaenopsis in the future. The beautiful and refreshing arrays of colors and patterns of these hybrids continue to be enjoyed and treasured by all phalaenopsis lovers. Plenty of new breeding directions are being pursued that will hopefully lead to a much broader color range with harlequins to include bright oranges and various "sunset" and "desert" tones.

Doritaenopsis Chain Xen Diamond 'Celebration' FCC/AOS

Gallery of Harlequins

Hybrids are listed by the year in which they were registered to demonstrate changes and evolution over time.

1983

Phalaenopsis Golden Peoker 'BL' HCC/AOS
Origin: *Phalaenopsis* Misty Green × *Phalaenopsis* Liu Tuen-Shen
Originator: Brother Orchid Nursery
Registered by Brother Orchid Nursery

Phalaenopsis Golden Peoker 'Nan-Cho' AM/AOS
Origin: *Phalaenopsis* Misty Green × *Phalaenopsis* Liu Tuen-Shen
Originator: Brother Orchid Nursery
Registered by Brother Orchid Nursery

Phalaenopsis Golden Peoker 'BL' HCC/AOS

Phalaenopsis Golden Peoker 'Nan-Cho' AM/AOS. Photo by Allen Black.

Phalaenopsis Ever-Spring King 'Lee' JC/AOS. Photo by Allen Black.

Phalaenopsis Ever-Spring Light

Phalaenopsis Hiroshima Fantasy 'Beautiful Dreamer' HCC/AOS. Photo by Eric Goo.

Doritaenopsis Ever Spring Prince 'Plum Flower'

Doritaenopsis Ever Spring Pioneer 'Champion'. Photo by Charlie Kovac.

Phalaenopsis Carolina Bronze Meteor 'Lenette' HCC/AOS. Photo by Allen Black.

1992

Phalaenopsis Ever-Spring King 'Lee' JC/AOS
Origin: *Phalaenopsis* Chih Shang's Stripes × *Phalaenopsis* Golden Peoker
Originator: Ever Spring Orchid Nursery
Registered by Ever Spring Orchid Nursery

Phalaenopsis Ever-Spring Light
Origin: *Phalaenopsis* Ever-Spring Star × *Phalaenopsis* Golden Peoker
Originator: Ever Spring Orchid Nursery
Registered by Ever Spring Orchid Nursery

1996

Phalaenopsis Hiroshima Fantasy 'Beautiful Dreamer' HCC/AOS
Origin: *Phalaenopsis* Golden Peoker × *Phalaenopsis equestris* var. *alba*
Originator: M. Kobayashi
Registered by M. Kobayashi

1997

Doritaenopsis Ever Spring Pioneer 'Champion'
Origin: *Phalaenopsis* Golden Peoker × *Doritaenopsis* Happy Valentine
Originator: Ever Spring Orchid Nursery
Registered by Ever Spring Orchid Nursery

Doritaenopsis Ever Spring Prince 'Plum Flower'
Origin: *Phalaenopsis* Golden Peoker × *Doritaenopsis* Taisuco Beauty
Originator: Ever Spring Orchid Nursery
Registered by Ever Spring Orchid Nursery

Phalaenopsis Carolina Bronze Meteor 'Lenette' HCC/AOS
Origin: *Phalaenopsis* Golden Peoker × *Phalaenopsis* James Burton
Originator: ABC Orchid Corp.
Registered by Lenette

Doritaenopsis Fangtastic Roslynn Greenberg 'Raspberry Delight' HCC/AOS

Phalaenopsis Haur Jin Diamond 'Montclair' HCC/AOS

1999

Doritaenopsis Fangtastic Roslynn Greenberg 'Raspberry Delight' HCC/AOS
Origin: *Phalaenopsis* Golden Peoker × *Doritaenopsis* Montclair King
Originator: Norman's Orchids
Registered by Norman's Orchids

Phalaenopsis Haur Jin Diamond
Origin: *Phalaenopsis* Golden Peoker × *Phalaenopsis* Ching Her Buddha
Originator: Haur Jin Orchids
Registered by Ching Ann

Doritaenopsis I-Hsin Marks. Photo by John Doherty.

Phalaenopsis Brother Jungle Cat. Photo by Allen Black.

Phalaenopsis Haur Jin Diamond 'Montclair' HCC/AOS
Origin: *Phalaenopsis* Golden Peoker × *Phalaenopsis* Chin Her Buddha
Originator: Haur Jin Orchids
Registered by Ching Ann

2001

Doritaenopsis I-Hsin Marks
Origin: *Phalaenopsis* I-Hsin Sentra × *Doritaenopsis* Leopard Prince
Originator: Chien
Registered by Chien

Phalaenopsis Brother Jungle Cat
Origin: *Phalaenopsis* Brother Fancy × *Phalaenopsis* Brother Kaiser
Originator: Brother Orchid Nursery
Registered by Selles

Phalaenopsis Tzeng-Wen Sentra

Phalaenopsis Tzeng-Wen Sentra 'Jia-Ho' AM/AOS

Phalaenopsis Tzeng-Wen Sentra
Origin: *Phalaenopsis* Golden Peoker × *Phalaenopsis* New Sentra
Originator: Ching-Tien Wong
Registered by Ching-Tien Wong

Phalaenopsis Tzeng-Wen Sentra 'Jia-Ho' AM/AOS
Origin: *Phalaenopsis* Golden Peoker × *Phalaenopsis* New Sentra
Originator: Ching-Tien Wong
Registered by Ching-Tien Wong

Phalaenopsis Yu Pin Pearl 'Peacock'
Origin: *Phalaenopsis* Ever-Spring King × *Phalaenopsis* Musashino
Originator: N. I. Chang
Registered by N. I. Chang

2002

Doritaenopsis Chain Xen Diamond 'Celebration' FCC/AOS
Origin: *Phalaenopsis* Golden Peoker × *Doritaenopsis* Judy Valentine
Originator: Fu-Liang Huang
Registered by Fu-Liang Huang

Phalaenopsis Yu Pin Pearl 'Peacock'

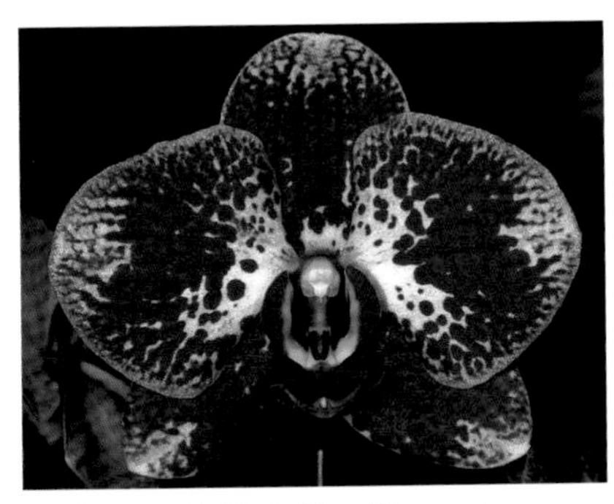

Doritaenopsis Chain Xen Diamond 'Celebration' FCC/AOS

Doritaenopsis Chain Xen Pearl 'Lucky Star'
Origin: *Doritaenopsis* Ching Hua Spring × *Doritaenopsis* Nobby's Pink Lady
Originator: Fu-Liang Huang
Registered by Fu-Liang Huang

Doritaenopsis Chain Xen Pearl 'Shih Hua'
Origin: *Doritaenopsis* Ching Hua Spring × *Doritaenopsis* Nobby's Pink Lady
Originator: Fu-Liang Huang
Registered by Fu-Liang Huang

Doritaenopsis Chain Xen Pearl 'Lucky Star'

Doritaenopsis Chain Xen Pearl 'Shih Hua'

Phalaenopsis Nobby's Shadowy 'Nobby'
Origin: *Phalaenopsis* Golden Peoker × *Phalaenopsis* Nobby's Fox
Originator: Nobby Orchids
Registered by Nobby Orchids

Phalaenopsis Oriental Fairy 'Montclair'
Origin: *Phalaenopsis* Ever-Spring Light × *Phalaenopsis* Ho's French Fantasia
Originator: Oriental Orchids
Registered by Oriental Orchids

Phalaenopsis Nobby's Shadowy 'Nobby'

Phalaenopsis Oriental Fairy 'Montclair'

Phalaenopsis Shin Yi Diamond

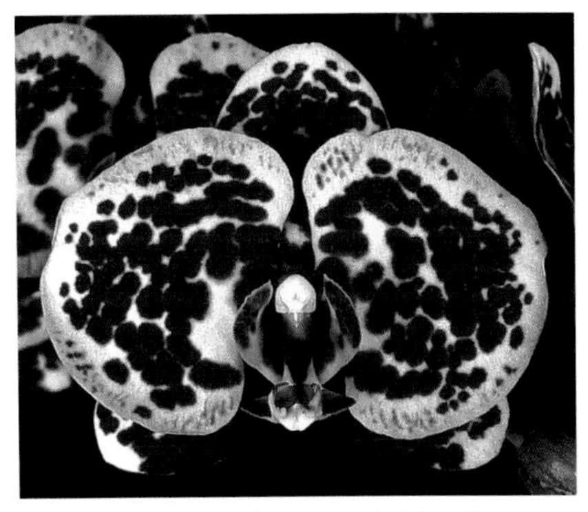

Phalaenopsis So Cha Gem 'Chin Jih' HCC/AOS. Photo by Eric Goo.

Phalaenopsis Shin Yi Diamond
Origin: *Phalaenopsis* Haur Jin Diamond × *Phalaenopsis* Chin Her Buddha
Originator: Sogo Team Co.
Registered by Sogo Team Co.

Phalaenopsis So Cha Gem 'Chin Jih' HCC/AOS
Origin: *Phalaenopsis* Ever-Spring King × *Phalaenopsis* Sogo Mini Dog
Originator: Ching Ann
Registered by Ching Ann

Phalaenopsis Taiwan Glory. Photo by Charlie Kovac.

Phalaenopsis Taiwan Glory
Origin: *Phalaenopsis* Ever-Spring King × *Phalaenopsis* Brother Danseuse
Originator: Orchis Flor.
Registered by Orchis Flor.

2003

Doritaenopsis Acker's Sweetie 'Dragon Tree Maple' SM/TOGA
Origin: *Phalaenopsis* Ho's French Fantasia × *Doritaenopsis* Taisuco Candystripe
Originator: Pi-Chiang Wang
Registered by Orchids by Acker's

Doritaenopsis I-Hsin Waltz 'Zephyrus'
Origin: *Doritaenopsis* I-Hsin Black Jack × *Doritaenopsis* Sinica Sunday
Originator: W. T. Chien
Registered by W. T. Chien

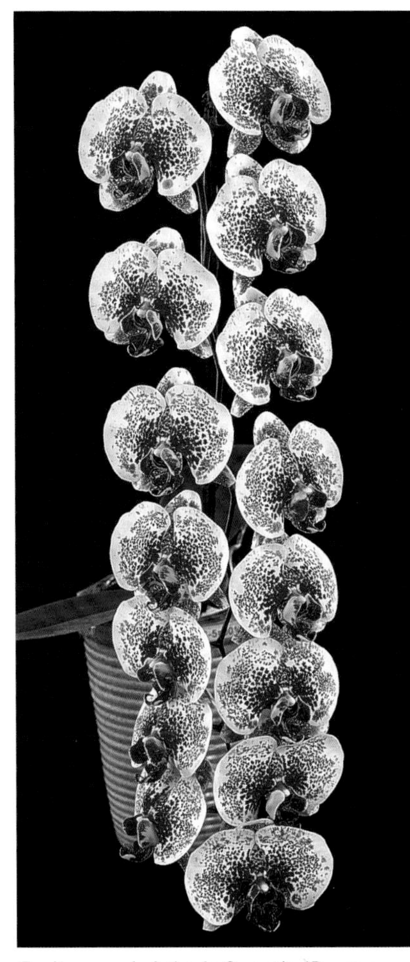

Doritaenopsis Acker's Sweetie 'Dragon Tree Maple' SM/TOGA. Photo by Marshall Ku.

Doritaenopsis I-Hsin Waltz 'Zephyrus'. Photo by John Doherty.

Phalaenopsis Brother Redland Spots

Phalaenopsis Sunrise Red Peoker. Photo by Allen Black.

Doritaenopsis Sogo Melody

Phalaenopsis Sunrise Red Peoker, peloric form. Photo by Allen Black.

Doritaenopsis Hurricane Katrina. Photo by Allen Black.

Doritaenopsis Joy Angel Voice. Photo by Charlie Kovac.

Phalaenopsis Brother Redland Spots
Origin: *Phalaenopsis* Golden Peoker × *Phalaenopsis* Brother Fancy
Originator: Brother Orchid Nursery
Registered by R. F. Orchids

Phalaenopsis Sunrise Red Peoker
Origin: *Phalaenopsis* Golden Peoker × *Phalaenopsis* Kuntrarti Rarashati
Originator: Sunrise Biotech
Registered by Sunrise Biotech

2004

Doritaenopsis Joy Angel Voice
Origin: *Doritaenopsis* Joy Philippine Davis × *Doritaenopsis* Chain Xen Pearl
Originator: J. Wu
Registered by J. Wu

2005

Doritaenopsis Sogo Melody
Origin: *Doritaenopsis* Chain Xen Pearl × *Phalaenopsis* Yu Pin Pearl
Originator: Sogo Team Co.
Registered by Sogo Team Co.

2006

Doritaenopsis Hurricane Katrina
Origin: *Doritaenopsis* Ever Spring Prince × *Doritaenopsis* Happy King
Originator: Allen Black
Registered by Allen Black

Doritaenopsis Taiwan Red Cat. Photo by Charlie Kovac.

Phalaenopsis I-Hsin Golden Sun 'IS186'. Photo by Marshall Ku.

Doritaenopsis Ching Hua Spring × *Doritaenopsis* Leopard Prince. Photo by John Doherty.

Phalaenopsis Diamond Beauty × *Phalaenopsis* Chin Ye Diamond. Photo by Charlie Kovac.

Doritaenopsis Taiwan Red Cat
Origin: *Doritaenopsis* Taiwan Smith × *Doritaenopsis* Kun-Cheng
Originator: Orchis Flor.
Registered by Orchis Flor.

Phalaenopsis I-Hsin Golden Sun 'IS186'
Origin: *Phalaenopsis* Taisuco Glory × *Phalaenopsis* Salu Peoker
Originator: I-Hsin Orchids
Registered by W. T. Chien

Unregistered

Unnamed *Doritaenopsis*
Origin: *Doritaenopsis* Ching Hua Spring × *Doritaenopsis* Leopard Prince
Originator: Unknown

Unnamed *Phalaenopsis*
Origin: *Phalaenopsis* Diamond Beauty × *Phalaenopsis* Chin Ye Diamond
Originator: Unknown

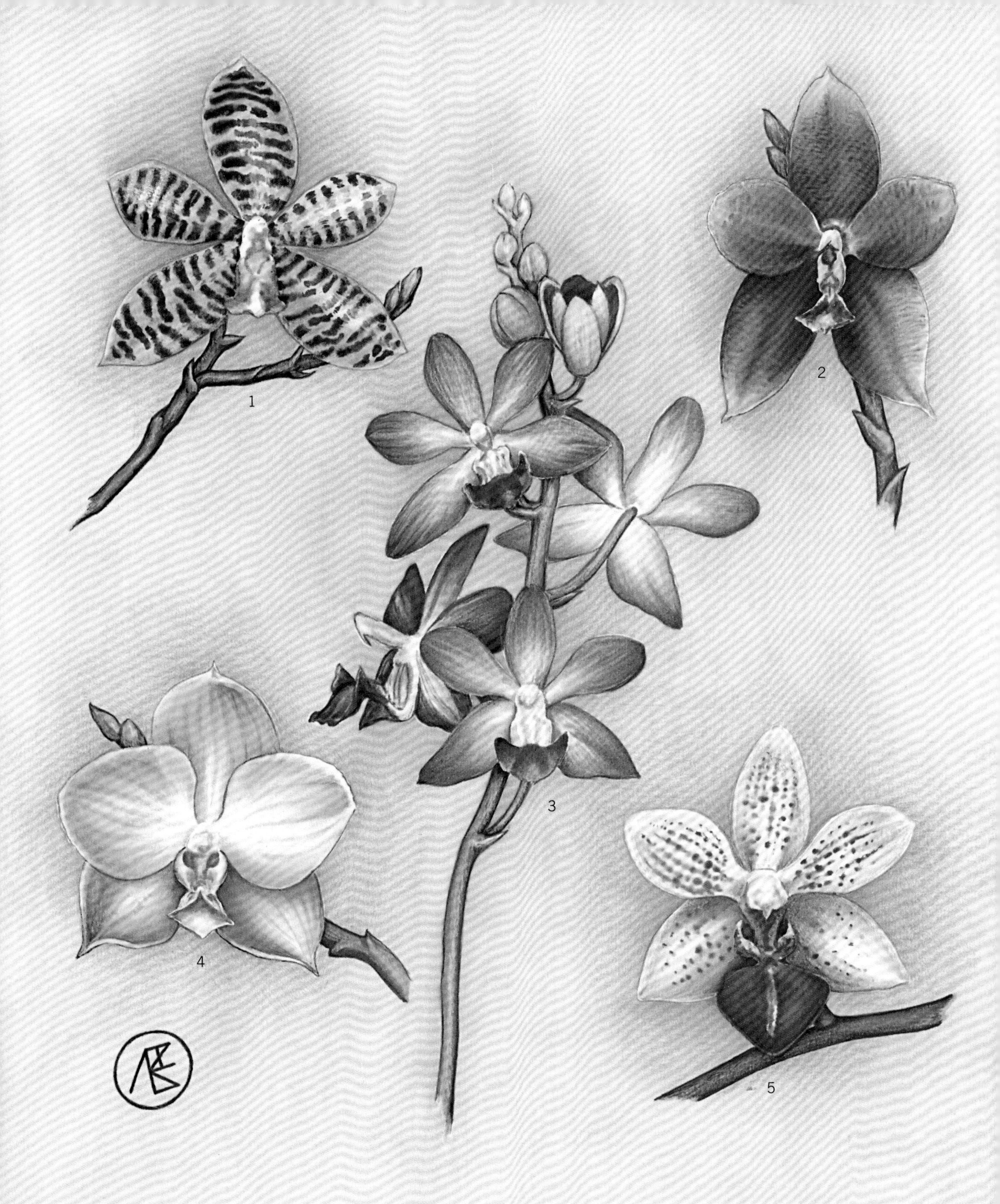

1
2
3
4
5

Chapter 7

Novelties, Multifloras, and Miniatures

Novelty Hybrids

Defining a novelty phalaenopsis can be a challenging task, because so much variety is possible within the group. A novelty phalaenopsis could be defined as "any phalaenopsis that is not a standard." In general, novelties have fewer and smaller flowers of usually quite heavy substance, in colors subtle to bright. Many are compact growers and are not as "complex" as the standard hybrids—that is, novelties are often primary hybrids or at least not far removed from the species. Many of the fragrant phalaenopsis belong to the novelty group, and their scent is one of the characteristics that contributes to their popularity. This is the most diverse category of phalaenopsis containing the widest range of colors and flower types.

Although they are sometimes not as grand as the standard hybrids in terms of flower size, novelties more than make up for it with their charming flowers on compact plants. They are ideal for growing under lights or on a windowsill. Because of their many endearing qualities, novelties have a special place in my collection and are among my favorites.

The species *P. violacea* and *P. bellina* have long been favorite parents in the production of novelties. They add flower substance, good color, and frequently fragrance to their offspring. Several successful crosses have been made with these species, but two that stand out are *P.* Luedde-violacea (*P. lueddemanniana* × *P. violacea*), registered in 1895, and *P.* Princess Kaiulani (*P. violacea* × *P. amboinensis*), registered in 1961. Today these hybrids are still being remade with some of the newer superior forms of the species. Some of the *P. bellina* hybrids include *P.* Valentinii (*P. cornu-cervi* × *P. violacea*), registered in 1959; *P.* Penang Girl (*P. violacea* × *P. venosa*), originated and registered by Ooi Leng Sun in 1984; *P.* Buena Jewel (*P. violacea* × *P.* Gelblieber),

Opposite: Novelty, multiflora, and miniature phalaenopsis: 1. mini hybrid, yellow with burgundy bars; 2. *Phalaenopsis* Penang Girl (*P. violacea* × *P. venosa*); 3. *Doritaenopsis* Kenneth Schubert (*Doritis pulcherrima* × *P. violacea*); 4. green hybrid; 5. *Phalaenopsis* Mini Mark (*P.* Micro Nova × *P. philippinensis*). Paintings by Liena Dieck.

Phalaenopsis Valentinii

originated by Barry Cohen and registered by N. LeJeune in 1992; and an unnamed and unregistered grex, *P.* 'Sweetheart' (*P. violacea* × *P.* Jungo Viotris). Other species that have also played key roles in developing these hybrids are *P. lindenii*, *P. mannii*, *P. mariae*, *P. pulchra*, *P. stuartiana*, and *P. sumatrana*.

Most early breeding for phalaenopsis produced hybrids that we could today call novelties since they were primary or close to primary hybrids and were developed to expand the color range. Among the premier orchid breeders in the world in the late 1800s was the firm Messrs. J. Veitch and Sons in England. This company produced an impressive array of *Phalaenopsis* hybrids using various species as parents. Some of their best known hybrids are listed in the accompanying table.

Phalaenopsis Penang Girl

Phalaenopsis 'Sweetheart'

Another pioneer in phalaenopsis breeding was Hans Burgeff, director of the University of Würzburg's botanical garden in Würzburg, Germany. He did a substantial amount of novelty phalaenopsis breeding in the mid-1950s (making 1000 crosses by 1958) but registered only a few of them. One of his best-known and highly regarded hybrids was *P.* Star of Rio (*P.* Bataan × *P. lueddemanniana*) that he named, but it was registered by Morgenstern in 1956. This grex has proved valuable as a parent and is found in the background of many hybrids.

Later additional novelty hybrids, registered in the 1950s to early 1970s, were produced by a cast of many

***Phalaenopsis* hybrids registered by Messrs. J. Veitch and Sons**

YEAR	HYBRID NAME	ORIGIN
1886	Harriettiae	*P. amabilis* × *P. violacea*
	Intermedia	*P. aphrodite* × *P. equestris*
1887	John Seden	*P. amabilis* × *P. lueddemannian*
	F. I. Ames	*P. amabilis* × *P. Intermedia*
	Leda	*P. amabilis* × *P. stuartiana*
1892	Artemis	*P. amabilis* × *P. equestris*
1895	Luedde-violacea	*P. lueddemanniana* × *P. violacea*
1896	Ariadne	*P. aphrodite* × *P. stuartiana*
	Cassandra	*P. equestris* × *P. stuartiana*
1897	Hebe	*P. equestris* × *P. sanderiana*
1898	Stuartiano-Mannii	*P. mannii* × *P. stuartiana*
1899	Hermione	*P. lueddemanniana* × *P. stuartiana*
	Mrs. J. H. Veitch	*P. lueddemanniana* × *P. sanderiana*
1900	Hymen	*P. lueddemanniana* × *P. mannii*

breeders including Amado Vasquez, Charles Beard, E. Iwanaga, F. Millington, Fields Orchids, Frederick Thornton, Gemstone, Henry Wallbrunn, Herb Hager, Hugo Freed, John Ewing, L. Kuhn, Lewis Vaughn, Mrs. Lester McCoy, Shaffer's Orchids, and Woodlawn. Some of their contributions are listed in the accompanying table.

Novelty *Phalaenopsis* hybrids registered in the late 1950s to early 1970s

YEAR	NAME	ORIGIN	BREEDER
1958	Golden Chief	*P.* Chieftain × *P. mannii*	Lewis Vaughn
1961	Doc Charles	*P. sanderiana* × *P. amboinensis*	J. H. Miller
1962	Enchantment	*P.* Summit Snow × *P. lueddemanniana*	Lewis Vaughn
	Lowana Goldlip	*P.* Grace Palm × *P. stuartiana*	Hugo Freed (Vasquez)
1963	Hawaiian Sunshine	*P.* Snowbird × *P. lueddemanniana*	Mrs. Lester McCoy
	Samba	*P.* Star of Rio × *P. amboinensis*	Gemstone
1964	Golden Sands	*P.* Fenton Davis Avant × *P. lueddemanniana*	Fields Orchids
1965	*Doritaenopsis* Bonita	*P. stuartiana* × *Doritis buyssoniana*	Lewis Vaughn
	Ambomanniana	*P. amboinensis* × *P. lueddemanniana*	Frederick Thornton
	Ambotrana	*P. sumatrana* × *P. amboinensis*	Frederick Thornton
	Janet Kuhn	*P.* Dos Pueblos × *P. fuscata*	Charles Beard
	Mambo	*P. amboinensis* × *P. mannii*	Frederick Thornton
	Tyler Carlson	*P.* Gladys Read × *P. lueddemanniana*	Shaffer's Orchids
1966	Helen Kuhn	*P.* Zada × *P. fuscata*	L. Kuhn
	Mannicata	*P. mannii* × *P. fuscata*	L. Kuhn
1967	Dos-Ambo	*P.* Dos Pueblos × *P. amboinensis*	E. Iwanaga
1968	Gold Nugget	*P.* Big Chief × *P. mannii*	Charles Beard
1969	Amber Sands	*P.* Susan Merkel × *P. fasciata*	Charles Beard
	Milstead	*P.* Thousand Oaks × *P. lueddemanniana*	F. Millington
	Renanthopsis Mildred Jameson	*Renanthera monachica* × *P. stuartiana*	Henry Wallbrunn
	Shapely Doll	*P.* Pink Symphony × *P. lueddemanniana*	Woodlawn
1970	Tuffy	*P.* Lowana Goldlip × *P. amboinensis*	Hugo Freed (Vasquez)
1971	Violet Charm	*P. violacea* × *P. mariae*	Hugo Freed (Vasquez)

Phalaenopsis gigantea hybrids

Phalaenopsis gigantea are anything but petite plants. In fact, because of the size of their leaves, which are from 2 to 3 ft. (60 to 90 cm) long, they were rarely thought to be a viable hybridizing choice as the results were believed to be unmanageable, large plants. Fortunately, curious breeders found out that the size of these plants could be tamed in its hybrids and that its flowers—large, brightly spotted, and leathery, with a citruslike fragrance—made it a parent worth considering.

Several grexes stand out in this group, include a few primary hybrids such as *P.* Mok Choi Yew (*P. gigantea* × *P. violacea*), originated and registered by C. Y. Mok in 1968; *P.* Joey (*P. gigantea* × *P. lueddemanniana*), originated by Wallbrunn and registered in 1973 by Fort Caroline's; *P.* David Lim (*P. amboinensis* × *P. gigantea*), originated by David Lim and registered by Y. Alsagoff

Preventing flowers from becoming trapped under leaves

Because novelty phalaenopsis have short inflorescences, or flowering spikes, their flowers can become trapped under their leaves. You can prevent this from happening to show off the flowers to their best advantage. With early attention and action, you can train the inflorescence so that the buds can develop above the leaves and the flowers are held just above the foliage.

In the Northern Hemisphere, most spiking phalaenopsis are standard types with long, arching inflorescences. However, older, mature novelty phalaenopsis can develop new buds that flower any time of the year. Detecting the young inflorescence early and taking appropriate action quickly are the keys to training the spike so that its flowers will show in the best possible way.

A new spike is easier to adjust than an old spike, because the new growth is more flexible (less stiff) than older spikes. To adjust a new spike that is growing under a leaf, carefully bend the spike around the edge of the leaf to allow it to emerge.

Working with the old spike is more difficult because it is less supple. Carefully fold the edge of the leaf just above the old spike behind the old growth, and then repeat this step with remaining leaves until the old spike is above all the leaves.

The spikes will develop new buds for flowering within the next two months. It is best to keep the plant in the same growing location while these buds develop to help the buds avoid changing orientation.

The young flower spike on the right is trapped under the leaf. Photo by Peter Lin.

An old spike (at left) and the new flower spike (at right). Photo by Peter Lin.

in 1974; and *P.* Jade Gold (*P. gigantea* × *P. venosa*), originated and registered by Lim in 1984.

Other more complex hybrids with *P. gigantea* in their background include *P.* Liu Tuen-Shen (*P. gigantea* × *P.* Golden Sands), originated and registered by Irene Dobkin in 1979; *P.* Fortune Buddha (*P.* Golden Buddha × *P.* Liu Tuen-Shen), originated and registered by Brother Orchid Nursery in 1983; *P.* Razzmatazz (*P.* Golden Gift × *P.* Mok Choi Yew), originated and registered by H. P. Norton in 1991; *P.* Orchidview Headliner (*P.* Mok Choi Yew × *P.* Hausermann's Goldcup), bred and registered by Norton in 1992; *P.* Brother Buddha (*P.* Fortune Buddha × *P.* Brother Angel), originated and registered by Brother Orchid Nursery in 1992; *P.* Formosa San Fan (*P.* Misty Green × *P.* Mok Choi Yew), originated and registered by Lin Ming Kung in 1993; and *P.* Brother Pirate King (*P.* Fortune Buddha × *P.* Brother Purple), originated and registered in 1998 by Brother Orchid Nursery. Some of these later hybrids are pushing the limits of what might be called "novel-

Phalaenopsis Formosa San Fan

Phalaenopsis Perfection Is 'Chen' FCC/AOS

ties," as their flower size and number are starting to approach standard phalaenopsis.

Probably the most famous hybrid with *P. gigantea* in its background is *P.* Golden Peoker (*P.* Misty Green × *P.* Liu Tuen-Shen), originated and registered by Brother Orchid Nursery in 1983. This hybrid is the backbone of harlequin hybrids and has produced many exceptional offspring, including one of my favorites, *P.* Perfection Is 'Chen' FCC/AOS (*P.* Golden Peoker × *P.* Black Eagle), registered by H. Ginsberg in 1999. Its waxy, long-lasting, heavily barred flowers are scented with a sweet citrus fragrance that can permeate an entire room.

Multiflora Hybrids

This group of compact-growing phalaenopsis, called multifloras, minis, miniatures, or pixies, have small flowers of less that 3 in. (7.5 cm) in width that are borne in profusion on branched inflorescences. These charming qualities make multifloras perfect choices for indoor windowsills or light gardens.

Most phalaenopsis hybridizing efforts of yesteryear and today have focused on increasing the flower size, which is frequently accompanied by larger plant size. Some phalaenopsis breeders, however, chose a different path, and that is where multiflora phalaenopsis come in. Years ago, when breeders had fewer large-flowered hybrids from which to choose, some of the earliest multifloras were, by necessity, crosses with some of the smaller flowered species. The breeder most often credited as the promoter, contemporary pioneer, and prime contributor to modern-day multiflora hybrids is Herb Hager, whose name appears frequently in any account of multiflora development.

Phalaenopsis equestris stands out as the species most often used for producing multifloras. In fact, more than 90 percent of all multiflora hybrids have *P. equestris* in their background, which amounts to almost 500 first-generation hybrids registered to date. Varieties of the species come in various shades of pink as well as the rarer white form. It is most valuable as a parent because of its diverse flower colors, diminutive plant habit, and ability to produce many flowers, sometimes on branched inflorescences. It can also pass on red lips, striping, and spotting. This species commonly produces peloric flowers in its offspring, which can be a plus or a minus, depending on the breeder's preferences. *Phalaenopsis equestris* readily produces keikis, or plantlets, so propagation is easy.

On the negative side, its flowers are usually relatively small, at 1 in. (2.5 cm) or so, open sequentially instead of all at once, are frequently crowded and presented in a whorl on its inflorescence instead of the more desired shingle effect, and are rarely very flat. A more recent clone, *P. equestris* 'Riverbend' AM/AOS, was a breakthrough; its strong flower color, good size (larger than 1 in.), and heavy substance are attributed to the fact that it is a tetraploid. It has become the clone of choice for many breeders. Other tetraploids of this species also hold promise for producing larger flowers with heavier substance.

Phalaenopsis equestris has a long history as a productive parent. *Phalaenopsis* Intermedia (*P. aphrodite* × *P. equestris*) was one of the earliest *Phalaenopsis* hybrids made by Veitch in 1886. A few other important primary hybrids of this species are *P.* Veitchiana (*P. equestris* × *P. schilleriana*), registered in 1872; *Doritaenopsis* Purple Gem (*Doritis pulcherrima* × *P. equestris*), registered by E. Iwanaga in 1963; and *P.* Kuntrarti Rarashati (*P. equestris* × *P. venosa*), registered by A. Kolopaking in 1986.

Doritaenopsis Purple Gem

Some newer hybrids using *P. equestris* are *P.* Little Steve (*P.* Steven Ai × *P. equestris*), introduced and registered by R. Takase in 1984, and *P.* Berries 'n Cream (*P.* Breckinridge Snow × *P. equestris*), developed and registered by Riverbend in 1987. Hawaiian breeder Ben Kodama developed an entire Hawaiian Series of various hybrids in the late 1980s to early 1990s that used *P. equestris* as a parent. *Phalaenopsis* Little Richard (*P.* Rich's Pride × *P. equestris*) was developed by Takase in 1990; *P.* Zuma's Pixie (*P.* Carmela's Pixie × *P. equestris*) was introduced and registered by Zuma Canyon in 1992; and Herb Hager registered *P.* Joyful (*P.* Gladrose × *P. equestris*) in 1992. In 1995, H. P. Norton introduced *P.* Tricki Woo (*P.* Mini Mark × *P. equestris*).

In 1998, Paphanatics registered its hybrid *P.* Small Steps (*P.* Orange Blaze × *P. equestris*). To produce waxy-flowered multifloras, *P. equestris* has been crossed onto some of the more modern hybrids to produce *P.* Brother Candytuft (*P.* Brother Grape × *P. equestris*). To this day, breeders still turn to superior clones of *P. equestris* to produce hybrids that are multifloras.

Another oldie but goodie is *P.* Cassandra (*P. equestris* × *P. stuartiana*), registered in 1896 by Veitch. This

Phalaenopsis Kuntrarti Rarashati 'Bunker Hill'. Photo by Allen Black.

Phalaenopsis Zuma's Pixie 'Taida Little Cutie'. Photo by Marshall Ku.

classic cross has been and still is an important contributor to the development of multifloras. Its highly desirable characteristic of multi-branching inflorescences is usually passed on to its offspring. One of its most successful progeny is *P.* Timothy Christopher (*P.* Cassandra × *P. amabilis*), developed and registered by J. Sandrik in 1982. A few other stars include *P.* Little Netsuke (*P.* Snow Leopard × *P.* Cassandra), developed and registered by E. Carlson in 1987; *P.* Carmela's Pixie (*P.* Terilyn Fujitake × *P.* Cassandra), introduced and registered by Carmela in 1990; *P.* Brother Sandra (*P.* Brother Yew × *P.* Cassandra), introduced and registered by Brother Orchids in 1993; and *P.* Sogo Lit-Angel (*P.* Cassandra × *P.* Su's Red Lip), developed and registered by Sogo in 1995.

Early pink-striped minis include *P.* Pink Profusion (*P.* Pink Mist × *P.* Marmouset), introduced and registered by H. D. Wright in 1960, and *P.* Peppermint (*P. lindenii* × *P.* Pink Profusion), introduced and registered by Hugo Freed in 1964. *Phalaenopsis* Peppermint led to *P.* Zuma Chorus (*P.* Music × *P.* Peppermint), introduced and registered by Zuma Canyon in 1982. Again using the favorite *P.* Cassandra as a parent, *P.* Little Hal (*P.* Cassandra × *P.* Peppermint) was produced by Herb Hager and registered by W. Sanders in 1978. Cassandra's contributions continue with *P.* Rainbow Chip (*P.* Cassandra × *P. equestris*), registered by R. Barstow in 1985, and *P.* Be Glad (*P.* Swiss Miss × *P.* Cassandra), a highly successful cross made by Hager and registered by him in 1978. This hybrid served as an important step in the development of a plethora of improved hybrid multifloras by contributing round flowers of good size and substance and fine presentation. One outstanding offspring was *P.* Be Tris (*P.* Be Glad × *P. equestris*), developed and introduced by Krull-Smith in 1989. A slightly improved version of this is *P.* Sogo Twinkle 'Stars' HCC/AOS (*P.* Be Tris × *P.* Sogo Tris), bred by the Sogo Team and registered by them in 1999. *Phalaenopsis* Ho's Amaglad (*P.* Be Glad × *P. amabilis*) was introduced and registered by Tin-Fan Ho in 1990. Hager contributed other hybrids, including *P.* Glad Melinda (*P.* Be Glad × *P.* Melinda Nan) in 1985 and *P.* Gladrose (*P.* Melinda Rose × *P.* Glad Melinda) in 1988. *Phalaenopsis* Glad Dawn (*P.* Be Glad × *P.* Dawn Treader) was bred and registered by Gold Country in 1997.

Phalaenopsis Sogo Twinkle 'Stars' HCC/AOS

The importance of *Phalaenopsis pulcherrima* in multiflora breeding

Another species that has played a key role in the development of multifloras is *P. pulcherrima*, still commonly known in the trade as *Doritis pulcherrima*. This species contributes an upright inflorescence, brilliant cerise and dark pink flowers, good flower count, and ease of propagation, because it readily forms basal keikis. However, it also contributes a few undesirable characteristics, including less than flat and sequential flowers, very long inflorescences, and average to poor flower substance.

One of the earliest successful hybrids from *P. pulcherrima* is *Doritaenopsis* Purple Gem (*Doritis pulcher-*

Doritaenopsis Siam Treasure

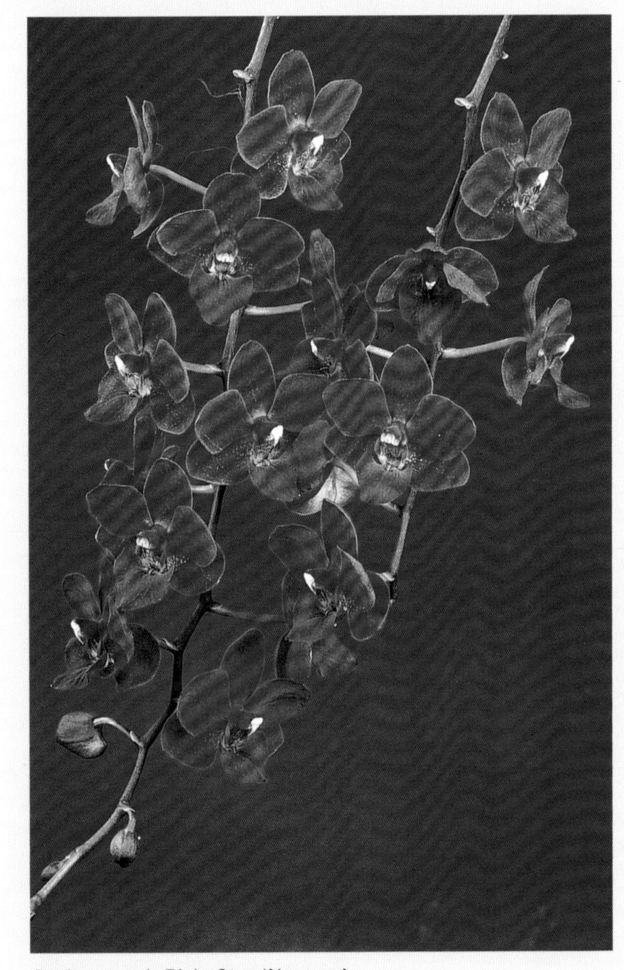

Doritaenopsis Pixie Star 'Norman'

Doritaenopsis Musick Surprise

rima × *P. equestris*). The plants of this cross are generally compact, and some clones have proven to be attractive as well. Recently, other superior hybrids have been created using this species and result in better flower form, including *Doritaenopsis* Fire Cracker (*D.* Red Coral × *Doritis pulcherrima*), developed and registered by Charles Beard in 1966; *Doritaenopsis* Jim (*Doritis pulcherrima* × *P. venosa*), developed and introduced by H. P. Norton in 1984; one of my personal favorites, *Doritaenopsis* Pixie Star (*Doritis pulcherrima* × *P.* Joyful), developed by Mark Pendleton and registered by Orchid Zone in 1997; and *Doritaenopsis* Joy Green Bee (*Doritis pulcherrima* × *P.* Timothy Christopher), developed and registered by J. Wu in 2004.

Following a line of breeding to produce small plants with petite flowers are hybrids such as *P.* Partris (*P. equestris* × *P. parishii*), developed and registered by Fred Thornton in 1965. Quite a bit later, another mini, *Doritaenopsis* Siam Treasure (*P. lowii* × *Doritis pulcherrima*), was originated by T. Lusup-anan and registered by S. Wannakrairoj in 1997. Using a newer species, *P. chibae*, breeders Fred and Mary Kaufmann have produced some charming small plants including *P.* Fantasy Musick (*P.* Micro Nova × *P. equestris*), registered in 2002, followed by *Doritaenopsis* Musick Surprise (*Doritis pulcherrima* × *P. chibae*), registered in 2003. An unusual and unique intergeneric cross, *Haraenopsis* Nanzhi Pink (*Phalaenopsis* Wedding Promenade × *Haraella retrocalla*), was developed by X. Ye and registered by A. Chen in 2005. This soft pink charmer breaks interesting new ground in mini breeding.

Other intergeneric crosses using *P. pulcherrima* as parent include hybrids *Beardara* Henry Wallbrunn (*Asconopsis* Irene Dobkin × *Doritis pulcherrima*), originated by Henry Wallbrunn and registered by Fort Caroline's in 1978, and *Doritaenopsis* Pico Lady Ruby (*Doritis pulcherrima* × *P.* Kuntrarti Rarashati), registered by Brother Orchid Nursery in 1995.

Beardara Henry Wallbrunn

Doritaenopsis Pico Lady Ruby 'Wickford' HCC/AOS

Most of the multifloras mentioned so far are white or various shades of pink. Some newer hybrids expand the color spectrum, including *P.* Gold Tris (*P.* Taipei Gold × *P. equestris*), registered by Brother in 1993, with its plethora of yellow flowers; *P.* Olympia's Golden Ember (*P.* Miniflash × *P. venosa*), with its stunning 2 in. (5 cm) yellow-striped red flowers, developed and registered by Bill Tippit in 1996; golden yellow *P.* Little Emperor (*P.* Sogo Lit-Angel × *P.* Golden Amboin), developed by Lee Shih Hua and registered by Norman's Orchids in 1999; *P.* Tying Shin Cupid (*P.* Sogo Lawrence × *P.* Kuntrarti Rarashati), produced and registered by Kuo Liang Hung in 2004, with gorgeous orange flowers of excellent shape and substance; and *Doritaenopsis* Tying Shin Champion (*D.* Tzu Chiang Orange × *P.* Kuntrarti Rarashati), whose clone 'Golden Amber' won the Bronze Medal at the 2006 Taiwan International Orchid Show.

The future of multifloras

Multifloras are receiving a new burst of interest from phalaenopsis breeders and commercial growers. Smaller, more compact plants with short blooming spikes seem to fit well with the space constraints of windowsill gardeners and home decorators. Europeans and Japanese orchid lovers are especially interested in these petite beauties. Sogo Team breeders worked with a European marketing group, Neon, to develop and introduce a mini phalaenopsis called Little Lady that blooms well in a 2¼ in. (5.5 cm) pot. A newer mini from Sogo, Table Dancer, blooms in a 3½ in. (9 cm) pot and produces a 4 to 12 in. (10 to 30 cm) inflorescence with flowers that last two months. Unfortunately for the North American market, this series may not be widely accepted because of its suggestive name.

Miniature Harlequins

Diminutive forms of harlequin hybrids are being developed in addition to the standard forms discussed in chapter 6. White hybrids include *P.* Hiroshima Fantasy (*P.* Golden Peoker × *P. equestris*), developed by Kobayashi and registered by him in 1996; *P.* Sogo Lovely (*P.* Timothy Christopher × *P.* Golden Peoker), developed and registered by Sogo in 2003; and *Doritaenopsis* Happy Helo (*P.* Timothy Christopher × *D.* Happy Ufo), developed and registered by Kun-Te Fang in 2004.

Doritaenopsis Taisuco Micky

Yellow mini harlequins include *D.* Chiada Gloria (*D.* Little Gem Stripes × *P.* Sunrise Red Peoker) and *P.* Chiada Ziv (*P.* Sogo Lisa × *P.* Sunrise Red Peoker), both developed and registered by National Chaiyi University in 2005.

Harlequins with dark pink flower bases include hybrids with *P. pulcherrima* (*Doritis pulcherrima*) in their background, such as *D.* Taisuco Micky (*P.* Golden Peoker × *D. pulcherrima*), developed and registered by Taiwan Sugar in 2000, and *D.* Sogo Chabstic (*P.* Golden Peoker × *D.* Anna-Larati Soekardi), bred and registered by Sogo in 2003.

Blue Hybrids

Blue is a desirable color for all flowers, including orchids. In the article "A Scientific Approach to Breeding Blue Orchids," (2005) Robert J. Griesbach presents a cogent, albeit complex, explanation of how blue pigments are formed in orchid flowers. The truth is that most of the contributions of "new" plants to horticulture, including those with color breakthroughs, have

Phalaenopsis violacea 'Blue Chip'

come from chance, and this has certainly been true in the orchid world. Although breeders take care in selecting the most promising parents, luck plays a major part in creating a winner.

Katherine Norton, wife of H. P. Norton, phalaenopsis breeder and owner of Orchidview nursery, provides an interesting account of the development of a blue phalaenopsis in an article entitled "Birth of the Blues" (from http://orchidview.com/Birth_of_the_Blues.htm). It is reproduced here with permission.

During a warm summer month in the early 1980s Michael Ooi toured the Eastern United States. Michael is from Malaysia and well known to most orchid fanciers. He had started his tour with a stop at the American Orchid Society Headquarters in Cambridge, Mass., and was working his way to Florida when he stopped by St. George, SC, to visit Jemmco Orchids.

Michael Osborne, a partner of Jemmco, was an old friend of Ooi's who had visited the Ooi orchid range in Buttersworth, Malaysia, frequently. The two young men had become fast friends.

Ooi had determined that the late Dr. Gavino Roto of Crestwood Orchids in Signal, Tenn., was a must on his list of interesting orchid growers who warranted a visit. The two young Michaels invited H. P. Norton, who had begun growing orchids only three years previously, to go on the trip. Little did Osborne, Ooi and H. P. realize as they set out on the trip that it would change the *Phal. violacea* world forever.

A special gift

The three drove from St. George to Atlanta and up to Chattanooga where they were fortunate enough to visit with Dr. Roto. Much would happen before they set out across the Smoky Mountains to Asheville, NC, and back to Charleston.

Phalaenopsis hybridizing was the main conversation for the four-day trip. Osborne had a multifaceted hybridizing program since Jemmco grew everything from Cattleyas for the cut flower market to the finest *Phalaenopsis* and *Paphiopedilum* compots being offered for sale at that time. Ooi lived in the heart of the region that is home to many *Phalaenopsis* species, therefore his knowledge of species was unparalleled.

During the trip H. P. explained that his goal was to breed large yellow phalaenopsis that flowered like standard white phalaelnopsis rather than the typical yellow novelties of the time, which had small yellow flowers with spots and bars and bloomed on short inflorescences. He claimed to have some like that in flasks—which was the wake up call for Ooi.

Half-joking, half-serious, Ooi kept asking H. P., "What are you going to give me to remember you by?" At the end of the week when Michael was departing, H. P. handed him a little four-ounce germination flask literally full of protocorms of one of his first yellow crosses.

About a month later, H. P. received a package from Malaysia containing 25 *Phal. violacea* (Borneo), which are now *Phal. bellina*, and 25 *Phal. violacea* (Malayan). It was impossible at that time to envision what this gift would mean to the world of *Phal. violacea*.

After flowering a majority of the *Phal. violacea* plants, the two best clones were chosen in 1982 to establish a long series of inbreeding. The best progeny were selected from each subsequent cross and used as the parents for the next grex. After more than eight successive crosses, with each subsequent cross producing darker magenta flowers than the previous grex, a startling breakthrough came in a cross made in 1996.

They couldn't believe their eyes

Flasks of 50 plants each of the now-famous N9670 *Phal. violacea* ('#1' and 'Harvey') were offered for sale in the Orchidview catalog for $75 and many flasks were taken to the IPA Symposium in Coral Gables, Florida. Susan and Todd of Miller's Tropicals of Miami bought one of the flasks. Later he told the Nortons that he thought at the time he should not spend that much on a violacea flask.

Miller's money was well spent, however, as he flowered the first *Phal. violacea* var. 'Indigo' from the flask. Miller said he could not believe his eyes when he saw the flower. He sent a digital photo of the flower to the Nortons, who had the same reaction. Subsequently, the Miller's flowered three 'Indigos' from the flask.

The cross has produced 25 blue *Phal. violaceas* thus far. There are at least 100 unbloomed seedlings from that 1996 cross remaining. When the Millers called with the good 'blue news' Norton went to his lab and replated every green dot in the only remaining mother flask.

Ken Avant in Kingston Springs, Tenn., bought a flask at a later IPA Symposium and flowered his first 'Indigo' in 2001. Being the gracious gentleman that he is, he sent pollen from 'Ken's #2' to Orchidview because the Nortons still had flowered only standard magenta *Phal. violaceas*. The pollen was used to make N0154 *Phal. violacea* 'Royalty' × 'Ken's Blue'.

The first flower from the N0154 cross surely has that 'WOW' factor. Cameras refuse to—or, maybe, just cannot—capture the Royal Purple color of the flowers. There is such fully saturated deep color that the green tips usually seen on the petals and sepals are not obvious. Even after mentioning all these attributes, we are saving the best for last—the iridescence. It shows so beautifully in the greenhouse light and is even more sparkling when taken outdoors into filtered sunlight.

Finally in September 2001 *Phal. violacea* 'Gulfstream Blue', the first 'Indigo' for Orchidview, opened on Friday, one day before monthly American Orchid Society judging in Atlanta. It was taken there simply to show it to the judges. They could not ignore it and gave the plant with one little blossom a JC/AOS. Since that time, the Nortons have flowered eighteen 'Indigo' *Phal. violaceas*.

As usual, the one little flower was pollinated and N0230 *Phal. violacea* 'Gulfstream Blue' × self was made. Mrs. Senchal Hatton, who bought the first little plant offered for sale from the cross, has now flowered her plant and, believe it or not, hers is 'Indigo'!

In 2004 the Nortons packed three 'Indigos' and headed to Indianapolis to display them at the IPA Symposium. The most outstanding, 'Rachel's Blue Eyes', opened on Friday just in time for AOS judging and received the IPA Symposium Best Phalaenopsis trophy.

On July 4, 2005, 'Blue Blood' opened. The Nortons were disappointed because they thought the flower would be past its prime on the 15th, opening day for the 11th IPA Symposium in Philadelphia. Not only was it not fading, but another 'Indigo', *Phal. violacea* 'Blue Chip' opened on the drive to Philadelphia, just as 'Rachel's Blue Eyes' had the year before on the way to Indianapolis. *Phal. violacea* 'Blue Chip' was also awarded the IPA Symposium Best Phalaenopsis trophy.

The birth of the blues

Hurricane Gaston came roaring ashore at Cape Romain Federal Wildlife Refuge east of Orchidview on August 29, 2004. It formed off the coast as a tropical depression and came onshore on Sunday morning as a hurricane. Trees were down and electrical power was off for eighteen hours.

When the Nortons finally were able to make their way to the greenhouse and start the generator they peeped in to see how the plants were faring. *Phal. violacea* 'Gaston Bleu' had just begun opening enough to show the deepest 'Indigo' color yet seen in this line of breeding. A professional photographer was called to record the beauty of the flower and the first true color pictures of the 'Indigo' violaceas were made. Until then it had proved difficult to capture the true indigo color, but Paul Alford was up to the task.

Since the Nortons have offered for sale all crosses made with progeny from Michael Ooi's gift, Phal. lovers worldwide have the opportunity to flower var. 'Indigo' *Phal. violacea*s in the near future. Michael certainly sent the Nortons something to remember him by. All this inbreeding has produced The Birth of the Blues.

Blue forms of various other phalaenopsis will continue to be desirable, since this color is so rare. *Doritaenopsis* Fire Cracker 'Blue Martini' (*D.* Red Coral var. *coerulea* × *Doritis pulcherrima* var. *coerulea*) is a recent offering in the blue line, as is a blue clone of *D.* Kenneth Schubert (*Doritis pulcherrima* × *P. violacea*) called 'First Rays', along with some selected forms of *D.* Siam Treasure.

Doritaenopsis Kenneth Schubert 'First Rays'. Photo by Allen Black.

Gallery of Novelties, Miniatures, and Multifloras

Hybrids are listed by the year in which they were registered to demonstrate changes and evolution over time.

1959

Phalaenopsis Valentinii
Origin: *Phalaenopsis cornu-cervi* × *Phalaenopsis violacea*
Originator: Unknown

1963

Doritaenopsis Kenneth Schubert 'First Rays'
Origin: *Doritis pulcherrima* × *Phalaenopsis violacea*
Originator: Clarelen
Registered by Clarelen

Doritaenopsis Purple Gem
Origin: *Doritis pulcherrima* × *Phalaenopsis equestris*
Originator: E. Iwanaga
Registered by E. Iwanaga

Phalaenopsis Valentinii

Doritaenopsis Purple Gem

Doritaenopsis Kenneth Schubert 'First Rays'. Photo by Allen Black.

1968

Asconopsis Irene Dobkin 'York' HCC/AOS
Origin: *Phalaenopsis* Doris × *Ascocentrum miniatum*
Originator: Frederick Thornton
Registered by Frederick Thornton

1970

Phalaenopsis Caribbean Sunset 'Sweet Fragrance'
Origin: *Phalaenopsis* Cassandra × *Phalaenopsis* Mambo
Originator: Fred K. Thornton
Registered by Fred K. Thornton

1978

Beardara Henry Wallbrunn
Origin: *Asconopsis* Irene Dobkin × *Doritis pulcherrima*
Originator: Henry Wallbrunn
Registered by Fort Caroline's

1984

Phalaenopsis Orchid World 'Bonnie Vasquez' AM/AOS
Origin: *Phalaenopsis* Malibu Imp × *Phalaenopsis* Deventeriana
Originator: Universal
Registered by Orchid World International

Phalaenopsis Penang Girl
Origin: *Phalaenopsis violacea* × *Phalaenopsis venosa*
Originator: Ooi Leng Sun
Registered by Ooi Leng Sun

Phalaenopsis Penang Girl 'Ching Ruey'
Origin: *Phalaenopsis violacea* × *Phalaenopsis venosa*
Originator: Ooi Leng Sun
Registered by Ooi Leng Sun

Asconopsis Irene Dobkin 'York' HCC/AOS

Phalaenopsis Caribbean Sunset 'Sweet Fragrance'

Beardara Henry Wallbrunn

Phalaenopsis Orchid World 'Bonnie Vasquez' AM/AOS. Photo by Allen Black.

Phalaenopsis Penang Girl

Phalaenopsis Penang Girl 'Ching Ruey'. Photo by Marshall Ku.

Phalaenopsis Kuntrarti Rarashati 'Bunker Hill'. Photo by Allen Black.

Phalaenopsis Little Mary 'Cherry Blossom'

Phalaenopsis Pago Pago 'First Love' AM/AOS

Phalaenopsis Kuntrarti Rarashati 'Joy'

1986

Phalaenopsis Kuntrarti Rarashati 'Bunker Hill'
Origin: *Phalaenopsis equestris* × *Phalaenopsis venosa*
Originator: Kolopaking
Registered by Kolopaking

Phalaenopsis Kuntrarti Rarashati 'Joy'
Origin: *Phalaenopsis equestris* × *Phalaenopsis venosa*
Originator: A. Kolopaking
Registered by A. Kolopaking

Phalaenopsis Zuma Aussie Delight. Photo by Allen Black.

Phalaenopsis Little Mary 'Cherry Blossom'
Origin: *Phalaenopsis* Mary Tuazon × *Phalaenopsis equestris*
Originator: T. Takase
Registered by T. Takase

Phalaenopsis Zuma Aussie Delight
Origin: *Phalaenopsis* Sweet Memory × *Phalaenopsis venosa*
Originator: Zuma Canyon
Registered by Zuma Canyon

Phalaenopsis World Class 'Big Foot' JC/AOS. Photo by Allen Black.

1988

Phalaenopsis Pago Pago 'First Love' AM/AOS
Origin: *Phalaenopsis venosa* × *Phalaenopsis* Lippeglut
Originator: Zuma Canyon
Registered by Zuma Canyon

1990

Phalaenopsis World Class 'Big Foot' JC/AOS
Origin: *Phalaenopsis* Mae Hitch × *Phalaenopsis* Kathy Sagaert
Originator: Carmela Orchids
Registered by Carmela Orchids

Phalaenopsis Zuma's Pixie 'Taida Little Cutie'
Origin: *Phalaenopsis* Carmela's Pixie × *Phalaenopsis equestris*
Originator: Pen-Chih Lai
Registered by Taida

1992

Phalaenopsis Buena Jewel
Origin: *Phalaenopsis violacea* × *Phalaenopsis* Gelblieber
Originator: Barry Cohen
Registered by N. LeJeune

Phalaenopsis Ho's Lovely Amethyst 'La Flora' AM/AOS
Origin: *Phalaenopsis* King Kamehameha × *Phalaenopsis* George Vasquez
Originator: Tin-Fan Ho
Registered by Tin-Fan Ho

Phalaenopsis Mini Mark 'Holm'
Origin: *Phalaenopsis* Micro Nova × *Phalaenopsis philippinensis*
Originator: Breckenridge
Registered by Breckenridge

1993

Phalaenopsis Ambo Buddha 'Phoenix' FCC/AOS
Origin: *Phalaenopsis* Brother Buddha × *Phalaenopsis amboinensis*
Originator: Brother Orchid Nursery
Registered by Brother Orchid Nursery

Phalaenopsis Ambo Buddha 'SW'
Origin: *Phalaenopsis* Brother Buddha × *Phalaenopsis amboinensis*
Originator: Brother Orchid Nursery
Registered by Brother Orchid Nursery

Phalaenopsis Zuma's Pixie 'Taida Little Cutie'. Photo by Marshall Ku.

Phalaenopsis Buena Jewel

Phalaenopsis Ho's Lovely Amethyst 'La Flora' AM/AOS. Photo by Marshall Ku.

Phalaenopsis Mini Mark 'Holm'. Photo by Mark Herzog.

Phalaenopsis Ambo Buddha 'Phoenix' FCC/AOS. Photo by Allen Black.

Phalaenopsis Ambo Buddha 'SW'

Phalaenopsis Formosa San Fan

Phalaenopsis Ho's Little Caroline

Phalaenopsis Formosa San Fan
Origin: *Phalaenopsis* Misty Green × *Phalaenopsis* Mok Choi Yew
Originator: Lin Ming Kung
Registered by Lin Ming Kung

Phalaenopsis Ho's Little Caroline
Origin: *Phalaenopsis* Be Glad × *Phalaenopsis* Carmela's Pixie
Originator: Tin-Fan Ho
Registered by Tin-Fan Ho

Doritaenopsis Taisuco Pixie 'Ching Ruey' AM/AOS. Photo by Marshall Ku.

Phalaenopsis Hannover Passion 'Ching Ruey'. Photo by Marshall Ku.

1994

Doritaenopsis Taisuco Pixie 'Ching Ruey' AM/AOS
Origin: *Doritaenopsis* Sun-Chen Beauty × *Phalaenopsis* Carmela's Pixie
Originator: Taiwan Sugar
Registered by Taiwan Sugar

Phalaenopsis Hannover Passion 'Ching Ruey'
Origin: *Phalaenopsis* Gelblieber × *Phalaenopsis mariae*
Originator: Cheng Hsien-I
Registered by Cheng Hsien-I

Doritaenopsis Pico Lady Ruby 'Wickford' HCC/AOS

Phalaenopsis Tsay's Evergreen 'Nobby's Jade' HCC/AOS. Photo by Allen Black.

1995

Doritaenopsis Pico Lady Ruby 'Wickford' HCC/AOS
Origin: *Doritis pulcherrima* × *Phalaenopsis* Kuntrarti Rarashati
Originator: Brother Orchid Nursery
Registered by Brother Orchid Nursery

Phalaenopsis Tsay's Evergreen 'Nobby's Jade' HCC/AOS
Origin: *Phalaenopsis* Sheba's Elf × *Phalaenopsis* Yungho Princess Gelb
Originator: Evergreen
Registered by Evergreen

Phalaenopsis Yungho Gelb Canary 'Yungho' AM/AOS
Origin: *Phalaenopsis* Gelblieber × *Phalaenopsis* Princess Kaiulani
Originator: Yung-Ho
Registered by Yung-Ho

1997

Doritaenopsis Pixie Star 'Norman'
Origin: *Doritis pulcherrima* × *Phalaenopsis* Joyful
Originator: Mark Pendleton
Registered by Orchid Zone

Doritaenopsis Siam Treasure
Origin: *Phalaenopsis lowii* × *Doritis pulcherrima*
Originator: T. Lusup-anan
Registered by S. Wannakrairoj

Phalaenopsis Chingruey's Morning 'Ching Ruey'
Origin: *Phalaenopsis* Penang Girl × *Phalaenopsis* Stone Morning
Originator: Ching Ruey Orchids
Registered by Ching Ruey Orchids

1998

Phalaenopsis An Tai Spot 'Splotchy' AM/AOS
Origin: *Phalaenopsis* Paifang's Queen × *Phalaenopsis* John Ewing
Originator: F. L. Chau
Registered by Sogo Team Co.

Phalaenopsis Nobby's Amy
Origin: *Phalaenopsis* Be Glad × *Phalaenopsis* Rothschildiana
Originator: Nobby Orchids
Registered by Nobby Orchids

Phalaenopsis Yungho Gelb Canary 'Yungho' AM/AOS

Doritaenopsis Siam Treasure

Phalaenopsis An Tai Spot 'Spotchy' AM/AOS. Photo by Eric Goo.

Doritaenopsis Pixie Star 'Norman'

Phalaenopsis Chingruey's Morning 'Ching Ruey'. Photo by Marshall Ku.

Phalaenopsis Nobby's Amy

Phalaenopsis Nobby's Amy 'Shih Hua'
Origin: *Phalaenopsis* Be Glad × *Phalaenopsis* Rothschildiana
Originator: Nobby Orchids
Registered by Nobby Orchids

1999

Phalaenopsis Little Emperor
Origin: *Phalaenopsis* Sogo Lit-Angel × *Phalaenopsis* Golden Amboin
Originator: Lee Shih Hua
Registered by Norman's Orchids

Phalaenopsis Perfection Is 'Chen' FCC/AOS
Origin: *Phalaenopsis* Golden Peoker × *Phalaenopsis* Black Eagle
Originator: Unknown
Registered by Howard Ginsberg

Phalaenopsis Sogo Twinkle 'Stars' HCC/AOS
Origin: *Phalaenopsis* Be Tris × *Phalaenopsis* Sogo Tris
Originator: Sogo Team Co.
Registered by Sogo Team Co.

2000

Doritaenopsis Chingruey's Goldstaff
Origin: *Phalaenopsis* Ambonosa × *Doritaenopsis* Taisuco Jewel
Originator: Ching Ruey Orchids
Registered by Ching Ruey Orchids

Doritaenopsis Taisuco Micky
Origin: *Phalaenopsis* Golden Peoker × *Doritis pulcherrima*
Originator: Taiwan Sugar Company
Registered by Taiwan Sugar Company

Phalaenopsis Nobby's Amy 'Shih Hua'. Photo by Allen Black.

Phalaenopsis Perfection Is 'Chen' FCC/AOS

Doritaenopsis Chingruey's Goldstaff. Photo by Marshall Ku.

Phalaenopsis Little Emperor

Phalaenopsis Sogo Twinkle 'Stars' HCC/AOS

Doritaenopsis Taisuco Micky

Phalaenopsis Taisuco Tunelip
Origin: *Phalaenopsis* Taisuco Suzanne × *Phalaenopsis* Carmela's Pixie
Originator: Taiwan Sugar Company
Registered by Taiwan Sugar Company

2001

Phalaenopsis Kung's Gelb Lishian
Origin: *Phalaenopsis* Yungho Gelbliambo × *Phalaenopsis* Hsu Li-Shian
Originator: Kung's
Registered by Kung's

2002

Phalaenopsis Fantasy Musick
Origin: *Phalaenopsis* Micro Nova × *Phalaenopsis equestris*
Originator: F & M Kaufmann
Registered by F & M Kaufmann

Phalaenopsis Joy Spring Canary 'Rainbow'
Origin: *Phalaenopsis* Buena Jewel × *Phalaenopsis* Yungho Gelb Canary
Originator: J. Wu
Registered by J. Wu

2003

Doritaenopsis I-Hsin Balloon 'KHM 1316'
Origin: *Phalaenopsis* Sogo Lisa × *Doritaenopsis* I-Hsin Gem
Originator: W. T. Chien
Registered by W. T. Chien

Doritaenopsis Musick Surprise
Origin: *Doritis pulcherrima* × *Phalaenopsis chibae*
Originator: F & M Kaufmann
Registered by F & M Kaufmann

Phalaenopsis Taisuco Tunelip

Phalaenopsis Kung's Gelb Lishian

Phalaenopsis Fantasy Musick

Phalaenopsis Joy Spring Canary 'Rainbow'

Doritaenopsis I-Hsin Balloon 'KHM 1316'. Photo by Marshall Ku.

Doritaenopsis Musick Surprise

2004

Doritaenopsis Musick Lipstick
Origin: *Phalaenopsis* Kuntrarti Rarashati × *Doritaenopsis* Abed-nego
Originator: F & M Kaufmann
Registered by F & M Kaufmann

Phalaenopsis Dragon Tree Eagle 'DT168'
Origin: *Phalaenopsis* Penang Girl × *Phalaenopsis* Black Eagle
Originator: Wang Bi-Jiang
Registered by Ching Ann

Phalaenopsis Memoria Chuck Noe
Origin: *Phalaenopsis cornu-cervi* × *Phalaenopsis* Kuntrarti Rarashati
Originator: Allen Black
Registered by Allen Black

Phalaenopsis Tying Shin Alice 'Hong'
Origin: *Phalaenopsis* Brother Skimmer × *Phalaenopsis* Kuntrarti Rarashati
Originator: Kuo Liang Hung
Registered by Tying Shin Orchid

2005

Doritaenopsis Tying Shin Phoenix 'Golden Cupid'
Origin: *Doritaenopsis* Tzu Chiang Orange × *Phalaenopsis* Sogo Lawrence
Originator: Kuo Liang Hung
Registered by Tying Shin Orchid

Doritaenopsis Tying Shin Phoenix 'Golden Leopard' BM/TOGA
Origin: *Doritaenopsis* Tzu Chiang Orange × *Phalaenopsis* Sogo Lawrence
Originator: Kuo Liang Hung
Registered by Tying Shin Orchid

Doritaenopsis Musick Lipstick

Phalaenopsis Dragon Tree Eagle 'DT168'. Photo by Marshall Ku.

Phalaenopsis Memoria Chuck Noe. Photo by Allen Black.

Phalaenopsis Tying Shin Alice 'Hong'. Photo by Marshall Ku.

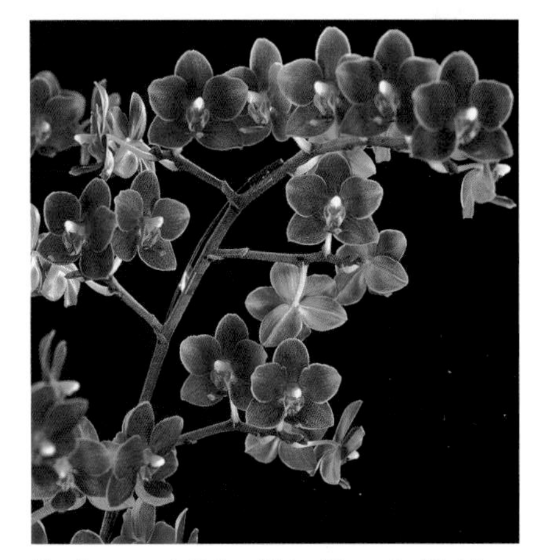

Doritaenopsis Tying Shin Phoenix 'Golden Cupid'. Photo by Marshall Ku.

Doritaenopsis Tying Shin Phoenix 'Golden Leopard' BM/TOGA. Photo by Marshall Ku.

Doritaenopsis Tying Shin Phoenix 'Golden Phoenix' SM/TOGA. Photo by Marshall Ku.

Doritaenopsis Tying Shin Phoenix 'T. S.' Photo by Marshall Ku.

Phalaenopsis Kunstler's Gem. Photo by Allen Black.

Doritaenopsis I-Hsin Black Valentine 'KHM 1566'. Photo by Marshall Ku.

Phalaenopsis Kenny Ewell. Photo by Allen Black.

Doritaenopsis I-Hsin Carnival 'KHM 1357'. Photo by Marshall Ku.

Doritaenopsis Tying Shin Phoenix 'Golden Phoenix' SM/TOGA
Origin: *Doritaenopsis* Tzu Chiang Orange × *Phalaenopsis* Sogo Lawrence
Originator: Kuo Liang Hung
Registered by Tying Shin Orchid

Doritaenopsis Tying Shin Phoenix 'T. S.'
Origin: *Doritaenopsis* Tzu Chiang Orange × *Phalaenopsis* Sogo Lawrence
Originator: Kuo Liang Hung
Registered by Tying Shin Orchid

Phalaenopsis Kunstler's Gem
Origin: *Phalaenopsis* Harford's Gem × *Phalaenopsis kunstleri*
Originator: Allen Black
Registered by Allen Black

2006

Doritaenopsis I-Hsin Black Valentine 'KHM 1566'
Origin: *Doritaenopsis* I-Hsin Black Jack × *Doritaenopsis* Chian Xen Sweet Valentine
Originator: I-Hsin Orchids
Registered by W. T. Chien

Phalaenopsis Kenny Ewell
Origin: *Phalaenopsis* Brother Purple × *Phalaenopsis* Kuntrarti Rarashati
Originator: Allen Black
Registered by Allen Black

Unregistered

Doritaenopsis I-Hsin Carnival 'KHM1357'
Origin: *Phalaenopsis* I-Hsin Salmon × *Doritaenopsis* Taisuco Pixie
Originator: I-Hsin Orchids

Unnamed *Doritaenopsis* hybrid (*Phalaenopsis* Veitchiana × *Doritaenopsis* Sogo Berry)

Phalaenopsis 'Sweetheart'

Unnamed *Phalaenopsis* hybrid (*Phalaenopsis equestris* × *Phalaenopsis viridis*). Photo by Allen Black.

Phalaenopsis 'KHM1412'. Photo by Marshall Ku.

Phalaenopsis violacea 'Blue Chip'

Unnamed *Phalaenopsis* hybrid (*Phalaenopsis venosa* × *Phalaenopsis hieroglyphica*)

Unnamed *Doritaenopsis*
Origin: *Phalaenopsis* Veitchiana × *Doritaenopsis* Sogo Berry
Originator: Unknown

Phalaenopsis 'KHM1412'
Origin: *Phalaenopsis* Graybeal's Trinity Bay × *Phalaenopsis* Caribbean Sunset
Originator: Unknown

Phalaenopsis 'Sweetheart'
Origin: *Phalaenopsis violacea* × *Phalaenopsis* Jungo Viotris
Originator: Unknown

Phalaenopsis violacea 'Blue Chip'
Origin: Unknown
Originator: H. P. Norton

Unnamed *Phalaenopsis*
Origin: *Phalaenopsis equestris* × *Phalaenopsis viridis*
Originator: Unknown

Unnamed *Phalaenopsis*
Origin: *Phalaenopsis venosa* × *Phalaenopsis hieroglyphica*
Originator: Unknown

Phalaenopsis and other orchids grow in an east-facing window in the author's home.

Chapter 8

Culture

In the 1948 edition of one of the first classic books on orchid growing in the United States, *American Orchid Culture*, Edward A. White states that *Phalaenopsis* are more particular than many other species regarding their environmental conditions. Some of the more obscure species such as *P. lobbii* can be a bit challenging, but most of the common species and just about all modern hybrids are considered to be among the easiest orchids to grow. Of course, they do have particular requirements that must be met to help them perform their best. These are detailed in this chapter, along with the simplest, most effective ways to provide them, based on my many years of experience growing phalaenopsis in windowsills, under lights, and in a greenhouse, and from information gathered from countless amateur and professional growers. The efforts you make to modify the growing environment so that phalaenopsis feel at home will pay off in healthy plants that provide plenty of flowers.

Light

Light is essential for all green plants. Along with water and carbon dioxide, light creates the raw materials plants use to produce their food via photosynthesis. For indoor gardeners who experience short days and low light levels during the winter, such as those who live in the northeastern and midwestern United States, Canada, England, and northern Europe, providing sufficient light can be the most challenging cultural requirement to meet. This is especially true with orchids such as vandas and some dendrobiums, which require high amounts of light. Fortunately, moth orchids are not nearly as demanding regarding their light needs and do well in indirect light. For this reason, healthy phalaenopsis can be grown indoors in windowsills, sun rooms, shaded greenhouses, and under artificial lights in most temperate climates.

Greenhouses are the most efficient collectors of natural light. The amount of light penetrating the greenhouse is determined by the glazing material used, the structure's geographical location, how it is sited, and whether it is shaded by surrounding trees, structures, or a commercial shading compound or fabric. Of course, the greenhouse option is also the most expensive one, and although a greenhouse is not necessary to grow phalaenopsis, it can be valuable for those species and hybrid *Phalaenopsis* with very tall inflorescences that are more difficult to accommodate in the confines of a windowsill or under fluorescent light or lamp setups.

For many orchid collectors, windowsills are the most readily available and cost-effective sources of light. Most phalaenopsis are right at home in such a growing spot. The amount of light that a windowsill can provide is determined by several factors:

The size of the window
The direction the window faces
How far the window is recessed
Whether a roof overhangs the window

How far the plants are placed from the window
The age and condition of the glass or other glazing material

The season of the year can make a great deal of difference regarding the amount of light available on the windowsill. During the winter, the sun is lower in the sky and the days are shorter. The opposite is true during the summer. As a result, a very bright window may be fine for certain orchids during the winter, but orchids may need to be be moved to another window during the summer because the winter location may be too hot and bright. In areas that experience snow for most of winter and bright sunny days, the intense light reflected from the snow can burn orchids, so some shading with sheers or blinds may be necessary.

The extent of the roof overhang also affects the amount of light the orchids will receive, and a bay window increases the size of the growing area and the amount of light that the plant receives, because light can penetrate from multiple angles. Keep windows clean, especially during the winter when the light intensity is low, so that orchids will receive as much light as possible. Also, keep in mind that tinted and reflective glass can dramatically reduce light intensity.

Window orientation and light level

The direction a window faces has a lot to do with the amount of light and the time of day that light will be provided to orchids. Some basic guidelines can help you find an appropriate place for a phalaenopsis. Window orientations are listed in the general order of preference (with North American orientations listed first).

South-facing window (all-day light). This brightest window provides a substantial amount of light all day and offers the most possibilities. It is an ideal location for phalaenopsis in the winter when the light is low in the sky and the day length is short. If the window is large and bright, the orchids can be placed back from the window, or the light from the window can be diffused with a sheer curtain. This exposure can get too hot and bright for phalaenopsis during the late spring through summer, and it is usually best to move them to a window with morning sunlight during these seasons.

East-facing window (morning sunlight). This light is bright, but not too hot. During the spring, summer, and fall this is usually an ideal exposure for phalaenopsis.

West-facing window (afternoon light). This orientation receives as much light as the east window and is also a good choice.

North-facing window (little direct sunlight). This exposure does not provide enough light to sustain healthy, strong growth and flowering of phalaenopsis. Use the location for low light plants such as ferns.

Comparing and calculating light availability

The Canadian Orchid Congress published a handy chart on the Web (http://www.canadianorchidcongress.ca) to help growers determine choice light sources for various orchids. Light requirements for phalaenopsis fit within the chart's medium light intensity category. This information states that moth orchids should be grown in an east- or west-facing windowsill that receives 2 to 3 hours of sun, and a south- or bright east-facing window during times of the year when light levels are low. In a greenhouse, moth orchids should receive about 25 percent of the summer light.

The calculation of watts per square meter (1 square meter equals about 10 square feet) with fluorescent lights is a way to measure recommended light levels. The greenhouse figures compare windowsill and fluorescent light levels with the equivalent percent of light of a greenhouse in full sun. To produce the amount of shading needed for a greenhouse, you would deduct the percent of summer light from 100 percent. For example, to determine the density of the shade cloth required to produce the medium light level (usually the best for phalaenopsis), you would subtract 25 percent from 100 percent with the result being a shading material with 75 percent shade density.

The Canadian Orchid Congress light recommendations for greenhouse and windowsills are applicable during the brighter times of the year (mid-spring to early fall). When the light intensity is naturally lower

Orchids grow inside in front of a south-facing sliding glass door at the author's home.

Measuring light in foot-candles

A foot-candle is a measurement of illumination whereby one unit is equal to the light of a candle at a distance of 1 foot (30 cm). One foot-candle is equal to one lumen per square foot.

To measure the light intensity accurately in foot-candles, you should use a light meter that includes measuring scales for natural and artificial light.

A less exact way of measuring light is the shadow method. If the shadow cast by your hand has very sharp and defined edges, the light is considered very bright, usually higher than 2000 foot-candles, and is likely to be too bright for phalaenopsis if they are exposed to it non-stop for several hours.

When the shadow is slightly diffused but still very visible, it is usually in the range of 1000 to 1500 foot-candles and is suitable for phalaenopsis.

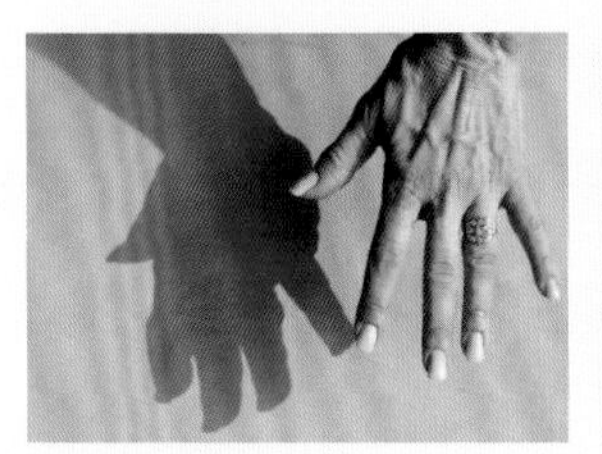

Sharp shadow cast by very bright light.

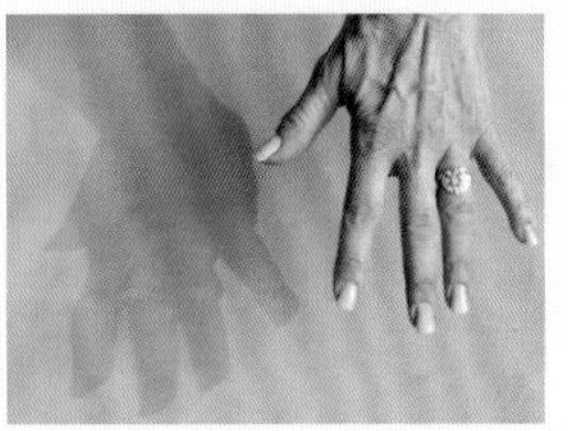

Diffused shadow cast by diffused light.

and day lengths are shorter, as in temperate climates, less shade is required in a greenhouse and for windowsill culture; a south-facing (all-day sunny) window is then usually the best choice, as long as precautions are taken in periods of extreme brightness.

Most commercial orchidists grow their plants in light intensities of 1000 to 1500 foot-candles. Amateurs frequently grow with less light—500 to 1000 foot-candles. The amount of light required by a phalaenopsis plant varies a great deal depending on its stage of growth. When the plant is in the vegetative stage, growing leaves and roots, and when flower induction is desired, the higher end of the light recommendations are most satisfactory; when the phalaenopsis is flowering and displayed inside the home, it can tolerate significantly lower light intensities (100 foot-candles or even less) and still continue to flower for an extended length of time. However, plants usually retain their flowers longest and will sometimes initiate new flower buds if they are provided with 1000 to 1500 foot-candles of light.

Discerning orchid light requirements

Phalaenopsis plants themselves are actually very good light indicators. They will tell you by their growth habits and leaf color whether they are receiving adequate, too little, or too much light. When phalaenopsis are receiving sufficient light, the mature leaves are usually a medium to light green, the new leaves are the same size or larger and the same shape as mature leaves, the foliage is stiff and compact, and the plants are flowering on schedule. If the phalaenopsis normally has some red, dark pink, or dark purple color in its flowers, it will also usually display this darker pigmentation on the undersides of the leaves.

Inadequate light results in succulent, floppy, dark green foliage with no flowering. Other symptoms include stretching, in which the distance between the new leaves on the stem of the phalaenopsis plant are farther apart than the older, mature leaves. New leaves also tend to be longer and thinner.

When a phalaenopsis receives too much light, its leaves turn a yellow-green or take on a reddish cast and may appear stunted. In extreme cases, the leaves show large circular or oval brown sunburn spots. These spots are caused by the leaf overheating, and although this leaf damage may not cause extreme harm to the plant if it affects only a small area, it does make the plant unsightly. Sunburn that occurs at the crown or the central growing point of the phalaenopsis can lead to the death of the plant.

Higher than recommended light intensities can sometimes be tolerated by phalaenopsis if the growing area's ventilation is increased to lower the elevated leaf temperatures that usually accompany brighter light conditions.

Viable alternatives to natural light

Artificial light sources make it possible for everyone without greenhouses or bright windowsills to enjoy growing phalaenopsis in their homes. Compact novelties, miniatures, and multifloras are particularly well suited to this method of growing.

The best artificial light sources for phalaenopsis are the various fluorescent and high intensity discharge (HID) lamps. Fluorescent light gardening is simple and economical. Individual fixtures in a variety of lengths are available from hardware stores and home centers. These units can be suspended from ceilings or installed in banks. In North America, 4 ft. (120 cm) long fixtures are the standard and are usually the best buy, and lamps or bulbs for these fixtures are readily available.

Commercially made, multiple-tiered light carts are versatile and practical. Most of the North American models are about 2 ft. (60 cm) wide by 4 ft. (120 cm) long, so their three shelves provide 24 square feet of growing area—with compact and multiflora phalaenopsis, this is enough space to keep at least one or more orchids in bloom year-round. For miniatures, a light cart provides a convenient growing space that is adequate for an entire collection. The growing structure can be placed in a heated garage, a basement, or a spare bedroom.

The best bulbs or lamps to use is a hotly debated topic. Years ago, the only real choices were "cool white" and "warm white" tubes. Some people still believe that a 50/50 mix of these tubes is the best option for growing orchids, because they are bright and inexpensive; when mixed with a little natural light, this combination works well.

A cart provides ample orchid growing space with a small floor footprint.

A race to produce the "best" plant bulb began when Sylvania introduced Gro-Lux tubes that were designed to provide light that closely replicate the spectrum of light that plants use in the photosynthesis process to produce their own food. The evolution of lamps has gone from the Gro-Lux to "wide-spectrum" types and today to the "full-spectrum" bulbs. The light cast by the full-spectrum lamp is said to be equal to that of natural sunlight. Another type of lamp, called a "power twist," has more convolutions in the tube, which supposedly increases the amount of light emitted by this lamp. I have grown orchids well under all these types of lamps.

Full-spectrum lamps are the best choice for showing off an orchid's true colors. When viewed under these lights, flower colors are rendered more accurately. The most economical and still satisfactory pick is the 50/50 ratio of warm white to cool white lamps. A compromise in terms of economy and light quality would be a mixture of one-quarter warm white bulbs, one-quarter cool white bulbs, and one-half wide- or full-spectrum lamps.

With energy costs soaring, it pays to invest in the most efficient light sources. New, high efficiency, 34-watt T8 fluorescent lamps are quickly replacing the standard 40-watt, T12 fluorescent lamps in the United States. These are already popular in Europe and are much more energy efficient, produce more light per watt, contain less harmful mercury, produce less heat, and are usually powered by silent, instant-start, flicker-free, electronic ballasts. Unlike the older lamps, these models burn at their full light output for a longer amount of time. These tubes are expected to become the commercial standard. Ballasts with the older fixtures with T12 tubes will not properly power the T8s. The T8s will burn in such units, but because the wattage of the ballast is higher than the T8s require, the lamps will age prematurely, evident from the black rings that will form at the ends.

Older light units that burn T12 lamps can be converted to light T8 lamps by replacing the ballasts with those designed for T8s. An electrician can do this or, if you are handy and can read simple wiring diagrams, you can do it yourself. The lamp holders in these older units will still work with the T8s, so they do not have to be replaced. However, the newer lamp holders are better designed and have a mechanism that locks the bulbs into place.

T5 tubes are the next generation of fluorescent technology. They are one step up again in energy efficiency and higher light output. I use a light unit that contains four, 54-watt, high output tubes, and I have been amazed at the light output of this unit. It produces 5000 foot-candles of light 6 in. (15 cm) from the tubes, with a modest heat output and no ballast buzz. These units are relatively expensive, however, and are not easily retrofitted into T12 or T8 units since they require different ballasts and the tubes are slightly shorter. T5s are a great choice as a "blooming light," where they are suspended 18 in. (45 cm) or so from the plants to allow the spikes to develop and to provide adequate light for leaves.

Another lighting option is high intensity discharge lamps (HID), which are the most efficient in their pro-

HID units provide intense light that allows plants to be placed away from them and still receive adequate illumination.

duction of light and are especially useful for allowing room for tall flower spikes of the standard sized phalaenopsis.

Both the ballasts and lamps of HIDs can produce quite a bit of heat, so the plants should not be located too close to the bulbs. Take precautions to ensure that the lamp or bulb is protected by a glass lens; otherwise an accidental splash of water from your hose or sprinkling can on the searing hot bulb could cause it to shatter. Since the ballasts are the primary source of heat with these systems, some growers remove the ballast from the light fixture and locate it away from the lights to another area where the heat can be used or dissipated. The higher wattage bulbs—400 to 600 watts—emit such an intense light that you should not look directly at the bulb after it is fully lit.

In some setups, the light fixture is mounted on a rail with a moving chain, and the unit moves back and forth over the growing area. This results in a larger growing area, lights the orchids more uniformly, and reduces the chance of the orchids getting burned from too much light or from bulb heat. Another alternative is a system with a rotating arm that lights a large circular area. Unfortunately, mechanical failure is a concern with both of these moving systems. If the track or rotating systems fails, plants can receive too much light or heat, causing leaf burn—or in extreme cases, the units can become jammed, which could result in a fire.

The two most frequently used lamps for HID systems are metal halide (MH) and high pressure sodium (HPS). HPS is slightly more energy efficient (produces more light per watt) than MH, but the light it emits is orange-yellow so the colors of the flowers and foliage are not true. MH produces a bluer light that is more pleasing to the eye and makes the flower and foliage colors look more natural. Either will grow orchids satisfactorily. Some manufacturers now produce lamps that combine the advantages of both.

Yet another alternative is the high intensity compact fluorescent lights. The fixtures for these look much like HID units. They do not produce quite as much light as HID, but they produce little heat, so there is much less likelihood of orchids being burned.

If you are a beginner light gardener, you can start with fluorescent light setups. They provide more uniform light than the HIDs and are easiest to purchase and most economical to install. Later, you can give the HID lamps a try.

Humidity

Phalaenopsis hail from the tropics, where high rainfall and humidity prevail. When they receive ample humidity, they grow lushly and their leaves have a healthy shine. Insufficient humidity can cause stunting, contribute to bud blast (when buds fall off the plant), cause leaves to become dehydrated and shriveled, and cause the edges of the flowers to become dry with a papery texture.

During the winter, homes with forced-air heating systems usually have a relative humidity of about 15 percent. Since this is the average humidity found in most desert areas, something has to be done to raise it to the 50 percent–plus humidity level that will better suit moth orchids. For greenhouses, this process is a relatively simple matter. Either the walkways can be regularly hosed down or foggers and commercial humidifiers can be connected to a humidistat so that the entire operation is automatic. Home growers require a different approach. High humidity levels that would be no problem in a greenhouse will cause paint, plaster, and wallpaper to peel off the walls inside a home. Humidity can be improved sufficiently in the growing area without causing damaging results, however.

Set up the growing area for your orchids in a naturally damp spot, such as a basement. Wherever orchids are grown, a room humidifier will likely be needed to boost the air moisture level, and an evaporative type is usually most practical. With these units, a pad is dampened by water in a reservoir; then a fan draws air across the pad and expels cool, humid air. This is usually the best choice for the in-home grower because, unlike the mist types, these units do not result in a white film from the minerals in the water being deposited on leaves and/or furniture.

Orchids can also be grown in a waterproof tray filled with pebbles. Water is added to the tray so that the level is just below the surface of the pebbles; the plants are placed on top of this bed of damp gravel. This system can be problematic, however, because the pots, especially the heavy clay types, frequently sink into the pebbles, resulting in the media in the pots getting soggy. After repeated waterings, the pebbles become clogged with algae and serve as a repository for insects, insect eggs, and various disease organisms. This can be avoided by placing inverted saucers under the pots to keep them above the water level.

A better approach, perhaps, is to add sections of plastic fluorescent light-diffusing grid (sometimes called egg crate diffusers and sold in home supply stores) to the trays, or purchase commercially produced plastic humidity trays. This material can be cut with a hacksaw to any size, is rigid enough to support the plants above the water, and will expose the water surface to the air so more evaporation and humidity result. The grating can be cleaned by removing and spraying it with warm water. To prevent algae or disease buildup, add a disinfectant such as Physan 20 to the water in the trays.

Humidity trays made from plastic are economical, lightweight, easy to clean, and small enough to fit on most windowsills.

Misting can also help increase humidity in a growing area but is effective only to a limited degree—because the water evaporates quickly, misting must occur several times per day. If a water source is mineral laden, the shiny leaves of an orchid can become encrusted with white mineral deposits; this is unsightly and hinders light penetration to the leaves. On the plus side, misting can clean the dust from the leaves and discourage mites.

Growing groups of plants, such as a variety of orchids and tropical plants, in the same area also creates more humidity, since the plants transpire and emit water vapor. Groups of plants placed close to an outside window during a cold winter day prove this, as a condensation pattern appears on the window from the warm moisture emitted from the plants.

Air Circulation

In most tropical lands where phalaenopsis reside, they luxuriate in incessant, but gentle, trade winds. Air movement in a growing environment ensures a more uniform air temperature and dramatically reduces disease problems by preventing the leaves from staying wet too long. It also evenly distributes the carbon dioxide gas that is used by the orchid plant in photosynthesis. The intention is not to create gale force winds in the growing area, but to produce a gentle breeze across the leaves.

Ceiling and oscillating fans are effective at providing airflow for both a hobby greenhouse and an indoor growing area. Ceiling fans move a large volume of air at a low velocity in a circular pattern, effectively preventing severe temperature stratification. They are inexpensive to operate (most use about the same electricity as a 100-watt bulb), are quiet, have variable speeds, and are easy to install. They stand up well to moist conditions, especially if you purchase the outdoor types. The air circulation pattern on most units can be adjusted so that they can either pull cool air up (the best summer setting) or push hot air down (the winter setting).

Oscillating fans are also a good choice, since they can cover large areas with a constantly changing air-

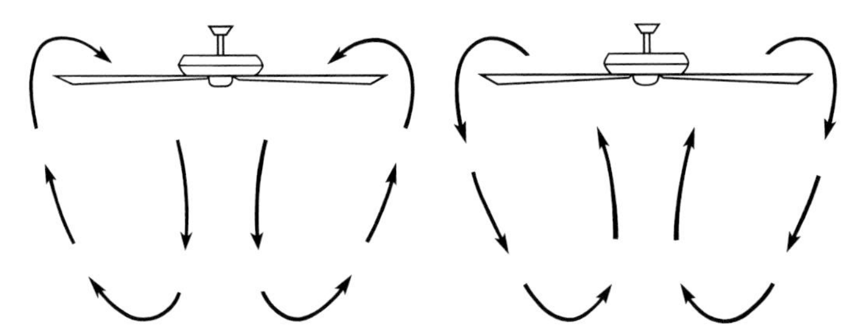

Preferred winter airflow pattern (push warm air down), and the preferred summer airflow pattern (pull cool air up). Drawing by Liena Dieck.

flow pattern without excessively drying the plants. Splurge for the better grade fans; inexpensive units frequently have plastic gears that strip easily, so the oscillating feature will not last long.

In a greenhouse, windowsill, or light cart, small hot or cold spots can develop, where just a touch of airflow is needed. This is where small muffin fans, frequently sold for electronic devices, are perfect for the job. They are efficient, quiet, and inexpensive to operate.

Temperature Requirements

Moth orchids love warmth. They are categorized as warm-growing orchids and prefer, on average, minimum night temperatures of 60° to 65° F (16° to 18° C). Phalaenopsis can tolerate a temperature of around 55° F (13° C) at night, for short periods, but this is not a good idea for more than a few days at a stretch. Continued periods of exposure to temperatures below 50° F (10° C), or a rapid drop in temperature, can lead to chilling injury, which results in yellow sunken spots on the leaves.

The assumption is that the daytime temperature will be 15° F (10° C) or more warmer than the nighttime temperature. In Taiwan, where breeders are trying to produce mature plants as quickly as possible, moth orchids will be grown at a daytime temperature of 82° F (28° C) or warmer to encourage growth. Home growers of already mature plants can back off these daytime temperatures by 10° F (7° C) or more, since rapid growth is not needed or desired.

If phalaenopsis are exposed to temperatures cooler than the recommended ranges, their growth will be slowed down, and in extreme cases, cooler temperatures can lead to bud blast (buds fall off before blooming). Also, cooler temperatures can reduce a plant's disease resistance. A short bout of high temperatures will not prove harmful, however, as long as the area's humidity stays high. Phalaenopsis can tolerate up to 90° to 95° F (32° to 35° C) for a few hours each day if they receive sufficient water. If their environment gets too hot, the orchids will show their displeasure with flower buds that wilt before they open, leaves that shrivel, and in extreme cases death. Hot, dry conditions also encourage infestations of mites. A maximum/minimum thermometer is a great help in recording day and evening temperatures to track temperature differentials.

A widely held misbelief that is perpetuated in popular orchid literature indicates that phalaenopsis (and other orchids) require a temperature differential of at least 10° to 15° F (7° to 10° C) between the warmer day temperature and the cooler evening temperature for a four- to five-week period to induce flowering. This has been proven false in a study and reported in a paper published in 2006 in the *Journal of Experimental Botany*. Matthew G. Blanchard and Erik S. Runkle of the Department of Horticulture at Michigan State University found that the only temperature requirement for flowering phalaenopsis is that the daytime and night-

A maximum/minimum thermometer is essential equipment for phalaenopsis growers.

time temperatures do not exceed 75° F (24° C). Their study proved that the orchids need about four weeks of this "cool" temperature for flower induction. If orchids are exposed to higher temperatures, particularly during the day, flowering can be delayed. In addition, high temperatures (above 78° F, or 28° C) during flower bud development can lead to flower abortion.

Growing Seedlings

Most moth orchids are purchased as flowering or flowering-sized plants; however, some of the more unusual species or hybrids that are difficult to find will sometimes be sold as a flask of baby plants or as seedlings that are a year or more away from flowering. Buying a flask of the newest and greatest hybrids can be a project for members of an orchid club, since many seedlings will result.

Transplanting seedlings from a flask

Several steps are required for transplanting seedlings from a flask of phalaenopsis.

Before purchasing the flask, check with the supplier to ensure that the seedlings are large enough to make it on their own outside the flask. Each seedling should have at least a few leaves, be about 2 in. (5 cm) long, and have strong, healthy roots. If the seedlings are mature enough to be transplanted, getting them out of the flask can be a challenge—like removing a toy ship from a bottle.

Because the leaves of the orchid seedlings are generally larger than the mouth of the bottle, you will probably need to break the bottle if it is glass (and most of them are) to extricate the babies. Wrap masking tape around the entire flask, and then wrap the flask in few layers of newspaper. Gently rap the covered flask with a hammer, trying not to shatter the glass more than necessary. Pour the seedlings into a bucket of warm water. Those that are reluctant to come out can be gently encouraged with a curved piece of wire, such as a section of coat hanger. Be careful not to break roots or get cut by the glass slivers. Let the glass fragments sink to the bottom of the bucket. Gently rinse the seedlings under warm water to remove any clinging media from the roots. You need not remove all of the agar growth medium—just most of it. Some growers treat these young seedlings with a mild fungicide/bactericide such as Physan 20 to prevent disease infections; others believe that these young plants are too tender for such treatment and opt not to treat them.

After they are rinsed, the seedlings are ready to be transplanted. Some growers use sphagnum moss while others use various fine seedling mixtures. Both work well, but sphagnum moss requires less frequent watering than the fine bark–coco chunk mixes.

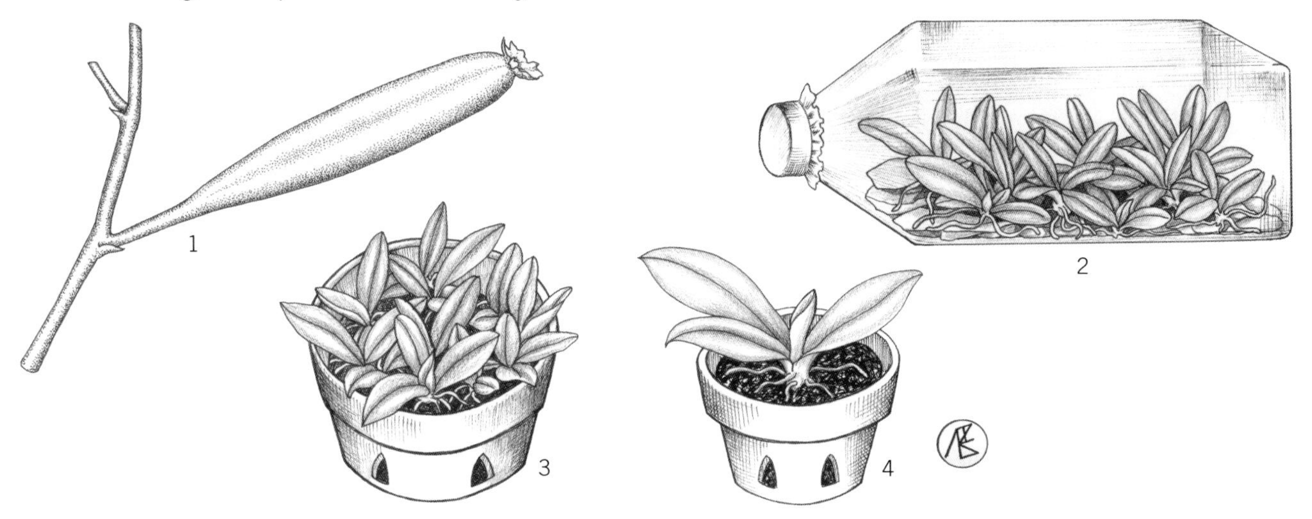

From seed to flask to pot: 1. The seed pod produces seeds that are sown in the flask. 2. The flask contains many phalaenopsis seedlings. 3. A community pot, or compot, is used for new transplants. 4. A transplanted seedling grows in its own container. Drawing by Liena Dieck.

The seedlings can be planted together in a community pot, or compot. Place each seedling about ½ in. (1 cm) from the other in a 4 in. (10 cm) pot. The potting material should be damp, and it should be packed firmly against the roots of the seedlings so they stay in place when watered. Next, water the seedlings gently but thoroughly from the top. Let the leaves dry off for a few hours. Then, either put the pot in a terrarium or propagator or cover it with a plastic bag with the top slightly open. This will provide the seedlings with a humid environment similar to that of the flask. Put the pot in a place that receives diffused, indirect sunlight. Seedlings require about half, or less, the light of mature plants. If the light is too strong, it can stunt their growth. For best growth, seedlings should be placed in a warm spot of about 80° F (26° C). If the growing area is not warm enough, place the pot on a seed starting mat with a built-in thermostat.

In several months, the seedlings should have grown large enough to transplant into a 6 in. (15 cm) compot, and the larger ones can be placed individually into 2½ in. (6 cm) pots. As the seedlings grow, they can be moved up to larger pots. Each orchid should reach a leaf span of 4 to 6 in. (10 to 15 cm) within a year or so from being initially being transplanted. If they are placed in ideal growing conditions, some of them bloom during this time. Although this may seem like a long time from flask to flower, phalaenopsis are one of the fastest of all orchids to grow and bloom.

Phalaenopsis growing conditions

Phalaenopsis health and appearance are closely dependent on their growing conditions. Keep several points in mind.

- If the air temperature is cool, moth orchids grow slower and need less water and light.
- If the humidity is high, they need more air circulation.
- If the light is very bright and/or the temperature is high, high humidity is required.
- When phalaenopsis are not actively growing because of lower light or temperatures, reduce or stop fertilizing the plants.
- If temperatures are high, the light and humidity should also be high, and the orchids will require more frequent watering.

Insects and Diseases

Fortunately for moth orchids, only a few pests bother with them and they are not difficult to identify and control. Although an invasion of some bug or disease will inevitably occur, you can prevent pest problems from getting out of hand with good general sanitation and a keen eye.

- Regularly inspect the tips of new growth and along the edges (margins) and midrib of the undersides of the leaves. This is where most insects hang out.
- Provide the best growing conditions possible. Stressed phalaenopsis are more susceptible to disease and insect infestations.
- Buy plants that are clean and healthy. Beware of the "bargain" or leftover plants; many have serious problems. Unless they are in excellent condition, stay away from them.
- Always isolate newly purchased phalaenopsis from your other plants for four to six weeks. During this time, inspect them for any signs of insects or disease.
- When repotting, always use new or cleaned and sterilized pots.
- Do not allow weeds to infest the pots of phalaenopsis; weeds can harbor insects.
- Keep the floor or ground in the growing area free of weeds, dead leaves, and spent flowers.

To prevent spreading diseases, sterilize your cutting tools before each use. For chemical sterilization, mix one part household bleach to nine parts water and soak your tools in this mixture for a few minutes before using them. Trisodium phosphate (TSP) can also be used to disinfect tools; this cleanser/degreaser is commonly used to prepare surfaces for painting and is available at most home supply and hardware stores in the paint section. The powdered product can be stirred into warm water until completely dissolved. Add another tablespoon or so be sure the solution is super-saturated. Most chemicals that are used to sterilize tools are highly corrosive; after using the tools, thoroughly rinse them with clean water or any metal parts will rust. Wear rubber gloves to protect your hands and avoid touching your eyes or face after handling the chemicals.

High heat is also a fast and clean way to sterilize tools. Use a compact propane torch or a small butane hand torch, such as the kitchen models sold to create the sugary crust on crème brûlée. Using a torch, you can flame the tool's cutting edges until they turn red hot. Let the tool cool before using. If you do not want to purchase a torch, you can use any open flame to sterilize your tools, such as a candle or gas lamp: swipe the blades of the tools across the flame for 5 to 10 seconds.

If you have tried several preventative and curative measures and an orchid does not recover, you may need to discard it. Once a phalaenopsis plant becomes too weakened by infection or a serious insect infestation, it will not likely recover, and in the process of your hoping for this to happen it can spread the problem to healthy plants.

A small, hand-held butane torch can be used to sterilize cutting tools.

A most important aspect of pest control is vigilance. Although most insects do reproduce faster than rabbits, infestations do not occur overnight; still, insect populations can get out of hand quickly if you do not regularly inspect your orchids. If you can detect the pests when they are few, you will be able to eradicate them more easily. Many pests, such as mites and thrips, are tiny and difficult if not impossible to see with the naked eye. Buy a 10× hand lens at a camera or stamp shop to make the task easier.

Common pests

When pests are first sighted, try to identify them promptly and properly so you can apply the most effective control. In many cases, especially if many pests are present, you will have to apply control measures repeatedly, every seven to ten days, at least three times. The creatures lay eggs that are resistant to the control measure and hatch after the control is applied. By repeating the control several times, you can kill the next generations of pests after they emerge from their eggs. You should also alternate the chemical controls you use so the pest does not develop resistance.

Aphids are probably the most ubiquitous insect pests. They come in many colors—green, red, pink, black, and yellow—and are usually found on the new, succulent growth, including the flower buds. They feed with syringe-like mouthparts and are particularly damaging to buds, causing them to be deformed when they open. Aphids are also effective carriers of disease, especially viruses. If clear, sticky droplets appear anywhere on a plant, look for aphids. This material, called honeydew, is actually aphid excrement. This sticky substance is also excreted by other piercing-sucking insects such as scale. Ants around your plants can be a sign of an insect infestation, because ants feed on honeydew.

The mealy bug's name pretty much describes this insect's appearance—a mealy or cottony mass. Mealy

Mealy bugs seek out hiding places in crevices of leaves, buds, and flowers.

bugs frequently hide out in the crevices of leaves, stems, and bud sheaths. One type is found on the roots. This bothersome pest has a waxy body that makes controls less effective. As a result, multiple insecticide treatments are usually necessary to get rid of it.

Thrips can be very destructive, especially to flower buds, maturing flowers, and young leaves; they can also carry diseases from plant to plant—especially viruses. These miniscule creatures look similar to small, long gnats and are difficult to see with the naked eye—a magnifying glass or similar lens comes in handy. Thrip damage is easy to detect: it shows up as light streaks on the flowers or stippling on the leaves. Affected flower buds are usually deformed.

Scale comes in various forms, but most have a shell that serves as a type of armor for the soft insect body underneath. This shell must be penetrated by a chemical or rubbed off before you can kill the insect. Scale are frequently found on the undersides of the leaves near the middle veins or on the edges of a leaf, and they also hang out on the flower stems. Scale is a very difficult insect to eradicate, but with persistence it can be controlled effectively.

Spider mites are not insects, but spiders, and are often found when growing conditions are hot and dry. They can be green or red, but in any color they are difficult to see because they are small. In extreme infestations, fine webbing will appear on the orchid leaves. Before the infestation gets this bad, however, the foliage will take on a stippling effect, which is a result of their feeding.

Snails and slugs are perhaps the most revolting of all orchid pests. These slimy creatures can do extensive damage to young orchid roots and stems and developing and maturing flowers. They usually feed at night, so if you suspect they are eating your plants, use a flashlight after dark to search for the culprits. Also, look on the bottom of the flower pots—a favorite hiding place. They love cool, damp spots. If they travel across dry surfaces, they leave a telltale slime trail.

Other unpopular beasts, cockroaches, also feed at

Spider mite damage appears as a stippling or silvery cast on phalaenopsis leaves.

Snails and slugs feed at night and leave evidence of their damage on the young, tender new leaf growth, root tips, and flower buds.

night and enjoy munching on flowers and flower buds. Controlling these insects usually requires use of chemicals.

Many of the chemical controls for insects and diseases can damage the plants to which they are applied if they are misused. To be on the safe side, always read the pesticide label to determine whether orchids are listed as a plant for which this chemical should not be used. When applying the pesticide, never use more than the dosage recommended. Apply it in the cool of the early morning and make sure that the potting media is damp. Pesticides can damage a moisture-stressed phalaenopsis, and this is especially true with emulsifiable concentrates (EC) under bright, warm conditions; soft new leaves and growing points can easily be burned or damaged.

More than once, to my great consternation, upon inspecting my plants in the morning, I discovered that mice had nibbled off the flower buds of some of my prized beauties right before they opened. Mice will also chew on young, succulent leaves and are usually most active in the late fall when they are searching out shelter for the winter. Luckily, these creatures can be easy controlled with snap traps.

Bees and pollinating insects are not harmful creatures, in the sense that they do not cause any physical damage to orchids, but if they land on the flowers and pollinate them, the flowers will soon collapse. To make orchids flowers last longer, keep pollinating insects out of the growing area.

Mouse damage on young leaves

Safe pest control measures

Some of the least toxic pest control solutions must be applied more frequently, since they kill on contact and are not residual or systemic. Most do not smell bad, an important feature for home grown plants. Some, such as orange oil, also serve as pest repellents.

Heavy-duty chemicals can be used when the infestation is more severe or when other controls have been ineffective. These are reasonably priced, readily available, systemic materials, which means they are absorbed into the plant sap and are somewhat residual. Although chemicals are highly effective, they are more toxic than some other solutions and many smell bad, so they should never be applied indoors. An emulsifiable concentrate (EC) is a clear liquid that turns a milky white when it is diluted before spraying. The petroleum distillate with which the concentrate is mixed can be phytotoxic (damaging to plants) if it is used in too high a concentration or if it is applied when the air temperature is too warm. Pesticides are also packaged in wettable powder (WP) form, which is preferred because it has less phytotoxicity, but it is more difficult to find in consumer-sized packaging.

The controls presented for each insect appear in their approximate order of safety. Many other products are available, but I have limited my suggestions to those that have worked well for me. Always start with the first line of defense. (To find more technical information on orchid pests and their controls, consult *Orchid Pests and Diseases*, an excellent booklet published by the American Orchid Society.)

Aphids

Wash them off with warm water.

Use insecticidal soap, an orange oil product, horticultural oil, or isopropyl alcohol.

If aphids cling to an orchid's flower buds, try repeatedly washing them off with warm water. Using any chemical may damage the delicate developing buds or flowers.

Mealy bugs

Use a cotton swab drenched with isopropyl alcohol.

Use insecticidal soap, horticultural oil, neem oil, or Imidacloprid (an active ingredient in many pesticides—do not apply these inside the house).

For orchids with mealy bugs on their roots, remove the orchid from the pot, soak the roots in a solution of insecticidal soap for a few hours, and then repot the plant in a clean new pot with new potting material.

Thrips

Use neem oil, horticultural oil, or insecticidal soap.

Use Imidacloprid.

Scale

Soak a cotton swab with isopropyl alcohol and wipe it across the insect's armored shell, making sure that you penetrate the shell.

Use an orange oil product, insecticidal soap, neem oil, horticultural oils, or Imidacloprid.

This pest is difficult to eradicate, so you will need to apply controls repeatedly to get rid of it. Before spraying, try to rub off the armored shells of the scale with your fingers or an old toothbrush. Then wash the leaf with mild soapy water before spraying with a control.

Pesticide notes

Do not spray household aerosol insect controls, such as those designed for killing ants, roaches, and wasps, on your phalaenopsis. These are intended to be used to kill insects outdoors and in the kitchen, and they contain petroleum distillates that can cause serious plant tissue damage if sprayed directly on your orchid plants.

All horticultural oils are not the same. Use superior oils; do not use dormant oils. The superior oils are much thinner and more refined and are meant to be used when the plants are actively growing. Some evidence suggests that horticultural oils may damage phalaenopsis roots, so try to target the spray toward the leaves. This can be problematic with mounted orchids rather than potted plants, because more roots are exposed in this method of growing.

Most chemical plant damage from pesticides, such as leaf burn, is usually caused not by the active ingredient of the pesticide but by its chemical carrier. To reduce the likelihood of this damage, try to obtain these materials in the wettable powder (WP) forms rather than as emulsifiable concentrates (EC). The wettable powders will not suffer degradation if they freeze and, more important, they are much less phytotoxic (plant damaging).

Always use the least poisonous solution. Read the label, and it will tell you its relative toxicity. Look for these words on the label, from the least to most toxic: *Caution*, *Warning*, *Danger*. Most of the pesticides you use should fall in the first two categories; if you must use those labeled *Danger*, use extreme care.

In most cases, repeated sprays will be necessary to control the pest—usually once every seven to ten days for a total of three to four sprayings to kill insects after they emerge from their eggs.

Apply the chemical where the insects are hiding—usually under the leaves and on new growth.

A teat sprayer, available from a feed store, is ideal for applying sprays to the undersides of leaves, where most insects hide. Photo by Marc Herzog.

Spider mites

Wash them off with a strong stream of warm water.

Use insecticidal soap, horticultural oils, or Acephate.

To prevent mite infestations, keep your orchids properly watered and in a growing area that is not too hot. If you decide to use Acephate, look for the wettable powder (WP) form.

Snails and slugs

Try some beer. The yeast in beer is a strong attractant to snails and slugs. Place a shallow platter of beer, about ½ in. (1 cm) deep, and wait for the creatures to belly up to the bar at nightfall. The next day, you will find them drowned in the brew. You can also put out pieces of lettuce in the evening, which will attract slugs and snails. The next morning, simply discard the lettuce, with feeding creatures attached.

If you use a commercial product, use one that is harmless to pets and other animals, such as a bait that uses the active ingredient iron phosphate, a chemical that occurs naturally in the soil.

Mice

Live traps and old-fashioned snap traps baited with peanut butter can be effective.

I do not recommend using poison baits. They can harm your pets, and the mice that eat this poison can end up in your pets' bellies, or in the walls of your house, where they decompose slowly.

Roaches

Use an orange oil product, which both repels and kills roaches. And it smells good.

Use roach aerosol sprays on the floor, not on plants.

Pests in the potting media

Fungus gnats come to mind. A simple, safe, and effective control is to drown them by submerging the pot and media in water for an hour or so. Before dunking the pot, wrap the top of it with a cloth to prevent the bark or other potting media from floating out of the container when submerged.

Common Diseases and Their Controls

Phalaenopsis are tough plants, and if they are grown in the correct cultural conditions and best preventative measures are in place, they will usually not suffer from fatal diseases. Still, all growers need to be aware of what can happen when diseases attack moth orchids. Diagnosing and treating diseases can be trickier than dealing with insects, because you cannot see a disease. Only the resulting damage, such as rotten plant centers or spots on the leaves, provides evidence of a disease. You might encounter several common types of disease.

Crown rot (bacterial brown spot)

Crown rot (*Pseudomonas*) is the plague for phalaenopsis. It begins as soft, sunken, slightly discolored spots on the leaves that later turn brown or black. In later stages, the lower leaves change rather rapidly from green to bright yellow and then fall off the stem. Though it is natural for some of the lower leaves of the orchid to turn yellow gradually as they age, with this disease, the yellowing occurs very quickly. Another hint of this disease at work is a lack of new leaves developing from the center, or crown, of the plant. If left unchecked, crown rot will attack the stem or crown of the plant and kill it.

To prevent crown rot, do not grow phalaenopsis too cool, and do not allow water to sit on the growing point of the plant for an extended period of time. Make sure your plants are spaced apart and that air movement is adequate so that the foliage and crown dry out between waterings and before nightfall or temperature drops.

If you observe disease symptoms on your plants, you must act quickly to remove the infected portions of the leaves before the disease progresses to the crown. With a sterile single-edge razor blade, cut off the diseased tissue about 1 in. (2.5 cm) into healthy tissue. After you remove all diseased tissue, remove the plant from the pot, drench the entire plant with a bactericide/disinfectant such as Physan 20, and then repot it in fresh media. Then wait and hope for the best. If you

A phalaenopsis plant with leaves killed by *Pseudomonas*

The plant after the diseased leaves and tissue have been removed. This plant has been drenched in a Physan 20 solution and repotted in fresh media.

Healthy new growths appear from dormant buds below the growing point.

are lucky, the disease will be killed before it spreads to the crown, and new healthy leaves will be produced.

If the disease reached the crown, but you were able to kill it with the bactericide and the roots are in good condition, you may eventually be rewarded with a new plant or two that will sprout from latent buds below the damaged area. A month or more may pass before the young sprout(s) appear. If no new sprouts appear within a month or so, and the roots are no longer sound, discard the plant.

You can use plant hormones to encourage latent buds to sprout at the base of the leaves. The most commonly available material comes in a paste form. It is applied and worked into the area at the base of the leaf where a dormant or an adventitious bud exists.

Soft rot

Soft rot (*Erwinia*) is a deadly bacterial leaf disease that can rapidly turn a stiff, dark green, healthy leaf into brown mush. Affected leaves show soft, somewhat circular, sunken brown spots that enlarge in circumference. You must act quickly. Cut off the diseased tissue with a sterile razor blade about 1 in. (2.5 cm) into healthy tissue. Apply a bactericide to the leaf, such as Physan 20, after surgery. Watch the plant closely for the next few days to make sure you have removed all the infected portions. If this disease gets to the crown or growing point of the plant, recovery is unlikely. Discard the plant in the trash, far away from healthy orchids, to avoid passing on the disease.

Petal blight

Petal blight (*Botrytis*) is a fungal disease that causes small, dark brown or black, circular specks on the flowers. These symptoms are most apparent on white and other lightly colored blossoms. Fortunately, this disease is not fatal, but it is disfiguring to the flowers it attacks. It becomes a problem most commonly when the humidity is high, temperatures are cool, and air circulation is inadequate. Once the spots appear on the flowers, they are there to stay. Using fungicides is not usually recommended for home growers. *Botrytis* is most simply prevented by providing orchids with adequate air circulation, less humidity, and higher temperatures. Increase the airflow so that the flowers barely move with the breeze. As a sanitation measure, remove the badly infected flowers.

Disease prevention and treatment

A few prophylactic measures can go a long way toward keeping your moth orchids healthy and beautiful.

- Buy only healthy, disease-free plants from a reliable grower or seller.
- Water orchids during the morning when the moisture will evaporate from the leaves before nightfall. Cool, damp leaves and water left in the crowns of the plants in the evening are an invitation to disease.
- Provide sufficient airflow to reduce the time moisture stays on the leaves and to remove stagnant air.
- Do not crowd plants, as this creates stagnant air pockets.
- Remove diseased leaves with a sharp, sterile blade.
- Sterilize your cutting tools each time before you use them on another plant.
- Do not reuse pots that have previously contained diseased plants.
- When you find a disease problem, treat it immediately; procrastinating could cost your orchid its life.
- Do not use media that retains an excessive amount of moisture, and do not overwater plants. Both of these practices can lead to root rots that make the plant more susceptible to other plant diseases.
- Many bacteria are spread through water, so avoid splashing water on the leaves.

You can take several steps to control disease problems.

- If your phalaenopsis plant is badly diseased, discard it. It is unlikely you will save it, and it could infect other healthy plants.
- If you find dark brown spots that look like disease and they are close to the end of the leaves, remove (cut off) the affected sections of the leaves with a sterile tool.
- As a general sanitation practice, after you have performed surgery or if your orchid has a disease spot that cannot be removed surgically, spray the leaves with a mild fungicide/bactericide such as Physan 20, Phyton 27, Natriphene, or RD-20 and hope for the best. An application of a hydrogen peroxide solution can also be effective in stopping the spread of disease.
- Reevaluate the area in which your orchids are growing to ensure that adequate air circulation is provided and that appropriate disease preventative measures are in place.

Most chemical pesticides are poisons and toxic to humans as well as insects and other animals. Read the precautions on the pesticide label and follow them carefully. Wear rubber gloves when mixing and spraying these materials.

Performing surgery—literally cutting out the infected parts of the plant—is the simplest and most effective way to stop the spread of disease. A sterile, single-edge razor blade is ideal for the job because it is extremely sharp and it can be disposed of after the operation. The sharpness is important so that you can remove as little of the healthy tissue as possible. Remove all the damaged or diseased areas by cutting the leaf off about 1 in. (2.5 cm) into healthy leaf tissue that shows no signs of the disease. Be careful not to cut into the diseased tissue and then into healthy tissue with the same blade or you will spread the disease. Some growers dress the edge of the cut with a simple fungicidal material such as sulfur or cinnamon, but this is not usually necessary.

Viruses

Orchid growers dread viruses because no practical cure is available to treat them. The most obvious symptom of a virus infection is streaking or color breaks in the flower. Most of us cannot reliably detect viruses. In 40 years of growing orchids, I have rarely seen (or, more accurately, positively identified) a virus on my phalaenopsis; of course, that does not mean my plants have never been afflicted by viruses, only that I did not detect them. Nevertheless, viruses are uncommon in orchids, especially if you buy high-quality plants or seedlings from reputable growers and suppliers and follow the appropriate cultural routines.

Potting Materials

Moth orchids do have special potting requirements, but after you have potted and repotted a few plants, you will realize that it can be a fun and rewarding part of orchid growing.

Choosing the best potting materials

Seldom are individual potting materials used alone; they are usually formulated into mixtures, so the final product will retain water, drain well, and last a reasonable length of time. Every phalaenopsis grower has favorite potting formulations—kind of like a favorite apple pie recipe. Your choice of the best potting material combinations depends on several factors.

How do you apply water? If you tend to be heavy-handed with the sprinkling can or hose, use materials that drain well and decompose slowly.

How mature are the plants? Large plants usually do best in coarser potting materials since they tend to be in larger pots that are slower to dry out.

What are the growing conditions? Plants grown in warmer areas dry out faster, so a mixture that holds moisture may be more desirable than one that dries out quickly. The opposite may be true in areas with cooler temperatures and lower light levels.

Mix components

Potting materials must provide support, drain rapidly, and retain some moisture. Moth orchids cannot tolerate being totally dry for long because they have no water-storage organs like some other orchids, such as cattleyas. Since they can usually go a year or longer between repotting, moth orchids require potting materials that are slow to decompose.

Various components can be used in phalaenopsis potting mixes (clockwise from lower left): coco chunks, charcoal, Spanish moss, sphagnum moss, aliflor (expanded clay), and diatomite.

No single potting material works best for every phalaenopsis. The accompanying table shows some of the most common materials with some of their pluses and minuses.

Potting recipes

Some specialists use complicated potting material formulations, but two basic mixtures work well for me and my phalaenopsis. These mixtures are based on the texture or particle sizes of the mix, which correlates to the size of the orchid plant and root system and the need for water retention. Keep your watering habits in mind: If your phalaenopsis tend to dry out too often, use plastic pots rather than clay and use the mix with smaller

Each orchid potting material has advantages and disadvantages.

POTTING MATERIAL	ADVANTAGES	DISADVANTAGES
aliflor (expanded clay)	Never decomposes and provides good aeration.	Heavy.
chunky peat moss	Retains moisture and mineral nutrients.	Can keep media too wet, increasing overwatering potential.
coco husk chunks	Retains moisture while providing sufficient air. Slower to decompose than bark.	Must be rinsed thoroughly to remove salt residue. Smaller grades may retain too much moisture.
coco husk fiber	Retains water well and decomposes slowly.	Does not drain as well as bark or coco husk chunks. Must be rinsed thoroughly to remove salt residue.
diatomite	Lightweight; retains water; provides good drainage and silica. Does not decompose.	Can retain salts after years of use.
fir bark	Easy to obtain, inexpensive, and available in many sizes.	Difficult to wet; decomposes quickly and unpredictably; can retain water and becomes acidic. In decomposition, can use a substantial amount of nitrogen.
gravel	Drains well and is inexpensive.	Heavy and holds no nutrients.
hardwood charcoal	Very slow to decompose and absorbs contaminants.	Holds little moisture and can be dusty to handle.
lava rock	Never decomposes and drains well.	Can retain salts and is heavy.
osmunda fiber	Retains moisture and is slow to decompose.	Very expensive and difficult to find.
perlite (sponge rock)	Lightweight, inexpensive, and provides good aeration and water retention.	Retains too much water if used alone. Can be very dusty.
redwood bark	Lasts longer than fir bark.	Difficult to find and expensive.
Spanish moss	Used for decorative purposes on top of potting material.	Can contain insects; inspect before using.
sphagnum moss	Retains water and air and is readily available.	Can retain too much water if packed tightly in the pot or after it starts to decompose—especially problematic in colder climates during the winter. Usually requires annual repotting.
sphagnum peat moss	Retains moisture and is readily available.	Becomes very acidic after a year. Can retain water too long, especially during the winter in colder growing conditions.
Styrofoam peanuts	Inexpensive, readily available, does not decompose, and drains rapidly.	Should not be used alone since it does not retain water or nutrients. Best used for drainage in bottom of pots. Can be too light for top-heavy plants.
tree fern fiber	Rapidly draining and slow to decompose.	Expensive; low water retention; difficult to find.

particles. If you tend to be a heavy waterer, consider using clay pots with a coarser potting material. If you live in a hot climate, pure, long-fibered sphagnum moss or a medium that contains some chunky peat might be your best choice.

Whatever potting material or mix you use, it should be wetted before you plant orchids into it (dampen it and let it sit overnight); otherwise, it will take a long time for it to retain water properly and the mixture (and your orchids) will dry out quickly.

Fine mix

This mix can be used for immature plants, miniature orchids, and small growing phalaenopsis such as some of the novelties. This mix is often used in pots up to 4 in. (10 cm).

- 4 parts fine grade coco husk chips (my preference), or fine grade fir bark, or fine grade redwood bark
- 1 part fine charcoal
- 1 part small grade aliflor (my preference) or horticultural grade perlite

Medium mix

This mix is for standard size phalaenopsis and larger specimens of other types in pots larger than 4 in. (10 cm).

- 4 parts medium coco husk chunks (my preference) or medium fir bark
- 1 part medium charcoal
- 1 part medium grade aliflor (my preference) or horticultural grade perlite

Ready-made mixes

Ready-made mixes are available from most orchid suppliers, including home improvement stores. Standard mixes are usually medium grade and are similar to those discussed here. Most contain fir bark, perlite, charcoal, and sometimes some peat moss.

Containers

Containers come in all shapes and sizes. Some are ornamental, while others have functional differences. The most common container is the plastic or clay pot. The big differences between standard garden pots and those used for orchids are the number and size of drainage holes in the container and its depth. Orchid pots have larger and more holes, both in the bottom and sides of the pot, to ensure better drainage. In addition, most of the pots are shallow and shorter, especially the 4 in.

Many containers are suitable for growing moth orchids. Look for pots with plenty of drainage holes or slits in the bottoms and sides.

(10 cm) or larger diameter pots. These are referred to in the trade as azalea pots, because azaleas, like phalaenopsis, prefer a well-draining container. Another advantage of this short, squatter pot is that it has a broader base and is more stable, which is especially useful for top-heavy phalaenopsis.

Most phalaenopsis growers prefer plastic over clay because the plastic containers can be found in a variety of sizes, are inexpensive, are easy to clean, do not readily accumulate salts, do not easily break, and retain moisture longer. Clay pots are heavier and more stable than plastic containers, and for growers who tend to overwater, clay can be easier to gauge moisture requirements. Clear or translucent plastic pots can also be used with pleasing results. You can see through the pot to examine the orchid's root system and judge the moisture level of the growing medium to determine when it is time to water. When exposed to light in transparent pots, the roots of moth orchids are green rather than white. Although the amount of photosynthesis performed by roots is negligible, Erik Runkle at Michigan State University states that phalaenopsis roots avoid darkness, so more roots can result on a plant in a transparent pot when compared to a plant in an opaque (conventional) pot.

Repotting Phalaenopsis Orchids

When roots are overflowing outside the pot and the potting material is getting soggy and drains poorly, it is time to think about repotting. Although exposed and wandering roots are not harmful to the plant, they can attach to other pots, and you can damage the roots as you try to untangle them. If the potting material becomes water-logged and the roots become deprived of air, root rot will result.

Using bark–coco chunk mixes

A step-by-step approach works well for repotting moth orchids in bark–coco chunk mixes.

1. If the plant is root-bound and/or has many roots protruding outside the pot, submerge the entire plant and pot in warm water for an hour or two. This will help loosen the roots from the container and will make the roots more supple so they will not be as likely to break when placed in a new container.
2. Remove the plant from the pot. If the roots adhere to the insides of the pot, you can use a thin (fillet) knife to circle the inside of the pot and loosen the roots. If the plant is potted in a clay pot and the roots adhere to the container, you may need to break the container to save as many healthy roots as possible. Since clay is inert and will not rot, you can ignore some of the shards that adhere to the roots and plant them along with the roots in the new container.
3. Remove the old, loose, rotted potting material and cut off soft, damaged, or dead roots and yellowed, dried up, or damaged leaves with a sharp, sterile blade.
4. Choose a pot one size larger than the pot from which the plant is removed. The roots should fill the pot without much open space. Potting in a pot that is too large can lead to moisture retention in the mix, which can cause roots to rot.
5. Make sure the pot is clean and free from algae or salt deposits. If the pot has been used, soak it overnight in a solution of one part household chlorine bleach and nine parts water. Then scrub and rinse it thoroughly before planting. (I have placed used plastic and clay pots in the dishwater to clean them. Put the plastic pots on the top shelf so they will not melt if the dishwasher has a heating element. Dampened clay or ceramic pots can also be sterilized in a microwave using a high power setting for a few minutes, or in a conventional oven at 350° F [176° C] for 10 or 15 minutes.)
6. Some orchidists like to add a coarse material such as broken clay pots or Styrofoam in the bottom of the pots to improve drainage. This is usually not necessary if you are using shallow (not standard or full taper) azalea pots.
7. Place all the orchid roots in the center of the pot on top of a little media. If some are too long, they can be pruned to fit with no harm.
8. Pour fresh, predampened potting material into the pot and shake it gently so that the media sifts down around the roots until the roots are totally buried in the media. The plant's lower leaves should rest on top of the potting material. Any covered leaves will rot. Potting up the plant too high in the pot it will inhibit new root growth. The finished surface of the mix should be about ½ in. (1 cm) below the inside rim of the pot to allow room for watering.
9. Firm the media with your thumbs and forefinger to force it into any remaining air pockets. The plant must be secure in the pot so it does not wobble; otherwise, new roots will not form properly.
10. Water the newly potted orchid thoroughly to wash out any fine-grade material that may plug the pot's drainage holes.

Using sphagnum moss

When potting in sphagnum moss, you can follow most of the same steps used for planting in bark–coco chunk mixes. However, sphagnum moss is a single planting medium, not a blend of materials. The moss of choice is

Tools of the trade

Of the many useful tools available for tending, repotting, and dividing phalaenopsis, a few are indispensable.

A single-edge razor blade is the perfect tool for making precise cuts, such as removing diseased tissue. The single-edge blade is much safer and easier to use than the double-edge types. They are also inexpensive, so you can toss them out after use.

Hand pruners are probably the heaviest duty tool you will use with moth orchids. They are ideal for cutting heavy stems and roots and for cutting bamboo stakes used for tying up phalaenopsis.

Light-duty bonsai pruners or scissors are handy for trimming diseased or damaged roots or spent flower spikes. The best ones have high carbon steel blades that stay sharp. These tools should not be allowed to stay wet for long, since their steel parts rust easily.

Lightweight scissors are perfect for delicate work such as cutting off spent flowers.

A fillet knife, a thin-bladed knife used to fillet fish, can be useful to slide down the inside wall of a pot to separate adhering roots—especially in clay pots.

Tools such as a small, serrated pruning saw; a single-edge razor blade; hand pruners; bonsai or other small scissors; and a fillet knife can be helpful to orchid growers.

the New Zealand and Chilean sphagnum moss, which is cleaner and springier than sphagnum produced in other areas.

1. Moisten the moss by running a handful of it under warm water. Then squeeze it out to the consistency of a damp sponge.
2. Since sphagnum moss retains much more moisture than bark–coco chunk mixes, you can add a drainage layer of Styrofoam peanuts to the bottom of the pot to enhance drainage.
3. Wrap the moss around the roots, and then place the bundled roots into the new pot. You may need to

1. A phalaenopsis plant out of its pot. Thin and/or dead roots should be pruned before repotting. 2. This plant has been repotted correctly in the center of the pot. 3. A cross section of a phalaenopsis plant repotted in sphagnum moss that fills the top two-thirds of the pot; Styrofoam peanuts fill the bottom third to improve drainage. A piece of broken pot can optionally be placed over the bottom drainage hole. Drawing by Liena Dieck.

add more moss to the pot. The moss should be packed firmly enough in the pot so the plant does not wobble.

4. After the potting is completed, the phalaenopsis leaves should not be buried in the moss or they may rot.

Mounting Phalaenopsis

In the wild, phalaenopsis are usually found growing in trees. You can mount them instead of growing them in pots to simulate their natural habitat and make them easy to maintain. Mounted orchids dry out quickly and require frequent watering and higher than average humidity to stay in good condition, however. Because the mounts drain so rapidly, the orchids need to be watered frequently, sometimes more than once a day during hot summer months. For these reasons, growing mounted moth orchids is most practical in a greenhouse or sunroom with gravel or paved floors that are not harmed by excess moisture. Some home growers do manage to grow healthy mounted phalaenopsis in a naturally humid part of the house, such as the kitchen or bathroom, where the plants can be periodically dunked in water-filled sinks.

Mounting phalaenopsis is a step-by-step process.

1. Place the orchid on a small handful of moistened, squeeze-dried sphagnum moss.
2. Center the plant and spread the roots around and inside the bundled sphagnum moss.
3. Use either stainless steel wire or clear fishing line (monofilament) to wrap around the top and bottom of the moss to hold it in place against a slab of tree fern or slow rotting wood such as redwood or cedar. You can also use onion bags or strips of nylon stockings to hold the plants in place. In several months, after the new roots have taken hold, the wire or line can be removed.
4. Place the crown of the plant so that it is pointing down (not up) so water will naturally drain away from this growing point.
5. Fashion some type of wire hook on the top of the slab for hanging. The finished mounted phalaenopsis is ready to hang in a bright place in a home greenhouse or windowsill.

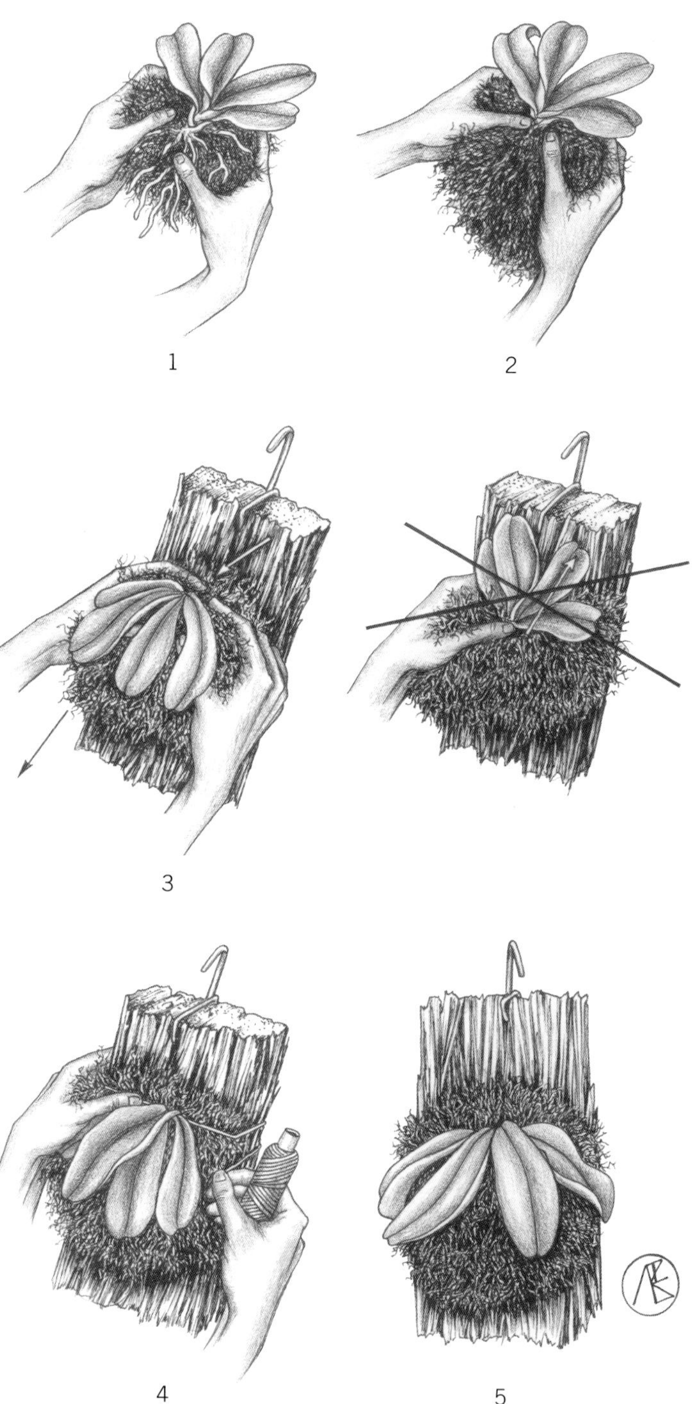

Mounting a moth orchid plant, step by step. Drawing by Liena Dieck.

Moth orchids can be placed in various mountings and containers, including 1. a wooden basket, 2. tree fern or coco pot, 3. tree fern totem, 4. strawberry jar, or 5. tree fern or wood slab. Drawings by Liena Dieck.

Moth orchids can also be planted in wooden baskets constructed of teak or other rot-resistant wood. Multiple plants can be grown together in tree fern or coco fiber containers, totems, large slabs of wood or totems, and strawberry jars.

Multiplying Moth Orchids

Commercial growers propagate massive numbers of moth orchids by seed and by mericloning. Both of these techniques are out of the realm of possibilities for all but the most dedicated phalaenopsis growers. Some propagation methods, however, are achievable with a modicum of skill and with easy to obtain and modestly priced equipment.

Division

Unlike *sympodial* orchids, such as cattleyas and oncidiums, with creeping horizontal stems or rhizomes that produce new growths each year, phalaenopsis are *monopodial*, which means they grow from only one point in the center of the plant. Sometimes another baby plant, or keiki, will sprout next to the mother plant, but this happens only with certain types of phalaenopsis, such as some of the species, primary hybrids, and novelties, or when the growing point is damaged physically or by

Dividing a phalaenopsis: 1. A keiki sprouts from the stem of the mother plant. 2. Cut the small plant away from the mother plant. 3. Leave the mother plant in its original pot. 4. Pot up the small plant. Drawings by Liena Dieck.

disease. This smaller plant can remain attached to its mother plant and the phalaenopsis will grow multiple crowns, or you can remove the smaller plant and pot it up separately.

If you do not divide it, you can produce quite a handsome show plant with multiple flower spikes. If you divide the plant, make sure the younger plant is well established with roots and leaves that are at least 2 in. (5 cm) long. To separate the small plant from the larger one, remove the entire plant from the pot and gently pull the two plants apart. Alternatively, you can carefully cut the smaller plant away from the mother plant with a very sharp knife or single-edge razor blade, while trying not to damage roots. Then repot the new plant and leave the mother plant in its original pot. If the small plant has few roots and is not stable in the pot, use rhizome clips to stabilize the plant while more new roots form.

Keikis will sometimes arise from dormant buds on the flower stem or inflorescence. They usually form when plants with an inflorescence are exposed to several weeks of high temperatures (above 80° to 85° F, or 27° to 29° C), which can abort flower buds and stimulate vegetative growth. If this happens, let the smaller plant grow for awhile until it produces several roots about 3 in. (7.5 cm) long. Cut off the plantlets with a sharp, sterilized blade, and pot them up.

You can also multiply phalaenopsis by encouraging the dormant buds along the flowering inflorescence to produce keikis. Hormone paste, such as Keikigrow Plus,

Keikis can form on the inflorescence. Drawing by Liena Dieck.

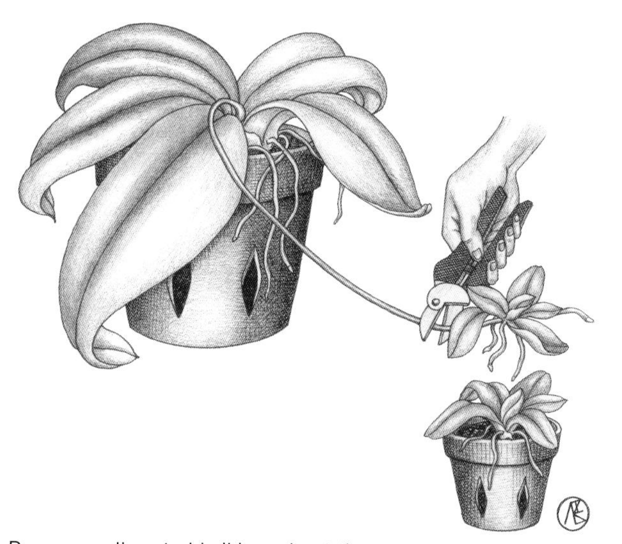

Remove well-rooted keikis and pot them up. Drawing by Liena Dieck.

is used to stimulate the vegetative growth of these buds. This method was developed by Jim Brasch, a plant scientist and owner of Canadian Plant Hormones.

Basic equipment is required for this procedure: tweezers, toothpicks, latex gloves, and a sharp knife or single-edge razor blade. No sterile procedure is necessary, but you should maintain normal sanitary practices around the plants. The knife and tweezers should be flamed or dipped in a disinfectant such as Physan 20 or a 1:9 mixture of household bleach to water. The toothpicks should be discarded after use on each plant.

1. After the last flower bud has been open for one week, apply the lanolin-based paste (lanolin sheds water) to nodes 2 through 4 (counted from the bottom of the inflorescence) on the orchid inflorescence.
2. Maintain a high relative humidity (greater than 60 percent), a temperature of at least 70° F (18° C), and good airflow.
3. Carefully split the bract (the small, pointed, modified leaf covering the bud) with the point of a sterile knife or razor blade on one or more of the nodes on the spike. Be careful not to damage the tender bud revealed under the bract.
4. Carefully remove the bract.
5. Apply a pea-sized portion of hormone paste to the bud and the tissue around it. Gently massage the paste into the area while wearing plastic gloves or similar protection. The bud will start to swell after about seven days.
6 A small keiki (baby plant) will appear about three months after application of the hormone paste. Leaf and root differentiation will begin at about four months. This time period will vary with some species and complex hybrids. High-nitrogen fertilizer is especially helpful at this time.

Root development generally follows leaf differentiation and usually requires no assistance. Keikis sometimes develop roots very slowly, however, and root growth can be encouraged by applying lanolin-based rooting hormone. When about four roots have each grown to 1 in. (2 cm) long, the keiki is ready for potting. It is usually not necessary to cut off the keiki with a blade; a brisk twist will usually cause it to separate without difficulty. The small scar left behind may be protected with a fungicide. With proper care, the new plant will flower in about 12 months.

Stem propagation

Stem propagation can also be used to create new plants. Orchid breeder Eric Goo offers several recommendations for how to accomplish this.

Choose the flasks and media

Many types of culture vessels (flasks) and media can be used for stem propagation. Eric uses 25×150 mm culture tubes (test tubes) to get the plants started. When the plants get too big for the culture tubes, they are potted (if they are large enough and have roots) or replated (reflasked) to larger flasks (500 ml).

Eric uses both a special orchid multiplication medium and a maintenance medium. (Contact Orchid Source Laboratory and Nursery [see "Sources and Suppliers"] for recommended media.) The multiplication medium contains plant growth stimulants to get the process started, and the maintenance medium is used after replating. He adds 5 grams (approximately 1.5 tsp.) of agar per liter of medium. The multiplication medium occasionally results in two to three plants per node, while the maintenance medium starts the stem propagation but is less likely to produce multiple plants per node.

Stem propagation of a moth orchid (left to right): 1. flower stem with swollen bud in flask, 2. cross section of a transplanted plantlet after it has sprouted and grown for several months in a flask, 3. established young plant. Drawings by Liena Dieck.

The media and culture vessels should be prepared a couple of weeks before cuttings are made. By making up the flasks ahead of time, any contamination that is present will probably grow to a visually discernable point. Flasks showing any type of contamination should not be used.

Remove the flower stem

The flower stem from the plant to be propagated should be mature, but not old. If the stem is very young, it will be soft and the sterilization process will kill a lot of tissue. Also, young stems tend to produce flower spikes rather than plantlets. Old stems are more difficult to sterilize and will be more likely to die.

Orchid growers can offer a variety of suggestions regarding the best time to harvest the stem cuttings. Depending on plant genetics and other factors, the optimum time to harvest the cuttings will vary from plant to plant, so some experimentation is required to obtain optimal results. Eric recommends that the stem remain on the plant until the first flower opens and that the stem be removed before the last flower opens.

The flower stem should be removed at its base (using sterile tools) and cut into segments with at least one node per segment. About ½ in. (1 cm) of stem should remain above the node and 1½ in. (3.5 cm) should remain below the node. The tip of the flower stem (or ends of any branches) can sometimes be successfully used as viable segments/nodes.

At this point, a sterile environment is required, and the use of rubber gloves is recommended—for your protection, not that of the plant.

Sterilize the stem

Perhaps the most difficult part of making a stem cutting is sterilizing the stem without killing it. Phalaenopsis flower stems are difficult to sterilize and you can expect about 65 to 95 percent success, but results will vary widely. Many types of contaminants can find their way into the flasks; some will overtake the culture and others will not.

A step-by-step sterilization procedure yields reasonably good results.

1. Prepare three sterilizing solutions.
   The first consists of 15-percent chlorine bleach to 85-percent water and the second consists of 50-percent bleach to 50-percent water. Add spreader sticker (a surfactant that increases the efficiency of the mixture) to each of these two solutions (about 1 drop for every 3 ounces of solution), and mix well.
   The third solution consists of 3-percent bleach and 97-percent sterile distilled water.
2. Use a toothbrush to scrub the segments thoroughly with the 50-percent solution. After scrubbing, immerse the segments in the 50-percent solution for about 2 minutes.
3. Rinse the segments in the 15-percent bleach solution.
4. Use a sterile scalpel to remove the bract from each node (this does not apply to the terminal segments). It is particularly important to remove all of the bract tissue to minimize contamination rates (Eric uses fine-pointed tweezers to accomplish this).
5. Immerse the segments in the 15-percent bleach solution for 15 minutes.
6. Remove the segments from the sterilizing solution and rinse with the 3-percent bleach solution. Use a sterile scalpel to cut off the damaged (bleach-soaked) tissue about a ¼ in. (5 mm) from each end. Eric cuts the bottom end diagonally to produce an elliptical (elongated) surface that increases the amount of surface area that will be in contact with the medium.

Flask the stem

Place the stem segments in the medium at a slight angle with the exposed node facing up. If the multiplication medium is used, having the node in contact with the upper surface of the medium seems to encourage the formation of multiple plantlets.

Wait and hope!

Wait six to eighteen months and pot up any stem cuttings that continue to grow and take root; throw out any cuttings that turn brown.

If a flower spike begins to form rather than a plant, let the spike harden, remove the segments from the flask, and cut the flower spike just above the first node that forms on it. Then place both pieces back into flasks. If the spike has more than one node on it, so much the better. Each section of the spike containing a node may also be flasked. This will significantly increase the probability of producing plants.

If any segments are temporarily removed from the medium for any reason (such as for replating to a larger flask), use a sterile scalpel to recut the bottom end and remove any dead or damaged tissue prior to putting it back into the medium. This procedure assures that good tissue is in contact with the medium, allowing the stem to absorb nutrients.

When replating, Eric generally waits until roots just start to emerge or until the leaves become large and very crowded in the test tube.

Watering Moth Orchids

Improper watering is probably the most common cause of phalaenopsis death. Learning how and when to water phalaenopsis is one of the more challenging aspects of growing them. Several factors affect how often you should water.

The type of pot and the potting media in which the orchid is placed affect how often phalaenopsis must be watered. Both clay and plastic pots can be used to grow orchids; they merely have different watering requirements. Potting material, such as bark, dries out much more slowly in plastic pots than in clay pots. With plastic, the potting material dries from the top down, so even though it may be dry on top, it may be damp 1 in. (2.5 cm) below the surface. With clay pots, the potting material dries out more uniformly because clay pots are porous, so they breathe and allow water to evaporate through the sides. Orchids in plastic pots will require watering less often than those in clay pots. For phalaenopsis that usually do best with constantly slightly damp media, plastic pots are a good choice. If you prefer the weight or look of clay pots, you can double pot your plants by inserting a plastic pot into a clay one.

Potting materials vary dramatically in terms of the amount of water they retain. Sphagnum moss, for example, is a water-absorbent plant harvested from bogs and is frequently used as a potting material for phalaenopsis, especially those grown in Taiwan. This material usually stays wet much longer than bark, which is not as water-retentive. Fresh potting material, especially bark, requires much more frequent watering for the first few weeks until it gets properly wetted or moistened. As it gets older, it retains water longer.

An overgrown or pot-bound orchid will dry out much more quickly than a plant that has plenty of space in the pot. When pot space is limited, less potting material is able to hold onto the water, so the overgrown plant quickly uses it up.

Plants and potting materials exposed to low humidity dry out more quickly than those in humid air, because more moisture is lost from the plant and the media when the air is dry. Warmer temperatures also increase water evaporation, because warmer air absorbs more moisture and because the plants are growing quicker in warmer temperatures and require more water. If phalaenopsis are grown in a cooler temperature, they need not be watered as often as those grown in warmer or dryer conditions.

The more ventilation your orchids receive, especially if air is vented to the outside or if the air is hot and dry as in most centrally heated homes, the quicker the water in the potting material evaporates. Gentle air movement is ideal, since it will keep the air fresh without drying out the plants or potting material excessively.

A proven watering technique

After choosing the appropriate potting material and growing environment, you must determine when and how much to water. The "pot-weighting method" relies on feel instead of precise weights and is easy to use for determining when to water.

First, thoroughly water the orchid in its pot. Then "weigh" the pot by picking it up. This lets you know how heavy it is when saturated with water. After a day or so, "weigh" it again. As the potting material becomes drier, you can feel the weight difference. "Weigh" the

Watering tips

A few tips can help you determine your orchids' watering needs.

Place phalaenopsis growing in the same media and pot type, and of the same size, in the same location. This strategy makes watering them easier, because they will all have similar moisture requirements. If mixed pot sizes or media types are stored in the same area, you will be tempted to water all of the orchids at once, which can result in overwatering.

Use warm water. Very cold water can cause root and bud shock, which sets back the phalaenopsis by slowing down its growth.

Always use a water breaker, a water diffuser attached to the front of a hose that softens the flow of water. For a few plants, a sprinkling can with a long spout and a rose (a water diffuser on the end of the spout) with many small holes works well. These devices allow thorough watering without washing out the potting material.

A huge selection of watering wands is available. Those with multiple settings on the head allow you to drench or mist without changing attachments. Regulating the flow of water is much easier with wands equipped with finger triggers than with those that have a switching on-and-off valve.

Keep the water breaker or end of the hose off the ground or floor. This commandment was handed to me by my first horticulture professor, D. C. Kiplinger, who preached that floors and soil are where the diseases and insects hang out, and a hose can be an all-too-effective way of spreading them.

When you water, water thoroughly. The water should pour out from the bottom of the pot. This method of watering ensures that the potting material is saturated, and it flushes out any excessive fertilizer salts.

Do not let the pots of phalaenopsis sit in water. If saucers are used under the orchid pots, keep them free of water. Excess standing water will prematurely rot the media and roots and will serve as a source of accumulating fertilizer salts and disease-causing organisms, such as bacteria, fungi, and viruses.

Water the phalaenopsis in the morning or early afternoon to give foliage plenty of time to dry before nightfall. Wet foliage or a puddle of water in the orchid crown in the evening is an invitation for disease.

plant every day until you judge that it is time to water, by looking at the surface and sticking your finger into the top 1 in. (2.5 cm) or so of the potting material to check for dampness. This process may sound tedious, but you will be amazed at how quickly you catch on. You will always know the right time to water. Just lift the pot, note its weight, and you have your answer. This method also works for orchids grown in sphagnum moss in translucent pots, plus you can see the darkness (wet) or lightness (dry) of the moss through the pot.

Determining whether watering is the problem

Overwatering and underwatering symptoms are often the same for phalaenopsis because the net effect of both practices is the same—damaged or destroyed root systems, resulting in the phalaenopsis becoming dehydrated. Look for signs of dehydration.

Droopy, soft, and puckered leaves
Slow, weak growth
Yellow and wilted bottom leaves
Bud blast (the buds fall off before opening)

To establish whether a phalaenopsis has been overwatered or underwatered, first remove it from its pot. Many beginner growers are reluctant to do this, but with care, removing an orchid from it pot should not disturb it to any degree, and inspecting the root system is an absolute necessity.

To determine whether you have underwatered or overwatered the orchid, you can follow a few steps.

1. Turn the orchid plant, in its pot, upside down.
2. For plants in clay pots, gently rap the pot against a hard object (such as the edge of your potting table) to loosen the potting material. For plants in plastic pot, squeeze the pot before turning it upside down.
3. Cup your hand over the surface of the pot to hold the loosened potting material as it falls out. Do this over a workbench or table covered with clean newspaper to catch the potting material.
4. If the potting material does not loosen easily, use a thin knife to circle the inside of the pot to loosen the material from the wall of the pot. In some situations, the material may be so packed into the pot that it will not come out easily.
5. When the plant is removed from the pot, evaluate the potting material and roots: Is it soggy? Does it have a bad (rotting or sour) smell? Are the roots dark and mushy? These are all signs of consistent overwatering. If the roots are dry and shriveled, not stiff and plump, and they have no or few growing root tips, the phalaenopsis probably has been receiving insufficient water. The potting material may be too coarse, making poor contact with the roots; otherwise, you have not watered the orchid frequently enough.
6. If the roots look healthy or only slightly damaged, pot up the orchid in fresh potting material.

If you find that the roots are badly damaged, you need to take action. The approach you take to remedy root damage depends on the severity of the orchid's situation. If the phalaenopsis still has a good number of healthy, firm roots, you can cut off all the soft, mushy roots with a sterile single-edge razor blade and repot the plant in fresh potting material. Go light on the watering for a few weeks to encourage new root development. Using a spray bottle, mist the orchid a few times a day to prevent the leaves drying out.

If the roots are almost all gone, emergency measures are called for and recovery is not guaranteed.

1. Cut off all the dead or damaged roots.
2. Spray what is left of the roots and crown with a disinfectant such as Physan 20. Let this air dry for a few hours.
3. Drench the roots with a liquid rooting hormone.
4. Let the liquid hormone dry on the roots for about an hour, and then repot the phalaenopsis in fresh, predampened potting mix or sphagnum moss.
5. Do not water the orchid for a day.
6. The next day, water once, and then put the potted phalaenopsis in an enclosed terrarium (such as a high-top propagator, a clear plastic box with vents at the top and a tray below to hold potting material, or an empty aquarium), with damp sphagnum moss or pebbles on the bottom to add humidity.
7. Close the top of the terrarium and place it in location with diffused light. In a greenhouse, this would be a shady spot with no direct sunlight. Under fluorescent lights, put the terrarium near the ends of the tubes, where less illumination occurs. If the terrarium is in the cool part of the greenhouse or growing area, put the entire unit on water-resistant soil or seedling heating mats. A mat with a built-in thermostat set to about 80° F (27° C) is perfect for providing bottom heat to stimulate root growth.
8. If you are concerned about disease, spray the orchid leaves with a disinfectant solution.
9. In this environment of 100 percent humidity, the leaves will not dehydrate, so the orchid will not be stressed while it reestablishes roots. Water the potting material only when it gets dry, keep the gravel or moss in the bottom of the terrarium damp, and

Recovering plant in a propagator

leave the phalaenopsis enclosed until new root growth is very apparent. This may take a few months.

This method does not guarantee recovery, but this procedure has been used to save damaged phalaenopsis that I considered "hopeless."

Water quality

Because water is by far the largest component of all living plants, providing high quality water to your orchids makes sense. Water chemistry is an involved science that is beyond the scope of this book, but some water quality parameters are easy to understand, and giving them attention will pay off in more healthy plants.

The first step is to have your water quality analyzed, which can be done by your municipality if you are using its water supply system or by a private service if you are using well water. Fertilizer manufacturers sometimes offer testing services, and various universities supply water testing services for greenhouse growers. Check with the school's horticulture or soil science (agronomy) department or the local county agriculture extension agent to determine whether these agencies can test your water.

When you receive the analysis, fill in the accompanying worksheet and compare how your values line up with the maximum tolerable amounts. The "Your tap water" column is for recording the results from your water test.

Water quality parameters worksheet

SUBSTANCE	IDEAL	MIN.	MAX.	YOUR TAP WATER
pH	6.6			
alkalinity ($CaCO_2$)	80–120 ppm			
nitrate (NO_3)			100 ppm	
total nitrogen				
boron (B)		0.2 ppm	0.8 ppm	
calcium (Ca)	30–50 ppm	30 ppm	50 ppm	
copper (Cu)		0	0.2 ppm	
iron (Fe)	1 ppm	2 ppm	2 ppm	
magnesium (Mg)	30–50 ppm	15 ppm	50 ppm	
manganese (Mn)	1 ppm	0.5 ppm	2 ppm	
molybdenum (Mo)		0	0.05 ppm	
sodium (Na)	>5 ppm	0	5 ppm	
soluble salts	0.3–1.0 mmhos/cm	0	1.5 mmhos/cm	
total dissolved solids (TDS)	>60 ppm			
sulfur (S)	10–80 ppm	15 ppm	25 ppm	
zinc (Zn)		1 ppm	2 ppm	
aluminum (Al)		0	5 ppm	
chloride (Cl)	0 ppm	0	140 ppm	
fluoride (Fl)		0	1 ppm	
sulfates (SO4)		0	414 ppm	
Total hardness ($CaCO_3$)				

pH is the measure of the relative acidity or alkalinity of the water. A 7.0 pH is neutral. Any value lower is acidic and any value higher is alkaline, or basic. pH is important because most nutrients needed by moth orchids are most soluble and available when the pH is slightly acidic—6.8 to 6.6.

Alkalinity, in addition to referring to pH levels above 7.0, refers to water's ability, or inability, to neutralize acids. The higher the alkalinity, the faster the pH of the media can increase. Alkalinity is the amount of calcium carbonate ($CaCO_2$), or dissolved limestone, in the water. Water with high alkalinity can cause white residue to appear on leaves; this type of water is usually referred to as "hard" water. Total hardness is a similar issue. For the most part, these numbers are not much to worry about for your plants. If they are high, some people opt to lower them by installing a water softener. To produce softer water, sodium is added, and this sodium-laced water is *deadly* to plants: if you use a water softener, make sure to install a pure water bypass for your phalaenopsis.

Nitrate and nitrogen's appearance in the test readings are not likely to be high enough from your water source to be of any significant nutrient value to your phalaenopsis.

Boron, copper, iron, manganese, molybdenum, and aluminum are called *trace elements* or *minor elements* and are useful to plants in very small concentrations; they are toxic at high levels. As long as these amounts are not above those recommended on the chart, they are of no concern.

Calcium, magnesium, and sulfur are considered major nutrients, but they are frequently incorrectly referred to as trace elements. They are required in lower amounts than nitrogen, phosphorus, and potassium, but in greater amounts than the trace elements, since they help with chlorophyll production and cell wall construction. The chart indicates that the amounts of calcium and magnesium recommended are higher than those of any of the other trace elements. If your water is lacking in these elements, you should consider using a fertilizer that contains these two in sufficient quantities.

Now for the bad guys: sodium, soluble salts, and TDS (total dissolved solids). The less you have of all three of these the better. Sodium is a salt and is toxic to plants. Soluble salts are the measure of all the salts in your water, and TDS is the sum of all the mineral components in your water. If your values are within the recommended ranges, you need not worry. If they are much above them, your moth orchids may survive, but they are not likely to thrive. You can reduce all three of these substances by diluting your tap water with rain water or distilled water. If you still need to get the values down, you can explore the possibility of purchasing a reverse osmosis water purification or deionization unit, which you can find advertised in orchid magazines and available from various water treatment companies.

Sulfates, chlorine, and fluoride are more concerns for human health than for phalaenopsis, so unless they are way off the chart, you need not be concerned. High levels can cause leaf tip–burn over time.

For more detailed information on this subject, you can consult the excellent articles on the Web by Bob Wellenstein: "Water Quality Issues for Slipper Orchid Growers" at http://ladyslipper.com/waterq.htm, and "Mineral Nutrition for Slipper Orchid Growers" at http://ladyslipper.com/minnut.htm. Both articles are focused on slipper orchids (*Paphiopedilum* and *Phragmipedium*), but the principal information is useful and pertinent for all orchids. Another fine resource is the booklet *Orchid Seedling Care* by Bob Gordon; he deals quite a bit with water quality issues directly relevant to phalaenopsis.

Using Fertilizers

Fertilizers will not save a dying phalaenopsis. In fact, if the plant's roots are damaged, a common problem that causes sickly looking plants, applying fertilizers can make things worse. If roots are not functioning well, they cannot absorb the fertilizer, and if the orchid does not use the fertilizer, its salts can accumulate in the orchid potting material. This buildup of fertilizer salts can further dehydrate and damage the remaining roots.

Fertilizers are most useful as a boost to help an already healthy orchid grow better. Fertilizer is not food;

plants produce their own food from sunlight, carbon dioxide, and water—the miracle of photosynthesis. Adding fertilizer merely provides minerals that your phalaenopsis can use to make photosynthesis more efficient. The number and types of fertilizers on the market can be daunting, and each package comes with a lot of mumbo-jumbo about why it is better than another. Fortunately, the choice is not nearly as complicated as some manufacturers seem to make it.

What to look for in orchid fertilizers

From my experience and by listening to other veteran orchid growers, I have come to some conclusions about fertilizers that apply to most phalaenopsis-growing situations.

Nitrogen sources are available in several different chemical forms. Although plants can use all forms, recent research indicates that the nitrate and ammoniacal forms, not urea, are more readily available, thus are usually the most beneficial to phalaenopsis. This is especially true where growing temperatures are lower and organisms that convert urea to a soluble form of fertilizer are not very active—in that case, the nitrogen is washed out of the pot before it reaches a form that the plant can use. The type of nitrogen material used will be spelled out on the fertilizer label. If you are using a proportioner or fertilizer injector to apply water-soluble fertilizer, aim for between 100 to 200 ppm of nitrogen. Use the lower figure when light and temperatures are low and the higher figure during optimum growing conditions. High amounts of nitrogen, much more than 20 percent, are not necessary to grow the best moth orchids, no matter what growth media is used. Too

OrchidMix™ Fertilizer
Pure Water Fertilizer
12-6-3

Total nitrogen	12.0%	Iron (Fe)	0.16%
12.5% nitrate nitrogen		Manganese (Mn)	0.08%
0.7% ammoniacal nitro.			
Available. Phosphate (P2O5)	6.0%	Zinc (Zn)	0.03%
Potash (K2O)	13.0%	Copper (Cu)	0.03%
Calcium (Ca)	7.0%	Boron (B	0.01%
Magnesium (Mg)	2.0%	Molybdenum (Mo)	0.01%

Derived from calcium nitrate, magnesium nitrate, potassium nitrate, and monopotassium phosphate.

Derived from iron EDTA, zinc sulfate, copper sulfate, boric acid, ammonium molybdate.

Plus traces of sulfur (S), chlorine (Cl), cobalt (Co), nickel (Ni), sodium (Na)
Potential Basicity 420# calcium carbonage equivalent per ton
Made in USA. Reg. in Ohio by Roberts Flower Supply
Use 1/4 teaspoon per gal. every other watering.

- Fertilizer brand name
- Fertilizer designed for a water source containing few nutrients
- First number (12) is nitrogen (12 lbs. per 100 lbs. of fertilizer); second number (6) is phosphorous (6 lbs.); third number is potassium. These are referred to as the "primary" or "macro" nutrients.
- The chemical form of the nitrogen component. It is most desirable that this be mostly in the nitrate form, not urea.
- Trace elements or micro elements, nutrients that are important but in very small amounts.
- Unless you know that your water has an adequate supply of magnesium and calcium, look for a fertilizer that contains them. Both these nutrients have been found to be very important for strong orchid growth.
- Actual compounds from which the nutrients are being derived.
- Fertilizers frequently contain very small amounts (traces) of other elements.
- This states whether the fertilizer has a basic or acid reaction.
- Where it is manufactured and what company distributes it.
- Dosage for fertilizer. Do not exceed recommendation.

A typical fertilizer label

much of any nutrient cannot be used by the plant and, as a result, it merely ends up as a pollutant inside and outside the pot.

At one time, a high phosphorus fertilizer was thought to be necessary for better phalaenopsis flowering, but these days, we know that this is not the case. Excess phosphorous, like too much nitrogen, just ends up not being used by the plant.

In most cases, a fertilizer with supplementary calcium (up to 15 percent) and magnesium (up to 8 percent) is a real plus. Have your water tested to determine whether it contains sufficient quantities of either of these nutrients; if enough is supplied in the water, you do not need to use fertilizers that contain them.

For most water sources, adding trace elements, including boron, copper, iron, manganese, molybdenum, and zinc, have been found to be beneficial to orchid growth. Check for these on the fertilizer label.

Before you purchase a fertilizer, read the label. In the United States, manufacturers are required by law to spell out the chemicals included in their fertilizer formulations.

Interpreting the Orchid Fertilizer Label

Fertilizers come in many forms—granule (which look like small bits of gravel), slow-release, and the commonly available water-soluble type. Most granule fertilizers are best suited for agricultural or lawn applications. Slow-release fertilizers are chemicals that have been encapsulated in a resinous perforated shell that slowly releases nutrients over time. Although some phalaenopsis growers use this type of fertilizer, it can partially wash out of the media, especially with some of the very porous potting materials that are frequently used with phalaenopsis. In addition, some orchid roots are very sensitive to fertilizer salts, so these fertilizer capsules can sometimes damage or burn their roots.

The most common form of fertilizer used with phalaenopsis is the water-soluble type, usually packaged as a concentrated liquid or in dry forms. Water-soluble fertilizers offer several advantages. They are readily available in a wide range of formulations. They are soluble in water and are easily and quickly absorbed by roots and, to a limited degree, even leaves of the various phalaenopsis. They are simple to use; they are dissolved in water and applied with a sprayer or sprinkling can. If the phalaenopsis are mounted on slabs or in baskets, they can be dunked in the fertilizer solution.

Water-soluble fertilizers do suffer from a few shortcomings, however. The nutrients do not last long in the media so the fertilizer needs to be applied once every two to three weeks (or constantly if you are using a low dosage type, such as one with 100 ppm of nitrogen). In addition, these fertilizers, in their original containers, are very concentrated and can damage phalaenopsis if they are not diluted correctly.

Fertilizer pros, cons, and application

TYPE	ADVANTAGES	DISADVANTAGES	APPLICATION
granule	Readily available, easy to use, and inexpensive.	Short term, lasting a few to several weeks. Can burn orchid roots. Often missing valuable trace elements.	Dry form applied on top or incorporated into media.
slow-release	Easy to use and long-lasting (three to nine months).	Can sometimes burn sensitive orchid roots. In coarse media, can be washed out with water. Relatively expensive.	Dry form applied on top or incorporated into media.
water-soluble	Readily available in a wide range of formulations. Easy to apply. Nutrients are instantly available for plants.	Must be applied frequently, every few weeks when plants are actively growing.	Diluted in water and applied by watering can or through a proportioning device.

The correct application rates or dosages of fertilizers vary. The safest procedure is to check the fertilizer container for recommended application rates. Never apply more than recommended or plant damage can result. During cooler conditions, you can reduce the recommended amount.

Fertilizer burn

When too much fertilizer of any type has been applied or if it is added when the media is dry, plant roots can become dehydrated by the moisture-robbing salts, resulting in fertilizer burn. This damage usually appears as brown or black root tips. To prevent fertilizer burn, do not apply more fertilizer than is recommended and fertilize only when the media is damp. It is also a good practice to "leach" your phalaenopsis plant every month or so. In other words, thoroughly drench the media in which the plant is growing once or twice with clear water that does not contain fertilizer to flush out any accumulating fertilizer salts.

Calendar of Care

While describing accurate phalaenopsis care month by month is difficult, because climates vary for phalaenopsis growers throughout the world, these approximate calendar dates should prove helpful for most phalaenopsis lovers in the Northern Hemisphere.

January (midwinter)

Cold, short days and low light are typical during this month, so phalaenopsis do not grow much vegetatively (leaves and roots) now. However, many are "spiking up" and getting ready to show off their splendiferous blooms. If temperatures are cool, be vigilant about not allowing cold water to remain on the crowns of the plants overnight. This will reduce problems with crown rot.

Keep the humidity high (50 to 70 percent) with

Tips for using fertilizers correctly

Knowing a few key tips may be helpful when fertilizing your phalaenopsis.

- When in doubt apply less, not more, fertilizer.
- Never apply more fertilizer than is recommended by the manufacturer.
- It is better to fertilize frequently at a more diluted rate than less often at a higher concentration. Some phalaenopsis growers find that fertilizing every time they water with a dilute amount of fertilizer works well. It is the most natural way to apply nutrients, rather than the "feast or famine" routine of fertilizing at a higher concentration every two or three weeks.
- Remember that fertilizers are a form of salt, and salts can damage or kill plants; in fact, salts have been used as weed killers. They will damage phalaenopsis at high concentrations.
- Very dark green leaves that are succulent and floppy can be a sign of too much fertilizer.
- When the phalaenopsis are actively growing, fertilize them. When they are not actively growing, do not fertilize them (or lower the rate).
- If the plant is diseased and in poor condition, do not fertilize it.
- If the plant is overfertilized, it will produce poor quality flowers.
- As water evaporates from the potting material, it leaves behind any solid minerals or salts that were dissolved in the water, including fertilizer salts. These salts can accumulate on the edges of the pots. Remove salt deposits with a damp cloth; otherwise, these deposits can burn the leaves of the phalaenopsis if they come in contact.
- Porous clay pots tend to accumulate more salt deposits on their edges than the plastic types. Dip the tops of the clay pots into about ½ in (1 cm) of melted paraffin before potting your phalaenopsis to prevent this.

good air movement. Maintaining sufficient humidity during the winter can pose a challenge, because air drying heating systems are usually running full blast. Dampen walkways in the greenhouse and increase humidity following the instructions in this chapter if plants are growing in windowsills or under lights.

If you are using well water on your orchids, warm it up to room temperature before watering the plants. Ice-cold water can cause forming buds to drop and may stunt new growth. Do not place moth orchids too close to the windows or the leaves could be damaged by the cold.

If orchids are growing in a greenhouse or on a windowsill while days are short, light intensity is low, and temperatures are cold, cut back the fertilizer to about half of the amount used during the rapid growth period in spring and summer. If your plants are growing under lights and temperatures are still in the 70s F (20s C) or higher during the day and mid-60s F (around 18° C) at night, you can continue the normal fertilizer regimen.

February (late winter)

In North America, February is usually a dark month, but days are growing longer and brighter, which should cause an increase in orchid growth. Toward the end of the month, increased light may require that you take care to keep orchids from being burned. Make sure orchids receive as much light as possible without burning them. Do not crowd the plants, and continue to provide good air circulation to prevent disease problems.

Most of the phalaenopsis will be showing buds and some should be blooming. Stake the inflorescences so the buds, and then flowers, orient themselves gracefully. Continue the fertilizing regimen outlined for January.

If orchids are growing under lights, take note of when you last changed the bulbs. Fluorescent lamps can lose up to 20 percent or more of their light output after several months of use.

March (early spring)

Finally, signs of spring appear with longer and brighter days. Apply shading if necessary; the increased light should not allow the heat in the greenhouse or windowsill to rise too much or orchids may suffer.

The light and warmth of this month mean an acceleration of orchid growth. New roots and leaves should be evident on plants. This is the beginning of the show for many phalaenopsis. As the days get brighter and warmer, resume a regular fertilizing schedule and maintain it through early fall.

This month and next are prime times to check out orchid shows in your area. Attending an orchid show is the most enjoyable way to learn which new varieties of phalaenopsis are being introduced. You can also get growing tips by attending classes at the shows and directly from orchid club members.

April (midspring)

By midspring, many phalaenopsis will be in glorious flower. You will probably need to increase the frequency of watering because of the new plant growth. Watch for insects. Warmer temperatures cause them to hatch and begin feasting on succulent new growth.

If you did not apply shading for the greenhouse last month, it may be needed now. In a sunny window, a gauze curtain can be added to soften the light for phalaenopsis.

Check out orchid shows in your area.

May (late spring)

Growth will continue at full speed this month—another prime time for phalaenopsis flowering.

This month and the next are ideal times to place orders for phalaenopsis to add to your collection. The outside temperatures make it a safe time to ship them, and when you receive the plants you can transplant them into your favorite potting mix in preparation for their summer flush of growth.

You will need to water and fertilize orchids more frequently. Increase ventilation in the growing area to remove excess hot air and prevent fungal disease spots on the flowers.

This is usually a good time to repot phalaenopsis after they have flowered.

June, July, and August (early to late summer)

Temperatures are heating up. This is paradise time for phalaenopsis except in very hot areas such as Arizona and Texas, where evaporative coolers are often installed to cool and humidify the air. In more temperate climates, warmer summer temperatures cause phalaenopsis to make their most rapid leaf and root growth, so your fertilizing program should now be in full swing.

Be sure orchids growing in windowsills or a greenhouse do not get too hot. Consider moving the orchids in a sunny windowsill to another spot that experiences less light and heat.

For phalaenopsis growing under lights, make sure the growing area receives plenty of ventilation, because it could get very warm under the lights. Provide plenty of air ventilation to help reduce leaf temperatures.

This is a prime time for insect problems. If the weather gets hot and dry, look out for mites. If weather is wet, slugs and snails can be a plague. Aphids and scale can show up at any time. If you need to spray the plants, do so in the morning when temperatures are cooler and be sure the phalaenopsis are well watered before you spray.

Phalaenopsis should be responding to your earlier repotting efforts with new root and leaf growth. Some of the novelty phalaenopsis are summer bloomers, so you can add more of these to your collection to expand the blooming season.

September (early autumn)

Cooler nights are beneficial for setting flower buds and spikes. You can remove some shade on the greenhouse in many parts of the Northern Hemisphere. Move phalaenopsis that require high amounts of light back to the windowsill with the most sun exposure.

Place orders for new phalaenopsis varieties from mail-order suppliers, because the outside temperatures are moderate to accommodate orchid shipping.

Carefully examine phalaenopsis plants to determine whether insects are present. Do this before the weather begins to get cold, so if you do detect insects or mites you can take the plants outdoors to treat them.

October (midautumn)

As days continue to shorten and the angle of sunlight gets lower in the sky, position the orchids in your windowsill and greenhouse so that they capture the most light. Clean glass or the glazing surface in greenhouses and windowsills. This can make a big difference in light transmission.

Get ready for winter. Insulate your greenhouse. Get a standby emergency electric or propane heater.

Orchid growth will start to slow from lower temperatures and light; reduce your watering and fertilizing accordingly.

November and December (late autumn to early winter)

Some flower spikes will start to appear, though low light, short days, and cold temperatures bring most phalaenopsis growth to a stop or at least a crawl. More new growth will appear on plants under lights than on plants in a greenhouse or in a windowsill because of the additional light and warmer temperatures that are provided.

In cold climates, November is the last month to purchase mail-order plants safely before temperatures sink to levels that increase the risk of freezing damage in transit. This a great time to visit orchid nurseries to pick out holiday presents for your orchid-growing friends (or yourself).

Water orchids in the early part of the day to ensure that no moisture remains on the leaves. In cold, damp weather, this moisture can cause a disease outbreak.

Staking, Displaying, and Enjoying Moth Orchids

The main purpose for growing moth orchids is to enjoy their unmatched beauty in your environment. This is your just reward for the months you have spent coddling them. Phalaenopsis deserve to look their best when they are putting on their show. Proper staking and grooming can make a big difference in how their flowers appear.

Spikes of orchid flowers can be heavy; if they are improperly staked, they will open at an awkward and disconcerting angle. This can distract from the beauty of the blossoms, because the most interesting and alluring perspective in which to observe phalaenopsis flowers is usually head-on.

Start the staking process before orchids are in flower to ensure that the flowers will be oriented correctly when they open. You can take a few steps to maintain a well-staked inflorescence.

A staked and tied developing phalaenopsis inflorescence

1. As soon as the inflorescence is about 12 in. (30 cm) long, insert a vertical bamboo stake (a green one that blends in with the inflorescence is best) close to where the spike originates at the base of the plant.
2. As you insert the stake, twist it to work it around roots to minimize damage to them.
3. Attach the first tie on the lower part of the spike close to the first node (the bump in the flower stem). Use twist ties, soft cotton string, small green cable ties, or hook and loop tape rather than wire, which could damage the stem.
4. Attach another tie a few inches higher on the flower spike.
5. Add more ties every few inches as the flower spike grows.
6. Place the last tie a few inches below the point at which the first flower buds form. This allows the spike to form a natural arch, with the first flower opening at the highest point and the others gracefully following suit below. Some growers help along the arching of the spike by wrapping green florist's wire around the arching portion of the inflorescence to form a curve.

Flower spikes always grow in the direction of the strongest light. After the flower spike reaches about 12 in. (30 cm) tall and buds are starting to form, never change the plant's orientation to the light source. If you do, the spike will try to reorient itself to the light, resulting in a twisted, distorted spike with flowers (that orient themselves to gravity) opening in all directions. When the flowers are fully open, they will keep their position, so you can then move the plant anywhere you want.

Phalaenopsis growers have lately discovered one of the best ways to attach developing upright flowering stems to bamboo or wood stakes: spring-operated baby hair clips. They are available in all colors, inexpensive, and frequently formed in whimsical shapes of butterflies, flowers, or dragonflies, which fit well with the tropical look.

Encouraging flowers to put on a repeat performance

If a phalaenopsis plant is strong and healthy, it will frequently produce a second flower spike after the first or primary one has stopped flowering. To encourage this to occur, cut the spent primary flower spike about ¼ in. (5 mm) above the node (the bump on the inflorescence or flower spike) immediately below where the first flower once opened. The second spike will probably be shorter than the first or primary spike and will produce fewer and smaller flowers.

This practice is not recommended for young or poorly established plants. For these plants, cut off the flower spike all the way down to its point of origination at the base of the plant. This will cause the orchid to transfer its energy from reproductive mode (producing flowers) to vegetative mode (producing leaves and roots). Foregoing this opportunity for a second blooming may be painful for you in the short term, but it will pay off next season when the better established, more vigorous phalaenopsis plant will reward you with more, and usually larger, flowers.

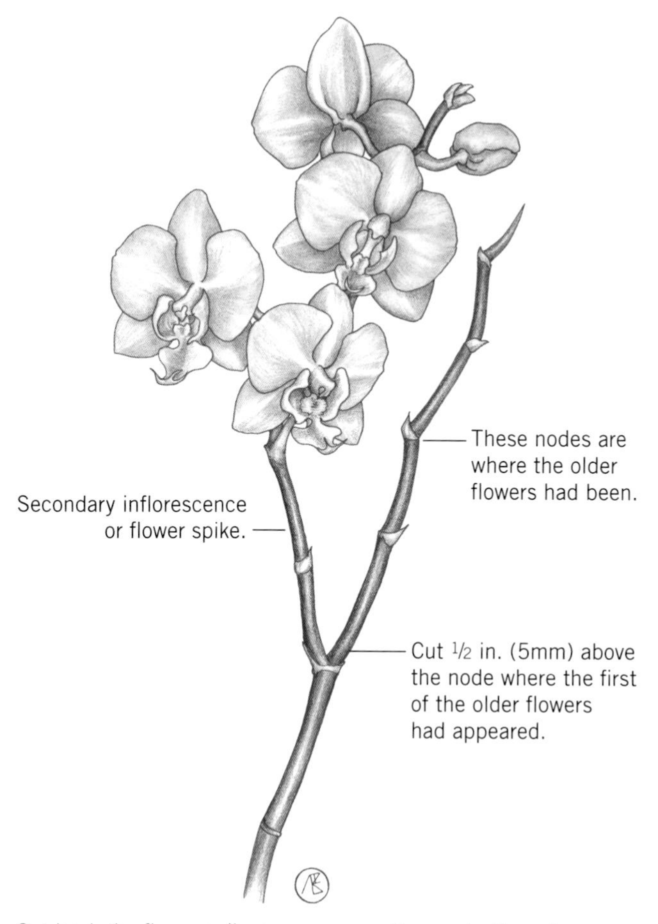

Cut back the flower spike to encourage the production of a secondary spike. Drawing by Liena Dieck.

Certain species *Phalaenopsis*, their primary hybrids, and many of the novelty *Phalaenopsis* hybrids continue to flower on their older flower spikes for years. Do not cut off the spikes of these moth orchids if they are firm and usually green. If and when they naturally shrivel and turn brown, you can safely remove them.

Helping orchids look their best

After orchids have grown for months in a windowsill, under lights, or in a greenhouse, they can look a little rough. The leaves can be dusty and/or blemished with chemical or mineral deposits, older leaves can be wilted or dead, and some of the tips of the leaves can be brown. You can dress them up to help them show off all of their naturally beautiful attributes.

Clean and shine the leaves with a paper towel dampened in whole milk, which contains the fat necessary to add the shine; mayonnaise, which is acidic and helps remove mineral spots; or a bit of mineral oil and water. If the leaves are blemished with mineral deposits, wipe them with a cloth damped with a mild vinegar solution. None of these solutions will harm the plants.

Carefully remove any dead or severely damaged leaves close to the stem. Trim off damaged tips of leaves with very sharp scissors or a single-edge razor blade. The sharper the cutting tool, the cleaner the cut and the less leaf tissue damage will result. When trimming, follow the natural shape of the leaf.

If you plan to bring the orchid to a show, tape the name of your orchid and your own name to the pot. Keep a record of which plants you have entered.

For orchids displayed in the home, protect your furniture by placing the pots on waterproof pads, such as cork platters. If pots are placed on saucers, be sure the saucers are waterproof and without leaks. Terracotta platters are porous, and moisture will seep through and can cause serious damage to unprotected wood furniture. Place felt or rubber protectors under cachepots, platters, or saucers so your furniture will not be scratched.

If the growing pot is encrusted or ugly, insert it into a larger ornamental pot or basket. Choose simple green, white, or neutral colors that do not compete with the flower colors. Place a layer of sheet moss or Spanish moss on the surface of the pot—a nice touch for covering up the sometimes unattractive potting material.

Place a blooming orchid where it gets bright light but not hot, late afternoon sun, so the flowers will last longer. Display the plant on a pedestal or elevate it in some way to present its flowers at eye level, usually the most attractive vantage point. Group orchids with other tropical foliage plants, which provide an attractive backdrop for the phalaenopsis flowers.

Think about how you will light your orchids to display them. Artificial lighting can play an important part in the appearance of an orchid, and track lights work well. Use halogen or other bulbs that produce white light or light as close to sunlight as possible so the orchid flower colors will be rendered accurately. Regular incandescent light produces a yellow to red light that makes reds glow but makes blues and greens appear dull.

Moth orchids make elegant corsages

In some quarters, it is passé to wear a corsage. What a pity! It is time to bring back this accessory. You can add a stylish touch to a special event with an easy-to-make phalaenopsis corsage that you can create in minutes. It is guaranteed to bring praising comments.

You will need green florist's tape, fine florist's wire, one or two phalaenopsis flowers, and a colored ribbon.

1. Choose mature flowers that have been open for several days and that have reached their full size, proper color, and substance.
2. To condition each flower, pick it off the inflorescence the night before the event and let it float, flower stem (peduncle) down, in a bowl of water. This will make it stiff and last longer.
3. Fashion a 4 to 6 in. (10 to 15 cm) piece of fine florist's wire into the shape of a hair pin. Wrap this wire with green florist's tape (A).
4. Gently push this wire through, but not penetrating, the base of the dorsal sepal of the flower to the back of the flower (B). Then take one end of the wire and wrap it around the peduncle and the other end of the wire (C).
5. If the wire cannot be easily passed through the base of the sepal, place the curved wire along the peduncle up against the back of the flower (D).
6. Then take one end of the wire and wrap it around the peduncle and the other end of the wire (E).
7. Wrap florist's tape over the exposed wire and peduncle (F).
8. Add a ribbon and another flower if you like. Voilà! You are ready to show off your elegant phalaenopsis flowers to admirers (G).

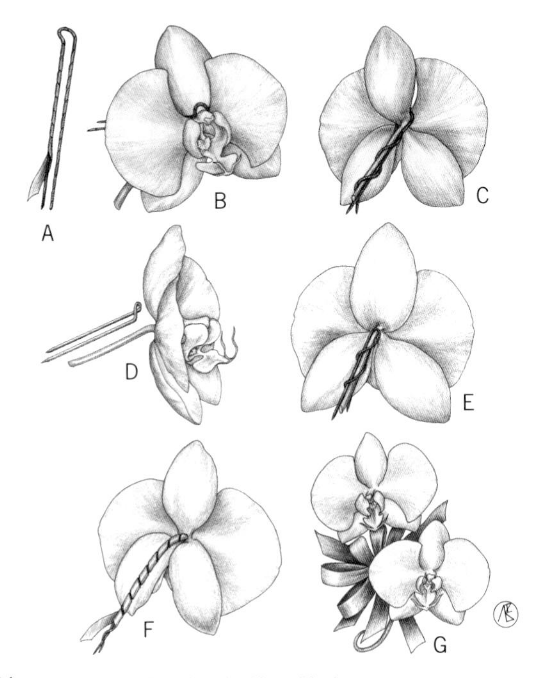

Making a corsage. Drawings by Liena Dieck.

Chapter 9

Selecting and Buying Moth Orchids

After deciding which phalaenopsis best fit your needs, you are ready to acquire plants. To find the closest orchid supplier, visit the American Orchid Society's Grower/Vendor Listing on the Web at http://www.orchidweb.org/aos/orchids/osd-listing.aspx. *Orchids*, the monthly publication of the American Orchid Society, also includes advertisements from various orchid growers.

After you have arrived at the greenhouse and are viewing the live plants, you still have a little research to do. All the plants around you should be healthy. If they are plagued with insects or disease, or in general do not look healthy, the phalaenopsis you choose will likely have these problems as well, whether or not you see evidence on the plant. If the plants in the greenhouse look good overall, you should look closely at the specific plants that interest you. Make sure they are clearly labeled. Gently lift up on the plant to determine how firmly it is rooted in the pot. If it wobbles around, indicating few roots, pass it up. Look for weeds in the pot. A few oxalis (cloverlike) weeds may be acceptable, but too many weeds is a sign of careless culture, and this will create trouble for you later because the only way you can totally remove these weeds is by removing them roots and all, and to do this you will need to remove and repot the plant as well. Examine the leaves. They should be free of disease and insect spots and should be a healthy green color.

Purchase Blooming-Sized Plants

If you are new to moth orchids, you should consider purchasing a plant that is as mature as possible. Better yet, buy it in bloom. You will pay more for a blooming plant, but you will be able to see and smell the flower, you will know how large it gets when it is mature, and it will bloom again sooner than a nonflowering plant.

If you decide to buy an immature plant, be aware that the designations that growers use to indicate the size or maturity of their plants—BS (blooming size) and NFS (near flowering size)—can vary significantly as to how long it will actually take until they flower. Here is a rule of thumb: NFS plants could bloom within twelve months, and BS plants could bloom within six months. Be sure your supplier agrees with these definitions. Before you buy, ask someone in the know how long before the plant blooms.

Caring for newly purchased moth orchids

A moth orchid you purchase will likely have been growing in the bright, humid environment of a commercial greenhouse. You bring the orchid into a home environment, which is usually less bright with lower humidity, so the plant is forced to make some adjustments. How you care for the plant depends on its stage of growth.

Clones versus hybrid seedlings

Taiwanese growers, the largest world suppliers of moth orchids, and many other the large producers in other parts of the world, sell primarily cloned plants. The techniques used for producing these plants in large quantities have reached a high level of dependability. Since only the best hybrids are cloned, the flowers of these orchids are usually of high quality. Many hybrids have won top awards in international orchid shows. Because of the success of cloning award-quality plants, home orchidists can purchase them at reasonable prices.

On the other hand, some orchidists strongly propose that hybrid seedlings should be the focus instead of, or at least in addition to, clones. These orchids are grown from seed produced from mating one promising hybrid with another. New and possibly better flower types may result from hybrid seedlings. Since sexual propagation is used to produce offspring, unlike clones that are produced asexually, the resulting plants and their flowers are variable. An example of this unpredictability is obvious when viewing a sampling of plants from one grex called *Phalaenopsis* Tsunami Warning. However, breeders must wait until an orchid flowers before they can judge the result.

Various flower colors of *Phalaenopsis* Tsunami Warning. Photo by Allen Black.

If the plant is in bloom

Knowing a few important points can make the flowers on your new phalaenopsis last longer.

Position the plant in a spot that is bright, but where it will not receive direct sunlight, except possibly in the morning. Too much harsh sunlight can bleach out the flowers.

Keep the plant on the cool side, in temperatures not exceeding 75° F (24° C). Flowers stay fresher longer this way.

Keep the plant well watered. Even though the orchid plant usually stops growing much when it is in bloom, the leaves and flowers still use and need water.

Do not let bees or flies enter the room where your orchids are blooming. If bees or flies pollinate the flowers, the flowers will soon collapse.

Do not place a plant close to ripe fruit. Fruit emits ethylene gas, which can cause flowers to collapse prematurely.

Keep plants away from strong fumes such as paint thinners or other pollutants. These can cause the blossoms to fade.

Do not spray flowers with water or place the blooming plant in a room that is highly humid with no air movement. This can cause spotting on the flowers from fungal diseases.

If the plant is not in bloom

Before you add a new, unblooming phalaenopsis to your collection, take a few measures to ensure the plant is healthy.

Look under the leaves and at the younger growth to make sure no insects are hiding there.

Isolate this new phalaenopsis from your collection for at least three weeks to allow time for hidden insect eggs to hatch and be treated.

Spray the plant thoroughly with an insecticidal soap. Use a paper towel to wipe off the excess spray. This will not only kill any soft-bodied insects but will also clean the leaves.

Consider repotting the phalaenopsis into your own potting mix. You can then rest assured that the potting mix is fresh and you will know its watering requirements.

Sources and Suppliers

Phalaenopsis hybrids are the most ubiquitous orchids in the world. You can find at least a small selection in many garden centers, building supply centers, discount box stores, home shows, Christmas stores, and even grocery stores. However, some of the more unusual or new hybrids will require some searching. Start with vendors at orchid shows and specialty orchid growers. Many of these growers have greenhouses you can visit. Some of the modest family-run businesses are not always open, so to avoid disappointment, contact the grower ahead of time. Some are mail-order or Internet-only businesses.

If you are not able to visit a grower in person, excellent mail-order suppliers carry all the newest hybrids.

Al's Orchid Greenhouse
204 Masons Lane SE
Leesburg, VA 20175
(703) 771-7753
Al@orchidexchange.com
http://www.orchidexchange.com

Al Pickrel and David Clark offer a broad selection of Phalaenopsis *hybrids and species.*

Baldan Orchids, Inc.
20075 SW 180 Avenue
Miami, FL 33187
(305) 232-8694
baldanorchids@aol.com
http://www.baldanorchids.com

This family business has been breeding and growing phalaenopsis for more than 30 years. It offers a broad range of hybrids and clones and is best know for its beautiful and wildly popular clone, Phalaenopsis *Baldan's Kaleidoscope 'Golden Treasure' AM/AOS.*

Bedford Orchids
630 Sherbrooke Street W
Suite 610
Montreal, QC, Canada H3A 1E4
(514) 866-6111 or fax (514) 878-3679
or
45 Shawsheen Road, Unit 15
Bedford, MA 01730-1936
orchids@orchidsatbedfordorchids.com
http://www.bedfordorchids.com

Howard Ginsberg specializes in reds, yellows, and novelties and offers a broad selection of some of the newest and best clones and hybrids from Taiwan on his web site. He also does some orchid breeding.

Big Leaf Orchids
4932 Longwood Court
Irving, TX 75038
(972) 659-1406 or fax (972) 594-2303
phal@bigleaforchids.com
http://www.bigleaforchids.com

Peter Lin is a passionate phalaenopsis grower. His web site hosts an informative "Phalaenopsis Forum" and offers many of the best of the small species, primary hybrids, and compact, multiflora phalaenopsis from Taiwan and other premier breeders. Peter has a fondness for fragrant phalaenopsis, as I do, and this is reflected in his broad selection of sweetly scented species and hybrids.

Canyon Creek Orchids
40 South 7440 East
Kanah, UT 84741
(435) 644-2146
Stockspallone@kanab.net

Owner A. Dean Stock is a founding member of the International Phalaenopsis Alliance and a retired cytogeneticist/medical geneticist/cancer researcher. His background serves him well as a cutting-edge phalaenopsis breeder, speciailizing in tetraploid yellows and reds. E-mail him for plant availability.

Carmela Orchids
P.O. Box 277
Hakalau, HI 96710
(808) 963-6189 or fax (808) 963-6125
carmelaorchids@hawaii.rr.com
http://www.carmelaorchids.net

This long-established and reputable Hawaiian orchid company offers a broad range of orchids, including a good selection of Phalaenopsis *clones and hybrids.*

Carter and Holmes Orchids
629 Mendelhall Road
P.O. Box 668
Newberry, SC 29108
(800) 873-7086 or fax (803) 276-0588
orchids@carterandholmes.com
http://www.carterandholmes.com

Mac Holmes is the second-generation owner of this respected orchid nursery that offers a large range of moth orchids at reasonable prices, including many of their own hybrids, although they are best known for their art shade cattleyas. With 18 greenhouses full of orchids, the nursery is worth a visit.

Chesterfield Orchid Company
P.O. Box 241
Crosswicks, NJ 08515
(609) 324-1081 or fax (267) 200-0639
CustomerCare@OrchidCo.com
http://www.orchidco.com

Chesterfield offers a selection of some of the newest Taiwanese hybrids. Some species are also available.

D & B Orchids
5608 Boat Club Road
Fort Worth, TX 76135
(817) 238-0234
buyorchids@dandborchids.com
http://www.dandborchids.com

Dottie and Berry Woodson are the proprietors, and Berry is the orchid breeder in the partnership. They offer stems propagations of selected forms of various phalaenopsis species and a range of hybrids.

The Dowery Orchid Nursery
4000 Dowery Lane
Hiwassee, VA 24347
dowery@psknet.net
http://www.doweryorchids.com

This small business, located in the Blue Ridge Mountains, specializes in hard-to-find and fine forms and species of many types of orchids, including phalaenopsis.

Ever Spring Orchids
2868 Pipeline Road
Winnipeg, MB, Canada R4A7A8
(204) 338-2340
grking@shaw.ca
http://www.everspringorchids.ca

Owner Jack Lin is from Taiwan and is familiar with that nation's phalaenopsis work. He and his family bring the best of Taiwanese hybrids and those from other breeders to their North American enterprise. Doritaenopsis with grex and clonal names Ever Spring originate from this nursery.

Gardener's Supply Company
128 Intervale Road
Burlington, VT 05401
(800) 427-3363 or fax (800) 551-6712
http://www.gardeners.com

This company does not sell phalaenopsis plants but offers well-designed, reasonably priced light carts and light fixtures, including those that are more energy efficient and difficult to find and that contain T8 fluorescent lamps, which are great for growing phalaenopsis.

Hoosier Orchid Company
8440 West 82nd Street
Indianapolis, IN 46278
(888) 291-6269 or fax (317) 291-8949
orchids@hoosierorchid.com
http://www.hoosierorchid.com

Hoosier sells a modest selection of phalaenopsis species.

Iowa Orchids, Inc.
3910 Columbia Street
Des Moines, IA 50313
(515) 265-6879 or fax (515) 244-1262
IowaOrchids@hotmail.com
http://www.orchidmall.com/iowaorchids

This small company offers an interesting list of small and economically priced hybrid Phalaenopsis *crosses from Brother Orchid Nursery in Taiwan.*

Krull-Smith
2815 West Ponkan Road
Apopka, FL 32712
(407) 886-4134 or fax (407) 886-0438
sales@krullsmith.com
http://www.krullsmith.com/index.htm

This orchid growing firm is renowned for offering elite hybrids and clones of a broad range of orchids, including phalaenopsis. Frank Smith is the breeder responsible for developing several of the newer red grexes mentioned in this book.

Lauray of Salisbury
432 Undermountain Road
Route 41
Salisbury, CT 06068
(860) 435-2263
jbecker@mohawk.net
http://lauray.com

Judy Becker, owner and operator of this second-generation business, is a highly knowledgeable American Orchid Society judge. Lauray offers a broad range of orchid species and hybrids, including a selection of phalaenopsis, and suitable orchid companions such as begonias, gesneriads, and succulents.

New Vision Orchids
12661 W SR 32
Yorktown, IN 47396
(765) 749-5809
newvisionorchids@aol.com

Owner Russ Vernon was a classmate of mine in the Horticulture Department at The Ohio State University and was an orchid fancier even before that time. He is also an orchid hybridizer and an American Orchid Society judge. One of his specialties is standard and novelty hybrid Phalaenopsis. *He sells plants and flasks of warm- and cool-growing orchids in a variety of genera.*

Norman's Orchids
11039 Monte Vista Avenue
Montclair, CA 91763-6116
(909) 627-9515, or fax (909) 627-3889
support@orchids.com
http://www.orchids.com

Norman's offers a user-friendly site for purchasing orchids online and features a broad range of orchids, but phalaenopsis are clearly the stars. You can search by various requirements, such as size of plant, light needs, color of flower, or fragrance, to find an orchid that fits your needs. You can keep orchid preferences stored in your wish list until you are ready to purchase.

Oak Hill Gardens
37W550 Binnie Road
P.O. Box 25
Dundee, IL 60118-0025
(847) 428-8500 or fax (847) 428-8527
oakhillgardens@sprintmail.com
http://www.oakhillgardens.com

Oak Hill offers a fine selection of phalaenopsis and other orchids at reasonable prices.

Odom's Orchids, Inc.
1611 South Jenkins Road
Fort Pierce, FL 34947
(772) 465-1386 or fax (772) 465-4479
Odoms-Orchids@worldnet.att.net
http://www.odoms.com

This large orchid establishment has more than 60,000 square feet of greenhouse space and offers a broad selection of orchids, including many fine Phalaenopsis *clones and some hybrids.*

Orchidaceae
2022 Wallula Avenue
Walla Walla, WA 99362
(509) 525-9566 or fax (509) 525-3835
sales@orchidaceae.com
http://www.orchidaceae.com

Mark Srull and Joan Batemen opened for business in 1998 and offer a select group of plants in various genera, including fine clones of phalaenopsis, on their web site. The greenhouses are open by appointment.

Orchid Konnection
6812 Gold Dust Trail
Dallas, TX 75252
(972) 407-1885
orchidkonn@msn.com
http://www.orchidkonnection.com

Meir Moses started as a hobbyist and his obsession grew until he started his own business in 1993. He searches out the best breeding from Taiwan and offers these seedling and clones on his web site. He specializes in the newest colors, including reds, yellows, and harlequins.

Orchids by Hausermann, Inc.
2 N134 Addison Road
Villa Park, IL 60181
(630) 543-6855 or fax (630) 543-9842
info@orchidsbyhausermann.com
http://www.orchidsbyhausermann.com

This venerable orchid seller offers a huge selection of orchids, including many species, meristems, and hybrid Phalaenopsis.

Orchid Source Laboratory and Nursery
(formerly G & B Orchid Laboratory)
2426 Cherimoya Drive
Vista, CA 92084
(619) 727-2611, (888) 727-2760, fax (760) 727-0017
orchidsource@gmail.com
http://orchidsource.com/index.html

This company is a fine resource for all types of micropropagation supplies. It deals primarily with commercial growers, but it does sell smaller retail-size quantities to phalaenopsis enthusiasts.

Orchidview
1018 Live Oak Avenue
Moncks Corner, SC 29461
(843) 761-2463
Katherine@orchidview.com
http://www.orchidview.com

H. P. Norton, notable American phalaenopsis breeder and owner of Orchidview, is probably best known for his work in producing prize-winning red and yellow Phalaenopsis *hybrids plus selecting for very blue forms of* P. violacea. *Orchidview offers flasks, compots, seedlings, and stem propagations of some very special phalaenopsis.*

OrchidWiz Encyclopedia 3.03
Alex Maximiano, Managing Director
235 NE 91st Street
Miami Shores, FL 33138
(305) 758-3596
alex@orchidwiz.com
http://www.orchidwiz.com/servlet/StoreFront

This phenomenal orchid database program is a feature-rich program that is intuitive and easy to use.

Owens Orchids
P.O. Box 365
Pisgah Forest, NC 28768
(828) 877-3313 or fax (828) 884-5216
owensorchids@citcom.net
http://www.owensorchids.com/

Owens offers a range of orchids, including the newest Phalaenopsis *clones, seedlings, and plugs.*

Parkside Orchid Nursery
2503 Mountainview Drive
Route 563
Ottsville, PA 18942
(610)847-8039
parkside@ptd.net
http://www.parksideorchids.com

This orchid specialist offers a myriad of orchid types, including a selection of Phalaenopsis *hybrids, with a free newsletter and web catalog.*

Plant Hormones Canada
James D. Brasch, PhD
P.O. Box 40583
Burlington, ON, Canada L7P 4W1
(905) 335-1713 or fax (905) 335-3071
jbrasch@cogeco.ca
http://www.orchidmall.com/hormones/index.htm

This source for Keikigrow Plus offers an assortment of other plant hormones and an informative CD on orchid propagation and conservation.

Porter's Orchids
10868 Royston Road
Grand Ledge, MI 48837
(888) 622-7643 or fax (517) 622-4188
orchidsuzi@portersorchids.com
http://www.portersorchids.com

Porter's offers a selection of hybrid Phalaenopsis *that are easy to grow and bloom and are well suited to home culture.*

Robert Bedard Horticulture
475 Blair Ranch Road
Scotts Valley, CA 95066
(831) 439-9484
rbedard@robert-bedard.com
http://www.robert-bedard.com/orchids/index.html

Robert Bedard does his own hybridizing and growing and offers an impressive selection of stem propagations, species, and hybrids. He focuses on vigorous, easy-to-grow selections. Robert has expanded on some of the work of Herb Hager, who developed many of the miniature and multiflora types.

Sedona Orchids
19985 S. W. 264 Street
Homestead, FL 33031-1659
(305) 248- 0522 or fax (305) 248-0522
sedorchid@aol.com
http://www.sedonaorchids.com

This nursery, formed in 1990 and owned by David Kridel, specializes in phalaenopsis and cattleya breeding and growing. The cultivar name 'Sedona' appears on many prize-winning phalaenopsis. The company sells it own crosses as well as those of others—both as clones and seedlings.

Sigma-Aldrich
P.O. Box 14508
St. Louis, MO 63178
(800) 325-3010 or fax (800) 240-4668
http://www.sigmaaldrich.com

This global company offers an impressive array of chemicals and related equipment and a complete range of culture containers, tissue culture media, and other supplies.

Sky Island Orchids
18650 NW Fairdale Road
Yamhill, OR 97148
(503) 852-7088
skyisl@macnet.com
http://www.skyislandorchids.com/default.htm

Husband and wife team Bill and Linda Mitchell are both American Orchid Society judges and started this orchid nursery in 1983. Bill breeds and grows an interesting array of phalaenopsis. Sky Island sell flasks, compots, and flowering size plants of their various crosses.

Sylvies Orchids
Amy Howard
3017 Linwood Drive
Sarasota, FL 34232
(941) 341-0949 or fax (941) 379-4949
orders@sylviesorchids.com
http://www.sylviesorchids.com

Sylvies is a wholesale and retail supplier of a broad range of orchids, including Phalaenopsis *clones and hybrids.*

Zephyrus Orchids
The Bloomin' Gardener
6673 8th Concession Rd
Maidstone, ON, Canada N0R 1A0
(519) 256-0999 or fax (519) 256-8884
nic@zephyrusorchids.com
http://www.zephyrusorchids.com

Zephyrus sells a broad range of some of the newest phalaenopsis cultivars. Founder John Doherty has a background in plant biotechnology.

Fragrant Phalaenopsis

Phalaenopsis Ambo Buddha 'Phoenix' FCC/AOS
Phalaenopsis amboinensis 'Queen' HCC/AOS
Phalaenopsis Arizona Gem 'Ruby Glow' HCC/AOS
Phalaenopsis Arizona Princess 'Purple Gem' HCC/AOS
Phalaenopsis Arizona Princess 'Spotted Beauty' AM/AOS
Phalaenopsis bellina
Phalaenopsis Bonnie Vasquez 'Zuma Creek' HCC/AOS
Phalaenopsis Brother Sara Gold 'Peach'
Phalaenopsis Buena Jewel
Phalaenopsis Caribbean Sunset 'Sweet Fragrance'
Phalaenopsis Carolina Red Magic 'Lenette' AM/AOS
Phalaenopsis Chingruey's Morning 'Ching Ruey'
Phalaenopsis Coral Isles 'Lung Ching' AM/AOS
Phalaenopsis Coral Isles 'Yung Ho'
Phalaenopsis cornu-cervi var. *alba* 'Jade'
Phalaenopsis Dragon Tree Eagle 'DT168'
Phalaenopsis Flight of Birds
Phalaenopsis Formosa San Fan
Phalaenopsis George Leather 'Peter Lin'
Phalaenopsis gigantea
Phalaenopsis Hannover Passion 'Ching Ruey'
Phalaenopsis Ho's Lovely Amethyst 'La Flora' AM/AOS
Phalaenopsis Joy Spring Canary 'Rainbow'
Phalaenopsis Kuntrarti Rarashati 'Bunker Hill'
Phalaenopsis Kuntrarti Rarashati 'Joy'
Phalaenopsis Luedde-violacea 'Ana Red' HCC/AOS
Phalaenopsis Malibu Imp 'Evergreen Hill' AM/AOS
Phalaenopsis mannii
Phalaenopsis Min-Chao Yeo-Man 'Hwa Yuan'
Phalaenopsis Orchid World 'Bonnie Vasquez' AM/AOS
Phalaenopsis Penang Girl
Phalaenopsis Penang Girl 'Ching Ruey'
Phalaenopsis Perfect Sara 'Orange Delight'
Phalaenopsis Perfection Is 'Chen' FCC/AOS
Phalaenopsis Phoenix Flame 'Orange Glow' AM/AOS
Phalaenopsis pulcherrima f. *alba*
Phalaenopsis Samba
Phalaenopsis schilleriana
Phalaenopsis Sogo Cock 'Joy'
Phalaenopsis Sogo Cock 'Oriental Beauty' AM/AOS
Phalaenopsis Sogo Cock 'Oriental Princess' HCC/AOS
Phalaenopsis Sogo Grape
Phalaenopsis Sogo Rose 'Joy'
Phalaenopsis 'Sweetheart'
Phalaenopsis Tabasco Tex 'Garnet Glow' AM/AOS
Phalaenopsis Tsay's Evergreen 'Nobby's Jade' HCC/AOS
Phalaenopsis Valentinii
Phalaenopsis venosa
Phalaenopsis violacea
Phalaenopsis violacea 'Blue Chip'
Phalaenopsis violacea 'Purity'
Phalaenopsis Yungho Gelb Canary 'Yungho' AM/AOS
Phalaenopsis Zuma Aussie Delight

Intergeneric Hybrids

The genus *Phalaenopsis* has been interbred with many other genera of orchids. Some of the esoteric crosses are seldom offered for sale. More new crosses will continue to be made since orchid breeders are a curious and adventuresome lot.

GENUS	CROSS
Aeridopsis (*Aerps.*)	*Aerides* × *Phalaenopsis*
Arachnopsirea (*Aps.*)	*Arachnis* × *Phalaenopsis* × *Sedirea*
Arachnopsis (*Arnps.*)	*Arachnis* × *Phalaenopsis*
Asconopsis (*Ascps.*)	*Ascocentrum* × *Phalaenopsis*
Beardara (*Bdra.*)	*Ascocentrum* × *Doritis* × *Phalaenopsis*
Bogardara (*Bgd.*)	*Ascocentrum* × *Phalaenopsis* × *Vanda* × *Vandopsis*
Bokchoonara (*Bkch.*)	*Arachnis* × *Ascocentrum* × *Phalaenopsis* × *Vanda*
Chinheongara (*Chi.*)	*Ascocentrum* × *Phalaenopsis* × *Rhynchostylis*
Cleisonopsis (*Clnps.*)	*Cleisocentron* × *Phalaenopsis*
Devereauxara (*Dvra.*)	*Ascocentrum* × *Phalaenopsis* × *Vanda*
Diplonopsis (*Dpnps.*)	*Diploprora* × *Phalaenopsis*
Dorandopsis (*Ddps.*)	*Doritis* × *Vandopsis*
Doredirea (*Drd.*)	*Doritis* × *Sedirea*
Doricentrum (*Dctm.*)	*Ascocentrum* × *Doritis*
Doriella (*Drlla.*)	*Doritis* × *Kingiella*
Doriellaopsis (*Dllps.*)	*Doritis* × *Kingiella* × *Phalaenopsis*
Dorifinetia (*Dfta.*)	*Doritis* × *Neofinetia*
Doriglossum (*Drgm.*)	*Ascoglossum* × *Doritis*
Dorisia (*Drsa.*)	*Doritis* × *Luisia*
Doristylis (*Dst.*)	*Doritis* × *Rhynchostylis*
Doritaenopsis (*Dtps.*)	*Doritis* × *Phalaenopsis*
Dorthera (*Dtha.*)	*Doritis* × *Renanthera*

GENUS	CROSS
Dresslerara (*Dres.*)	*Ascoglossum* × *Phalaenopsis* × *Renanthera*
Edeara (*Edr.*)	*Arachnis* × *Phalaenopsis* × *Renanthera* × *Vandopsis*
Ernestara (*Entra.*)	*Phalaenopsis* × *Renanthera* × *Vandopsis*
Eurynopsis (*Eunps.*)	*Eurychone* × *Phalaenopsis*
Hagerara (*Hgra.*)	*Doritis* × *Phalaenopsis* × *Vanda*
Haraenopsis (*Hnp.*)	*Haraella* × *Phalaenopsis*
Hausermannara (*Haus.*)	*Doritis* × *Phalaenopsis* × *Vandopsis*
Himoriara (*Hmra.*)	*Ascocentrum* × *Phalaenopsis* × *Rhynchostylis* × *Vanda*
Isaoara (*Isr.*)	*Aerides* × *Ascocentrum* × *Phalaenopsis* × *Vanda*
Laycockara (*Lay.*)	*Arachnis* × *Phalaenopsis* × *Vandopsis*
Lichtara (*Licht.*)	*Doritis* × *Gastrochilus* × *Phalaenopsis*
Luinopsis (*Lnps.*)	*Luisia* × *Phalaenopsis*
Lutherara (*Luth.*)	*Phalaenopsis* × *Renanthera* × *Rhynchostylis*
Macekara (*Maka.*)	*Arachnis* × *Phalaenopsis* × *Renanthera* × *Vanda* × *Vandopsis*
Meechaiara (*Mchr.*)	*Ascocentrum* × *Doritis* × *Phalaenopsis* × *Rhynchostylis* × *Vanda*
Meirmosesara (*Mei.*)	*Ascocentrum* × *ParaPhalaenopsis* × *Phalaenopsis* × *Vanda*
Moirara (*Moir.*)	*Phalaenopsis* × *Renanthera* × *Vanda*
Morieara (*Moi.*)	*Doritis* × *Neofinetia* × *Phalaenopsis* × *Rhynchostylis*
Nakagawaara (*Nkgwa.*)	*Aerides* × *Doritis* × *Phalaenopsis*
Neostylopsis (*Nsls.*)	*Neofinetia* × *Phalaenopsis* × *Rhynchostylis*
Owensara (*Owsr.*)	*Doritis* × *Phalaenopsis* × *Renanthera*
Parnataara (*Parn.*)	*Aerides* × *Arachnis* × *Phalaenopsis*
Paulara (*Plra.*)	*Ascocentrum* × *Doritis* × *Phalaenopsis* × *Renanthera* × *Vanda*
Pepeara (*Ppa.*)	*Ascocentrum* × *Doritis* × *Phalaenopsis* × *Renanthera*
Phalaenidium (*Phd.*)	*Kingidium* × *Phalaenopsis*
Phalandopis (*Phdps.*)	*Phalaenopsis* × *Vandopsis*
Phalanetia (*Phnta.*)	*Neofinetia* × *Phalaenopsis*
Phaleralda (*Pld.*)	*Esmeralda* × *Phalaenopsis*
Phaliella (*Phlla.*)	*Kingiella* × *Phalaenopsis*
PhalPhalaenopsis (*Phph.*)	*ParaPhalaenopsis* × *Phalaenopsis*
Pooleara (*Polra.*)	*Ascocentrum* × *Ascoglossum* × *Phalaenopsis* × *Renanthera*
Renanthopsis (*Rnthps.*)	*Phalaenopsis* × *Renanthera*
Rhynchonopsis (*Rhnps.*)	*Phalaenopsis* × *Rhynchostylis*
Rhyndoropsis (*Rhdps.*)	*Doritis* × *Phalaenopsis* × *Rhynchostylis*
Richardmizutaara (*Rcmza.*)	*Ascocentrum* × *Phalaenopsis* × *Vandopsis*
Roseara (*Rsra.*)	*Doritis* × *Kingiella* × *Phalaenopsis* × *Renanthera*

GENUS	CROSS
Sappanara (*Sapp.*)	*Arachnis* × *Phalaenopsis* × *Renanthera*
Sarconopsis (*Srnps.*)	*Phalaenopsis* × *Sarcochilus*
Sediropsis (*Sdp.*)	*Phalaenopsis* × *Sedirea*
Sidranara (*Sidr.*)	*Ascocentrum* × *Phalaenopsis* × *Renanthera*
Sladeara (*Slad.*)	*Doritis* × *Phalaenopsis* × *Sarcochilus*
Stamariaara (*Stmra.*)	*Ascocentrum* × *Phalaenopsis* × *Renanthera* × *Vanda*
Sutingara (*Sut.*)	*Arachnis* × *Ascocentrum* × *Phalaenopsis* × *Vanda* × *Vandopsis*
Trautara (*Trta.*)	*Doritis* × *Luisia* × *Phalaenopsis*
Trevorara (*Trev.*)	*Arachnis* × *Phalaenopsis* × *Vanda*
Trichonopsis (*Trnps.*)	*Phalaenopsis* × *Trichoglottis*
Uptonara (*Upta.*)	*Phalaenopsis* × *Rhynchostylis* × *Sarcochilus*
Vandaenopsis (*Vdnps.*)	*Phalaenopsis* × *Vanda*
Vandewegheara (*Vwga.*)	*Ascocentrum* × *Doritis* × *Phalaenopsis* × *Vanda*
Waibengara (*Wai.*)	*Aerides* × *Ascocentrum* × *Phalaenopsis* × *Rhynchostylis* × *Vanda*
Wilkara (*Wlk.*)	*Ascocentrum* × *Neofinetia* × *Phalaenopsis*
Yapara (*Yap.*)	*Phalaenopsis* × *Rhynchostylis* × *Vanda*
Yeepengara (*Ypga.*)	*Aerides* × *Phalaenopsis* × *Rhynchostylis* × *Vanda*
Yithoeara (*Yit.*)	*Aerides* × *Ascocentrum* × *Doritis* × *Phalaenopsis* × *Rhynchostylis* × *Vanda*

Illustrated Hybrids by Registration Year

DATE	GENUS	GREX	CULTIVAR	REGISTERED BY
1895	*Phalaenopsis*	Luedde-violacea	'Ana Red' HCC/AOS	Veitch
1959	*Phalaenopsis*	Valentinii		Unknown
1963	*Doritaenopsis*	Kenneth Schubert	'First Rays'	Clarelen's
	Doritaenopsis	Purple Gem		E. Iwanaga
	Phalaenopsis	Samba		W. Sanders
1965	*Doritaenopsis*	Memoria Clarence Schubert		Fields Orchids
1967	*Phalaenopsis*	Coral Isles	'Lung Ching' AM/AOS	Frederick Thornton
1968	*Asconopsis*	Irene Dobkin	'York' HCC/AOS	Frederick Thornton
	Phalaenopsis	Lipperose		F. Hark
1969	*Phalaenopsis*	Spotted Moon	'Jo Ann' HCC/AOS	Charles Beard
1970	*Phalaenopsis*	Caribbean Sunset	'Sweet Fragrance'	Frederick Thorton
1974	*Phalaenopsis*	George Vasquez	'An Lin'	Hugo Freed
	Phalaenopsis	Seventh Heaven		Jones and Scully
1977	*Phalaenopsis*	Golden Buddha		P. Lista
1978	*Beardara*	Henry Wallbrunn		Fort Caroline's
	Phalaenopsis	Tabasco Tex	'Garnet Glow' AM/AOS	W. B. Smith
1983	*Doritaenopsis*	Happy Valentine	'Fangtastic'	Morita Inc.
	Phalaenopsis	Fortune Saltzman	'Maple Bridge' AM/TCA	Brother Orchid Nursery
	Phalaenopsis	Golden Peoker	'BL' HCC/AOS	Brother Orchid Nursery
	Phalaenopsis	Golden Peoker	Nan-Cho AM/AOS	Brother Orchid Nursery
1984	*Phalaenopsis*	Orchid World	'Bonnie Vasquez' AM/AOS	Orchid World International
	Phalaenopsis	Spirit House	'D & B' AM/AOS	Stewart, Inc.
	Phalaenopsis	Zuma Garnet	'Plantation' HCC/AOS	Zuma Canyon
1985	*Phalaenopsis*	Bonnie Vasquez	'Zuma Creek' HCC/AOS	Zuma Canyon
	Phalaenopsis	Hilo Lip	'Winter Frost'	G & D Kobayashi
1986	*Phalaenopsis*	Kuntrarti Rarashati	'Bunker Hill'	Kolopaking

DATE	GENUS	GREX	CULTIVAR	REGISTERED BY
1986	*Phalaenopsis*	Kuntrarti Rarashati	'Joy'	A. Kolopaking
	Phalaenopsis	Little Mary	'Cherry Blossom'	T. Takase
	Phalaenopsis	Zuma Aussie Delight		Zuma Canyon
1988	*Phalaenopsis*	Brother Girl		Brother Orchid Nursery
	Phalaenopsis	Flight of Birds		Carter and Holmes
	Phalaenopsis	Pago Pago	'First Love' AM/AOS	Zuma Canyon
1989	*Phalaenopsis*	Chih Shang's Stripes	'Marginata'	M. Lin
1990	*Phalaenopsis*	Baldan's Kaleidoscope		Baldan's
	Phalaenopsis	Ever-Spring Spot	'Montclair'	Ever Spring Orchid Nursery
	Phalaenopsis	World Class	'Big Foot' JC/AOS	Carmela Orchids
	Phalaenopsis	Zuma's Pixie	'Taida Little Cutie'	Taida
1991	*Doritaenopsis*	Hybridizer's Dream		Carmela Orchids
	Phalaenopsis	Dotty Woodson	'Orchidland'	Woodson
	Phalaenopsis	Ember	'Blumen Insel' AM/AOS	Zuma Canyon
	Phalaenopsis	Venimp	'Sedona'	J. G. Martin
1992	*Phalaenopsis*	Brother Mirage		Brother Orchid Nursery
	Phalaenopsis	Buena Jewel		N. LeJeune
	Phalaenopsis	Carolina Red Magic	'Lenette' AM/AOS	Lenette
	Phalaenopsis	Ever-Spring King	'Lee' JC/AOS	Ever Spring Orchid Nursery
	Phalaenopsis	Ever-Spring Light		Ever Spring Orchid Nursery
	Phalaenopsis	Mini Mark	'Holm'	Breckenridge
1993	*Phalaenopsis*	Ambo Buddha	'Phoenix' FCC/AOS	Brother Orchid Nursery
	Phalaenopsis	Ambo Buddha	'SW'	Brother Orchid Nursery
	Phalaenopsis	Formosa San Fan		Lin Ming Kung
	Phalaenopsis	Ho's Little Caroline		Tin-Fan Ho
	Phalaenopsis	Jungle Cat	'Bloody Mary'	Norman's Orchids
	Phalaenopsis	Taisuco Chinfang		Taiwan Sugar Company
1994	*Doritaenopsis*	Taisuco Pixie	'Ching Ruey' AM/AOS	Taiwan Sugar Company
	Phalaenopsis	Chromium Emperor	'Rising Sun' AM/AOS	A. Klehm
	Phalaenopsis	Hannover Passion	'Ching Ruey'	Cheng Hsien-I
1995	*Doritaenopsis*	Lonnie Morris	'Nationwide' AM/AOS	H. P. Norton
	Doritaenopsis	Pico Lady Ruby	'Wickford' HCC/AOS	Brother Orchid Nursery
	Phalaenopsis	Brother Lawrence	'Montclair'	Brother Orchid Nursery
	Phalaenopsis	Brother Passat		Brother Orchid Nursery
	Phalaenopsis	George Leather	'Peter Lin'	Orchid Hatchery
	Phalaenopsis	Katie Morris	'Burnished Copper' HCC/AOS	H. P. Norton
	Phalaenopsis	Katie Morris	'Caroline'	H. P. Norton

DATE	GENUS	GREX	CULTIVAR	REGISTERED BY
1995	*Phalaenopsis*	Katie Morris	'Dixie Sunset'	H. P. Norton
	Phalaenopsis	Min-Chao Yeo-Man	'Hwa Yuan'	C. N. Wan
	Phalaenopsis	Summer Garnet	'Neo' HCC/AOS	Orchid Plantation
	Phalaenopsis	Tsay's Evergreen	'Nobby's Jade' HCC/AOS	Evergreen
	Phalaenopsis	Yungho Gelb Canary	'Yungho' AM/AOS	Yung-Ho
1996	*Doritaenopsis*	Minho Princess		Sogo Team Co.
	Doritaenopsis	Minho Princess	'Watercolor Princess' HCC/AOS	Sogo Team Co.
	Phalaenopsis	Ben Goo	'Radiant Ruby' HCC/AOS	Eric Goo
	Phalaenopsis	Florida Heat	'Gemma' HCC/AOS	Krull-Smith
	Phalaenopsis	Hiroshima Fantasy	'Beautiful Dreamer' HCC/AOS	M. Kobayashi
	Phalaenopsis	Jackie Debonis		Norman's Orchids
	Phalaenopsis	Sogo Grape		Sogo Team Co.
1997	*Doritaenopsis*	Ever Spring Pioneer	'Champion'	Ever Spring Orchid Nursery
	Doritaenopsis	Ever Spring Prince	'Harlequin'	Ever Spring Orchid Nursery
	Doritaenopsis	Ever Spring Prince	'Plum Flower'	Ever Spring Orchid Nursery
	Doritaenopsis	Leopard Prince	'Brennan's Orchids' HCC/AOS	Sogo Team Co.
	Doritaenopsis	Leopard Prince	'KH4338'	Sogo Team Co.
	Doritaenopsis	Leopard Prince	'KHM430'	Sogo Team Co.
	Doritaenopsis	Pixie Star	'Norman'	Orchid Zone
	Doritaenopsis	Siam Treasure		S. Wannakrairoj
	Doritaenopsis	Sogo Manager	'Neo' HCC/AOS	Sogo Team Co.
	Doritaenopsis	Sogo Manager	'Nina'	Sogo Team Co.
	Doritaenopsis	Taida Salu		Taida
	Phalaenopsis	Brother Sara Gold	'Peach'	Sogo Team Co.
	Phalaenopsis	Brother Sara Gold	'Sogo F-623'	Brother Orchid Nursery
	Phalaenopsis	Carolina Bronze Meteor	'Lenette' HCC/AOS	Lenette
	Phalaenopsis	Chingruey's Morning	'Ching Ruey'	Ching Ruey Orchids
	Phalaenopsis	Cygnus		Kokubunji
	Phalaenopsis	Malibu Imp	'Evergreen Hill' AM/AOS	Hugo Freed
	Phalaenopsis	Mary Lilian Taylor	'Desert Orange' AM/AOS	G. R. Taylor
	Phalaenopsis	Mary-Tauscher-Goo	'The Queen' HCC/AOS	Eric Goo
1998	*Doritaenopsis*	Brother Little Hatter		Brother Orchid Nursery
	Phalaenopsis	An Tai Spot	'Splotchy' AM/AOS	Sogo Team Co.
	Phalaenopsis	Brother Oconee	'Maria Teresa'	Brother Orchid Nursery
	Phalaenopsis	Brother Pirate King		Brother Orchid Nursery
	Phalaenopsis	Lawless Red Peppers		Brother Orchid Nursery
	Phalaenopsis	Nobby's Amy	'Shih Hua'	Nobby's Orchids
	Phalaenopsis	Phoenix Flame	'Orange Glow' AM/AOS	Phoenix Orchids, Eric Goo

DATE	GENUS	GREX	CULTIVAR	REGISTERED BY
1999	*Doritaenopsis*	Chian-Huey Red Rose		J. S. Wu
	Doritaenopsis	Fangtastic Roslynn Greenberg	'Raspberry Delight' HCC/AOS	Norman's Orchids
	Doritaenopsis	I-Hsin Black Valentine	'KHM 1566'	W. T. Chien
	Doritaenopsis	Jack Beckwith		H. P. Norton
	Doritaenopsis	Mepkin Bells	'Katherine'	H. P. Norton
	Doritaenopsis	Montclair Valentine	'Picotee'	Norman's Orchids
	Doritaenopsis	Scarlet in Snow		Ming-Rong Tsay
	Doritaenopsis	Sinica Sunday	'KHM364'	Shen Nung Agr.
	Doritaenopsis	Taisuco Bloody Mary		Taiwan Sugar Company
	Phalaenopsis	Arizona Gem	'Ruby Glow' HCC/AOS	Phoenix Orchids-Eric Goo
	Phalaenopsis	Black Ball		Sogo Team Co.
	Phalaenopsis	Brecko Dawnphil		Breckenridge
	Phalaenopsis	Haur Jin Diamond		Ching Ann
	Phalaenopsis	Haur Jin Diamond	'Montclair' HCC/AOS	Ching Ann
	Phalaenopsis	Little Emperor		Norman's Orchids
	Phalaenopsis	Nobby's Amy		Nobby Orchids
	Phalaenopsis	Perfection Is	'Chen' FCC/AOS	Howard Ginsberg
	Phalaenopsis	Purple Majesty	'Burgundy Beauty' AM/AOS	Eric Goo
	Phalaenopsis	Ruth Tauscher	'Garnet Beauty' HCC/AOS	Eric Goo
	Phalaenopsis	Shenandoah Fire	'Ember'	Brennan's
	Phalaenopsis	Sogo Cock	'Joy'	Sogo Team Co.
	Phalaenopsis	Sogo Cock	'Oriental Beauty' AM/AOS	Sogo Team Co.
	Phalaenopsis	Sogo Cock	'Oriental Princess HCC/AOS	Sogo Team Co.
	Phalaenopsis	Sogo David	'Peachy'	Sogo Team Co.
	Phalaenopsis	Sogo Twinkle	'Stars' HCC/AOS	Sogo Team Co.
2000	*Doritaenopsis*	Brother Success		Brother Orchid Nursery
	Doritaenopsis	Chingruey's Goldstaff		Ching Ruey Orchids
	Doritaenopsis	Hsinying Mount	'Ching Ruey'	Ching Hua
	Doritaenopsis	Taisuco Micky		Taiwan Sugar Company
	Phalaenopsis	Arizona Princess	'Purple Gem' HCC/AOS	Phoenix Orchids, Eric Goo
	Phalaenopsis	Brother Dendi	'Mary' HCC/AOS	Brother Orchid Nursery
	Phalaenopsis	Brother John		D. Diehm
	Phalaenopsis	Sogo Lion	'Amber'	Sogo Team Co.
	Phalaenopsis	Sogo Rose	'Joy'	Sogo Team Co.
	Phalaenopsis	Taisuco Tunelip		Taiwan Sugar Company
2001	*Doritaenopsis*	I-Hsin Marks		W. T. Chien
	Doritaenopsis	Kiss Me Kate	'Carol'	H. P. Norton
	Phalaenopsis	Brother Jungle Cat		J. & L. Selles

DATE	GENUS	GREX	CULTIVAR	REGISTERED BY
2001	*Phalaenopsis*	I-Hsin Sunflower	'KHM-95-1'	W. T. Chien
	Phalaenopsis	I-Hsin Sunflower	'M' AM/AOS	W. T. Chien
	Phalaenopsis	Krull's Red Hot	'Red Leather'	H. P. Norton
	Phalaenopsis	Kung's Gelb Lishian		Kung's
	Phalaenopsis	Taida Lovely	'M'	Taida
	Phalaenopsis	Taisuco Date	'F. L.'	Taiwan Sugar Company
	Phalaenopsis	Taisuco Rosemary		Taiwan Sugar Company
	Phalaenopsis	Tzeng-Wen Sentra		Ching-Tien Wong
	Phalaenopsis	Tzeng-Wen Sentra	'Jia-Ho' AM/AOS	Ching-Tien Wong
	Phalaenopsis	Wes Addison	'Ruby Glow' HCC/AOS	Phoenix Orchids, Eric Goo
	Phalaenopsis	Yu Pin Pearl	'Peacock'	N. I. Chang
2002	*Doritaenopsis*	Chain Xen Diamond	'Celebration' FCC/AOS	Fu-Liang Huang
	Doritaenopsis	Chain Xen Pearl	'Lucky Star'	Fu-Liang Huang
	Doritaenopsis	Chain Xen Pearl	'Shih Hua'	Fu-Liang Huang
	Doritaenopsis	Happy King		H. P. Norton
	Doritaenopsis	Taisuco Sunset		Taiwan Sugar Company
	Doritaenopsis	Yu Pin Lover		N. I. Chang
	Phalaenopsis	Canyon Sun		A. D. Stock
	Phalaenopsis	Fantasy Musick		F & M Kaufmann
	Phalaenopsis	Gene Wentz		K & D Emig
	Phalaenopsis	Joy Spring Canary	'Rainbow'	J. Wu
	Phalaenopsis	Nobby's Shadowy	'Nobby'	Nobby Orchids
	Phalaenopsis	Oriental Fairy	'Montclair'	Oriental Orchids
	Phalaenopsis	Shin Yi Diamond		Sogo Team Co.
	Phalaenopsis	So Cha Gem	'Chin Jih' HCC/AOS	Ching Ann
	Phalaenopsis	Taiwan Glory		Orchis Flor.
2003	*Doritaenopsis*	Acker's Sweetie	'Dragon Tree Maple' SM/TOGA	Acker's
	Doritaenopsis	Bill Tippit	'Purple Glow' HCC/AOS	Eric Goo
	Doritaenopsis	I-Hsin Balloon	'KHM1316'	W. T. Chien
	Doritaenopsis	I-Hsin Waltz	'Zephyrus'	W. T. Chien
	Doritaenopsis	Jiuhbao Red Rose	'Brilliant'	JiuhBao Orchids
	Doritaenopsis	Memorial Bud Terrell	'Red Beauty' HCC/AOS	Eric Goo
	Doritaenopsis	Musick Surprise		F & M Kaufmann
	Doritaenopsis	Ruey Lih Beauty	'Formosa'	Ching Ann
	Doritaenopsis	Sau Goo	'Orange Beauty' HCC/AOS	Eric Goo
	Phalaenopsis	Brother Redland Spots		R. F. Orchids
	Phalaenopsis	Cris Lee	'Red Beauty'	Eric Goo

DATE	GENUS	GREX	CULTIVAR	REGISTERED BY
2003	*Phalaenopsis*	H. P. Norton	'Kathy' AM/AOS	Krull-Smith
	Phalaenopsis	I-Hsin Gold Dust	'Neo' AM/AOS	W. T. Chen
	Phalaenopsis	Memoria Flora Ho	'Gold Emerald' HCC/AOS	Eric Goo
	Phalaenopsis	Perfect Sara	'Orange Delight'	Nobby Orchids
	Phalaenopsis	Sherri Pantano	'Red Beauty' AM/AOS	Phoenix Orchids, Eric Goo
	Phalaenopsis	Sherri Pantano	'Tangelo'	Eric Goo
	Phalaenopsis	Sunrise Red Peoker		Sunrise Biotech
2004	*Doritaenopsis*	Joy Angel Voice		J. Wu
	Doritaenopsis	Musick Lipstick		F & M Kaufmann
	Doritaenopsis	Tying Shin Phoenix	'Golden Cupid'	Tying Shin Orchid
	Doritaenopsis	Tying Shin Phoenix	'Golden Leopard' BM/TOGA	Tying Shin Orchid
	Doritaenopsis	Tying Shin Phoenix	'Golden Phoenix' SM/TOGA	Tying Shin Orchid
	Doritaenopsis	Tying Shin Phoenix	'T. S.'	Tying Shin Orchid
	Phalaenopsis	Bev Tall	'Carnelian Queen' AM/AOS	Eric Goo
	Phalaenopsis	Chingruey's Stripes	'Ching Ruey'	Ching Ruey Orchids
	Phalaenopsis	Dragon Tree Eagle	'DT168'	Wang Bi-Jiang
	Phalaenopsis	Memoria Chuck Noe		Allen Black
	Phalaenopsis	Memoria Winona Brown Weeks		Wickford Orchids
	Phalaenopsis	Tying Shin Alice	'Hong'	Tying Shin Orchid
2005	*Doritaenopsis*	Brother Sheridan		Wickford Orchids
	Doritaenopsis	Happy Ending		Allen Black
	Doritaenopsis	Sogo Melody		Sogo Team Co.
	Doritaenopsis	Taida Fortune	'Taida Golden Girl'	Taida
	Phalaenopsis	Hilo Gold	'Mary' HCC/AOS	Eric Goo
	Phalaenopsis	Kunstler's Gem		Allen Black
	Phalaenopsis	Memoria Don Tauscher	'Purple Beauty' AM/AOS	Eric Goo
	Phalaenopsis	Memoria Phoebe Kwock	'Bold Beauty' HCC/AOS	Eric Goo
	Phalaenopsis	Tsunami Warning		Allen Black
	Phalaenopsis	Yellow Brite Lites	'Neo' HCC/AOS	Coqui (Carmela)
2006	*Doritaenopsis*	Firepower	'Cinnamon Glow'	Eric Goo
	Doritaenopsis	Flash Point	'Orange Glow'	Eric Goo
	Doritaenopsis	Hurricane Katrina		Allen Black
	Doritaenopsis	Taiwan Red Cat		Orchis Flor.
	Phalaenopsis	Frog Hollow Fantasia	'Montclair'	Frog Hollow Orchids
	Phalaenopsis	Kenny Ewell		Allen Black
	Phalaenopsis	Orchidview Tabasco		H. P. Norton

Illustrated Hybrids by Originator

ORIGINATOR	NAME
A. D. Stock	*Phalaenopsis* Canyon Sun
A. Klehm	*Phalaenopsis* Chromium Emperor 'Rising Sun' AM/AOS
A. Kolopaking	*Phalaenopsis* Kuntrarti Rarashati 'Bunker Hill'
	Phalaenopsis Kuntrarti Rarashati 'Joy'
ABC Orchid Corp.	*Phalaenopsis* Carolina Bronze Meteor 'Lenette' HCC/AOS
Allen Black	*Doritaenopsis* Happy Ending
	Doritaenopsis Hurricane Katrina
	Phalaenopsis Kenny Ewell
	Phalaenopsis Kunstler's Gem
	Phalaenopsis Memoria Chuck Noe
	Phalaenopsis Tsunami Warning
B. Woodson	*Phalaenopsis* Dotty Woodson 'Orchidland'
Baldan Orchid Nursery	*Phalaenopsis* Baldan's Kaleidoscope
Barry Cohen	*Phalaenopsis* Buena Jewel
Bracey	*Phalaenopsis* Samba
Breckenridge Orchids	*Phalaenopsis* Brecko Dawnphil
	Phalaenopsis Mini Mark 'Holm'
Brennan's Orchids	*Phalaenopsis* Shenandoah Fire 'Ember'
Brother Orchid Nursery	*Phalaenopsis* Brother Jungle Cat
	Doritaenopsis Brother Little Hatter
	Doritaenopsis Brother Sheridan
	Doritaenopsis Brother Success
	Doritaenopsis Pico Lady Ruby 'Wickford' HCC/AOS
	Phalaenopsis Ambo Buddha 'Phoenix' FCC/AOS
	Phalaenopsis Ambo Buddha 'SW'
	Phalaenopsis Brother Girl

ORIGINATOR	NAME
Brother Orchid Nursery	*Phalaenopsis* Brother John
	Phalaenopsis Brother Lawrence 'Montclair'
	Phalaenopsis Brother Mirage
	Phalaenopsis Brother Oconee 'Maria Teresa'
	Phalaenopsis Brother Passat
	Phalaenopsis Brother Pirate King
	Phalaenopsis Brother Redland Spots
	Phalaenopsis Brother Sara Gold 'Peach'
	Phalaenopsis Brother Sara Gold 'Sogo F-623'
	Phalaenopsis Fortune Saltzman 'Maple Bridge' AM/TCA
	Phalaenopsis Golden Peoker 'BL' HCC/AOS
	Phalaenopsis Golden Peoker Nan-Cho AM/AOS
C. N. Wan	*Phalaenopsis* Min-Chao Yeo-Man 'Hwa Yuan'
Carmela Orchids	*Doritaenopsis* Hybridizer's Dream
	Phalaenopsis Lawless Red Peppers
	Phalaenopsis World Class 'Big Foot' JC/AOS
	Phalaenopsis Yellow Brite Lites 'Neo' HCC/AOS
Carter and Holmes	*Phalaenopsis* Flight of Birds
Charles Beard	*Phalaenopsis* Spotted Moon 'Jo Ann' HCC/AOS
Cheng Hsien-I	*Phalaenopsis* Hannover Passion 'Ching Ruey'
Ching Ann	*Doritaenopsis* Ruey Lih Beauty 'Formosa'
	Phalaenopsis So Cha Gem 'Chin Jih' HCC/AOS
Ching Hua	*Doritaenopsis* Hsinying Mount 'Ching Ruey'
Ching Ruey Orchids	*Doritaenopsis* Chingruey's Goldstaff
	Phalaenopsis Chingruey's Morning 'Ching Ruey'
	Phalaenopsis Chingruey's Stripes 'Ching Ruey'
Ching-Tien Wong	*Phalaenopsis* Tzeng-Wen Sentra
	Phalaenopsis Tzeng-Wen Sentra 'Jia-Ho' AM/AOS
Clarelen Orchids	*Doritaenopsis* Kenneth Schubert 'First Rays'
	Doritaenopsis Memoria Clarence Schubert
D. Diehm	*Phalaenopsis* Brother Dendi 'Mary' HCC/AOS
Dogashima	*Doritaenopsis* Happy Valentine 'Fangtastic'
E. Iwanaga	*Doritaenopsis* Purple Gem
Eric Goo	*Doritaenopsis* Bill Tippit 'Purple Glow' HCC/AOS
	Doritaenopsis Firepower 'Cinnamon Glow'
	Doritaenopsis Flash Point 'Orange Glow'
	Doritaenopsis Memorial Bud Terrell 'Red Beauty' HCC/AOS

ORIGINATOR	NAME
Eric Goo	*Doritaenopsis* Sau Goo 'Orange Beauty' HCC/AOS
	Phalaenopsis Arizona Gem 'Ruby Glow' HCC/AOS
	Phalaenopsis Arizona Princess 'Purple Gem' HCC/AOS
	Phalaenopsis Arizona Princess 'Spotted Beauty' AM/AOS
	Phalaenopsis Ben Goo 'Radiant Ruby' HCC/AOS
	Phalaenopsis Bev Tall 'Carnelian Queen' AM/AOS
	Phalaenopsis Cris Lee 'Red Beauty'
	Phalaenopsis Mary Tauscher-Goo 'The Queen' HCC/AOS
	Phalaenopsis Memoria Don Tauscher 'Purple Beauty' AM/AOS
	Phalaenopsis Memoria Flora Ho 'Gold Emerald' HCC/AOS
	Phalaenopsis Memoria Phoebe Kwock 'Bold Beauty' HCC/AOS
	Phalaenopsis Phoenix Flame 'Orange Glow' AM/AOS
	Phalaenopsis Purple Majesty 'Burgundy Beauty' AM/AOS
	Phalaenopsis Ruth Tauscher 'Garnet Beauty' HCC/AOS
	Phalaenopsis Sherri Pantano 'Red Beauty' AM/AOS
	Phalaenopsis Sherri Pantano 'Tangelo'
	Phalaenopsis Wes Addison 'Ruby Glow' HCC/AOS
Ever Spring Orchids	*Doritaenopsis* Ever Spring Pioneer 'Champion'
	Doritaenopsis Ever Spring Prince 'Harlequin'
	Doritaenopsis Ever Spring Prince 'Plum Flower'
	Phalaenopsis Ever-Spring King 'Lee' JC/AOS
	Phalaenopsis Ever-Spring Light
	Phalaenopsis Ever-Spring Spot 'Montclair'
Evergreen	*Phalaenopsis* Tsay's Evergreen 'Nobby's Jade' HCC/AOS
F. Hark	*Phalaenopsis* Lipperose
F. L. Chau	*Phalaenopsis* An Tai Spot 'Splotchy' AM/AOS
F & M Kaufmann	*Doritaenopsis* Musick Lipstick
	Doritaenopsis Musick Surprise
	Phalaenopsis Fantasy Musick
Fred K. Thornton	*Asconopsis* Irene Dobkin 'York' HCC/AOS
	Phalaenopsis Caribbean Sunset 'Sweet Fragrance'
	Phalaenopsis Coral Isles 'Lung Ching' AM/AOS
Frog Hollow Orchids	*Phalaenopsis* Frog Hollow Fantasia 'Montclair'
Fu-Liang Huang	*Doritaenopsis* Chain Xen Diamond 'Celebration' FCC/AOS
	Doritaenopsis Chain Xen Pearl 'Lucky Star'
	Doritaenopsis Chain Xen Pearl 'Shih Hua'
Fu-Sheng Huang	*Phalaenopsis* Sogo Cock 'Joy'
	Phalaenopsis Sogo Cock 'Oriental Beauty' AM/AOS

ORIGINATOR	NAME
G. R. Taylor	*Phalaenopsis* Mary Lilian Taylor 'Desert Orange' AM/AOS
H. P. Norton	*Doritaenopsis* Jack Beckwith
	Doritaenopsis Kiss Me Kate 'Carol'
	Doritaenopsis Lonnie Morris 'Nationwide' AM/AOS
	Doritaenopsis Mepkin Bells 'Katherine'
	Phalaenopsis 'Blue Chip'
	Phalaenopsis Katie Morris 'Burnished Copper' HCC/AOS
	Phalaenopsis Katie Morris 'Caroline'
	Phalaenopsis Katie Morris 'Dixie Sunset'
	Phalaenopsis Orchidview Tabasco
H. Tanaka	*Phalaenopsis* Hilo Lip 'Winter Frost'
H. Wallbrunn	*Beardara* Henry Wallbrunn
Haur Jin Orchids	*Phalaenopsis* Haur Jin Diamond
	Phalaenopsis Haur Jin Diamond 'Montclair' HCC/AOS
Hawaiian Hybrids	*Phalaenopsis* Hilo Gold 'Mary' HCC/AOS
Hugo Freed	*Phalaenopsis* George Vasquez 'An Lin'
	Phalaenopsis Malibu Imp 'Evergreen Hill' AM/AOS
I-Hsin Orchids	*Doritaenopsis* I-Hsin Balloon 'KHM1316'
	Doritaenopsis I-Hsin Black Valentine 'KHM 1566'
	Doritaenopsis I-Hsin Carnival 'KHM1357'
	Doritaenopsis Sinica Sunday 'KHM364'
	Phalaenopsis I-Hsin Golden Sun 'IS186'
J. G. Martin	*Phalaenopsis* Venimp 'Sedona'
J. S. Wu	*Doritaenopsis* Chian-Huey Red Rose
J. Wu	*Doritaenopsis* Joy Angel Voice
	Phalaenopsis Joy Spring Canary 'Rainbow'
Jean Chin-Shang	*Phalaenopsis* Taisuco Chinfang
Jiuhbao Orchids	*Doritaenopsis* Jiuhbao Red Rose 'Brilliant'
Jones and Scully	*Phalaenopsis* Seventh Heaven
K & D Emig	*Phalaenopsis* Gene Wentz
Kokubunji	*Phalaenopsis* Cygnus
Krull-Smith	*Phalaenopsis* Florida Heat 'Gemma' HCC/AOS
	Phalaenopsis H. P. Norton 'Kathy' AM/AOS
	Phalaenopsis Krull's Red Hot 'Red Leather'
Kung's	*Phalaenopsis* Kung's Gelb Lishian
Kuo-Liang Hung	*Doritaenopsis* Tying Shin Phoenix 'Golden Cupid'
	Doritaenopsis Tying Shin Phoenix 'Golden Leopard' BM/TOGA
	Doritaenopsis Tying Shin Phoenix 'Golden Phoenix' SM/TOGA

ORIGINATOR	NAME
Kuo-Liang Hung	*Doritaenopsis* Tying Shin Phoenix 'T. S.'
	Phalaenopsis Tying Shin Alice 'Hong'
Lee Shih Hua	*Phalaenopsis* Little Emperor
Lin Ming Kung	*Phalaenopsis* Formosa San Fan
M. Kobayashi	*Phalaenopsis* Hiroshima Fantasy 'Beautiful Dreamer' HCC/AOS
M. Lin	*Phalaenopsis* Chih Shang's Stripes 'Marginata'
Mark Pendleton	*Doritaenopsis* Pixie Star 'Norman'
Ming-I Chuang	*Phalaenopsis* Taisuco Date 'F. L.'
Ming-Rong Tsay	*Doritaenopsis* Scarlet in Snow
N. I. Chang	*Doritaenopsis* Yu Pin Lover
	Phalaenopsis Yu Pin Pearl 'Peacock'
Nobby Orchid Nursery	*Phalaenopsis* Nobby's Amy
	Phalaenopsis Nobby's Amy 'Shih Hua'
	Phalaenopsis Nobby's Shadowy 'Nobby'
	Phalaenopsis Perfect Sara 'Orange Delight'
Norman's Orchids	*Doritaenopsis* Fangtastic Roslynn Greenberg 'Raspberry Delight' HCC/AOS
	Doritaenopsis Montclair Valentine 'Picotee'
	Phalaenopsis Jackie Debonis
	Phalaenopsis Jungle Cat 'Bloody Mary'
Ooi Leng Sun	*Phalaenopsis* Penang Girl
	Phalaenopsis Penang Girl 'Ching Ruey'
Orchid Plantation	*Phalaenopsis* Summer Garnet 'Neo' HCC/AOS
Orchid World International (Universal's)	*Phalaenopsis* Orchid World 'Bonnie Vasquez' AM/AOS
Orchis Flor.	*Doritaenopsis* Taiwan Red Cat
	Phalaenopsis Taiwan Glory
Oriental Orchids	*Phalaenopsis* Oriental Fairy 'Montclair'
P. Lista	*Phalaenopsis* Golden Buddha
Pen-Chih Lai	*Doritaenopsis* Taida Fortune 'Taida Golden Girl'
	Phalaenopsis Taida Lovely 'M'
	Phalaenopsis Zuma's Pixie 'Taida Little Cutie'
Sogo	*Doritaenopsis* Leopard Prince 'Brennan's Orchids' HCC/AOS
	Doritaenopsis Leopard Prince 'KH4338'
	Doritaenopsis Leopard Prince 'KHM430'
	Doritaenopsis Minho Princess
	Doritaenopsis Minho Princess 'Watercolor Princess' HCC/AOS
	Doritaenopsis Sogo Manager 'Neo' HCC/AOS
	Doritaenopsis Sogo Manager 'Nina'
	Doritaenopsis Sogo Melody

ORIGINATOR	NAME
Sogo	*Phalaenopsis* Black Ball
	Phalaenopsis Shin Yi Diamond
	Phalaenopsis Sogo Cock 'Oriental Princess HCC/AOS
	Phalaenopsis Sogo David 'Peachy'
	Phalaenopsis Sogo Grape
	Phalaenopsis Sogo Lion 'Amber'
	Phalaenopsis Sogo Rose 'Joy'
	Phalaenopsis Sogo Twinkle 'Stars' HCC/AOS
Stewart, Inc.	*Phalaenopsis* Spirit House 'D & B' AM/AOS
Sunrise Biotech	*Phalaenopsis* Sunrise Red Peoker
T. Lusup-anan	*Doritaenopsis* Siam Treasure
T. Takase	*Phalaenopsis* Little Mary 'Cherry Blossom'
Taida	*Doritaenopsis* Taida Salu
Taisuco (Taiwan Sugar Company)	*Doritaenopsis* Taisuco Bloody Mary
	Doritaenopsis Taisuco Micky
	Doritaenopsis Taisuco Pixie 'Ching Ruey' AM/AOS
	Doritaenopsis Taisuco Sunset
	Phalaenopsis Taisuco Rosemary
	Phalaenopsis Taisuco Tunelip
Tin-Fan Ho	*Phalaenopsis* Ho's Little Caroline
	Phalaenopsis Ho's Lovely Amethyst 'La Flora' AM/AOS
Tom Harper	*Phalaenopsis* Carolina Red Magic 'Lenette' AM/AOS
Veitch	*Phalaenopsis* Luedde-violacea 'Ana Red' HCC/AOS
W. T. Chien	*Doritaenopsis* I-Hsin Balloon 'KHM1316'
	Doritaenopsis I-Hsin Marks
	Doritaenopsis I-Hsin Waltz 'Zephyrus'
	Phalaenopsis I-Hsin Gold Dust 'Neo' AM/AOS
	Phalaenopsis I-Hsin Sunflower 'KHM-95-1'
	Phalaenopsis I-Hsin Sunflower 'M' AM/AOS
Wang Bi-Jiang	*Doritaenopsis* Acker's Sweetie 'Dragon Tree Maple' SM/TOGA
	Phalaenopsis Dragon Tree Eagle 'DT168'
Wickford Orchids	*Phalaenopsis* Memoria Winona Brown Weeks
Yung-Ho	*Phalaenopsis* Yungho Gelb Canary 'Yungho' AM/AOS
Zuma Canyon	*Phalaenopsis* Bonnie Vasquez 'Zuma Creek' HCC/AOS
	Phalaenopsis Ember 'Blumen Insel' AM/AOS
	Phalaenopsis Pago Pago 'First Love' AM/AOS
	Phalaenopsis Zuma Aussie Delight
	Phalaenopsis Zuma Garnet 'Plantation' HCC/AOS

Bibliography

Allikas, Greg, and Ned Nash. 2000. *Orchids*. San Diego, California: Thunder Bay Press.

American Orchid Society. 2002. *American Orchid Society Handbook on Judging and Exhibition*, 11th ed. Delray Beach, Florida: American Orchid Society.

Bachner, Martin. 1976. *Phalaenopsis* Joseph Hampton: Progenitor Supreme. *American Orchid Society Bulletin* 45 (6): 521–23.

Baker, Margaret L., and Charles O. 1991. *Orchid Species Culture: Pescatorea, Phais, Phalaenopsis, Pholidota, Phragmipedium, Pleione*. Portland, Oregon: Timber Press.

Bassin, Harvey. 1986. *Phalaenopsis* Deventeriana 'Treva'. *American Orchid Society Bulletin* 55 (4): 347–50.

Bechtel, Helmut, Phillip Cribb, and Edmund Launert. 1986. *The Manual of Cultivated Orchid Species*, Rev. ed. Cambridge, Massachusetts: The MIT Press.

Blanchard, Matthew, Roberto Lopez, Erik Runkle, and Yin-Tung Wang. 2005. The orchid grower. *Greenhouse Grower* (October): 86–89.

Blanchard, Matthew C., and Erik S. Runkle. 2006. Temperature during the day, but not during the night, controls flowering of *Phalaenopsis* orchids. *Journal of Experimental Botany* 57 (15): 4043–49.

Bray, Helga, and Joseph Helga. 2005. Wildcatt Orchids Database, March 2005 version. http://www.wildcattdata.com/NewWeb/. Accessed March 2005.

Burian, Rick, ed. 2004. *An Orchidist's Lexicon*, 2nd ed. Portland, Oregon: Oregon Orchid Society.

Carri-Raven Riemann. 2007. The mini but mighty multifloral *Phalaenopsis*. *Phalaenopsis, Journal of the International Phalaenopsis Alliance* 16 (3): 13–25.

Christenson, Eric A. 2001. *Phalaenopsis: A Monograph*. Portland, Oregon: Timber Press.

Conkin, Doug. 2002. Pilgrimage to the Holy Grail: the development of modern yellow *Phalaenopsis* in America. *Orchid Digest* 66 (4): 229–36.

Cootes, Jim. 2001. *The Orchids of the Philippines*. Singapore: Times Editions.

Davis, Diane, and Phyllis Finklestein. 1990. *Phalaenopsis* Lipperose and its influence on modern pink hybridizing. *American Orchid Society Bulletin* 59 (4): 352–60.

Evans, Anabel. 2007. Phalaenopsis steal the show in Taiwan. *Floriculture International* (May): 18–22.

Fighetti, Carlos. 2004. Passing the torch. *Phalaenopsis, Journal of the International Phalaenopsis Alliance* 13 (3): 20–31.

Fitch, Charles Marden. 2002. *Growing Orchids Under Lights*. Delray Beach, Florida: American Orchid Society.

Fitch, Charles Marden, ed. 2004a. *The Best Orchids for Indoors*. Brooklyn, New York: Brooklyn Botanic Garden.

———. 2004b. *The Gardener's Guide to Growing Orchids*. Brooklyn, New York: Brooklyn Botanic Garden.

Freed, Hugo. 1968. Breeding pink *Phalaenopsis*. *Orchid Digest* 32 (9): 262–65.

———. 1970. *Orchids and Serendipity*. Englewood Cliffs, New Jersey: Prentice-Hall, Inc.

———. 1972. *Phalaenopsis violacea* Breeding Has Come of Age. *Orchid Digest* 36 (1): 4–7.

———. 1973a. Breeding Novelty Phalaenopsis. *Orchid Digest* 37 (1): 5–10.

———. 1973b. The spectacular eye-catchers: peppermint-striped *Phalaenopsis. American Orchid Society Bulletin* 44 (2): 103–8.

———. 1975. The exquisite semi-alba *Phalaenopsis. Orchid Digest* 39 (1): 4–6.

———. 1978. The twelve most important white *Phalaenopsis* stud plants. *American Orchid Society Bulletin* 47 (12): 1104–11.

———. 1979. *New Horizons in Orchid Breeding.* Pomona, California: Day Printing Corp.

———. 1984a. Novas of the *Phalaenopsis* world 1. *American Orchid Society Bulletin* 53 (9): 927–35.

———. 1984b. Novas of the *Phalaenopsis* world 2. *American Orchid Society Bulletin* 53 (10): 1029–34.

———. 1984c. Novas of the *Phalaenopsis* world 3. *American Orchid Society Bulletin* 53 (11): 1145–50.

Frowine, Steven A. 2007. *Miniature Orchids.* Portland, Oregon: Timber Press.

———. 2005a. *Fragrant Orchids.* Portland, Oregon: Timber Press.

———. 2005b. *Orchids for Dummies.* Hoboken, New Jersey: Wiley.

Gian-Quey, Fon. 2003. *New Phalaenopsis of Taiwan III.* Taiwan: Sogo Orchids.

Ginsburg, Howard S. 2006. Golden Peoker: golden parent. *Orchid Digest* 70 (3): 160–69.

———. 2000. Breeding trends in red *Phalaenopsis. Orchids* 69 (11): 1050–61.

———. 2001. Multifloral *Phalaenopsis*: an overview. *Orchid Digest* 65 (1): 27–34.

Goo, Eric. 2002. Color them red. *Phalaenopsis, Journal of the International Phalaenopsis Alliance* 12 (Fall): 22–27.

Gordon, Bob. 1994. *Beginner's Guide to Growing Phalaenopsis*, Rev. ed. Running Springs, California: Laid-Back Publications.

———. 1985. *Culture of the Phalaenopsis Orchid.* Rialto, California: Laid-Back Publications.

———. 1988. *Phalaenopsis Culture: A Worldwide Survey.* Rialto, California: Laid-Back Publications.

———. 1991. *Orchid Seedling Care.* Rialto, California: Laid-Back Publications.

Griesbach, R. J. 2005. A scientific approach to breeding blue orchids. *Orchids* 74 (5): 376–79.

———. 2000. Potted *Phalaenopsis* orchid production: history, present status, and challenges for the future. ASHA-2000 Symposium. Beltsville, Maryland: Floral and Nursery Plant Research, U.S. National Arboretum.

Gruss, Olaf, and Manfred Wolff. 1995. *Phalaenopsis.* Stuttgart, Germany: Eugen Ulmer Gmbh & Co.

Hamilton, Robert M. 1977. *When Does It Flower?* British Columbia, Canada: Robert M. Hamilton.

Hardy, Sandy. 2002. IPA profile: H. P. Norton. *Phalaenopsis, Journal of the International Phalaenopsis Alliance* (12 (1): 12–21.

Harper, Tom. 2004a. *Phalaenopsis* culture: advice for growing 20 species. *Orchids* 73 (2): 118–27.

———. 1991. Multiflora *Phalaenopsis*: the contributions of *Phalaenopsis equestris* in breeding multifloras. *American Orchid Society Bulletin* 60 (2): 106–14.

———. 1996. Recent trends in phalaenopsis breeding. *Orchids* 65 (4): 366–71.

———. 2002. Color them red. *Phalaenopsis, Journal of the International Phalaenopsis Alliance* (12): 28–39.

———. 2004b. Unmasking the harlequins. *Phalaenopsis, Journal of the International Phalaenopsis Alliance* 14 (1): 26–39.

Hetherington, Ernest. 1995. Keith Schaffer and Schaffer's orchids. *Orchid Digest* 59 (1): 12–13.

Kobayashi, Gregory.1989. *Phalaenopsis* Hilo Lip 'Lightfoot'. *Orchid Digest* 53 (4): 148–51.

Koch, Alan. 2003. *Phalaenopsis equestris* and the genius of Herb Hager. *Phalaenopsis, Journal of the International Phalaenopsis Alliance* 13 (1): 28–42.

Koopowitz, Harold. 2001. Understanding orchid roots. *Orchid Digest* 65 (4): 155–56.

Koopowitz, Harold, and Norito Hasagawa. 1985. Golden Buddha—golden parent. *American Orchid Society Bulletin* 54 (11): 1308–13.

Kranz, Frederick H., and Jacqueline L. 1971. *Gardening Indoors Under Lights: A Complete Guide*. New York: The Viking Press.

Lin, Peter. 2003. *Phalaenopsis gigantea*, giant of the genus. *Phalaenopsis, Journal of the International Phalaenopsis Alliance* 12 (3): 24–30.

Livingston, Bill. 2002. Hybridizing with *Phalaenopsis* species. *Orchid Digest* 66 (4): 207–17.

Logan, Harry B., and Lloyd C. Cosper. 1949. *Orchids Are Easy To Grow*. Englewood Cliffs, New Jersey: Prentice-Hall Inc.

Lopez, Roberto, Erik Runkle, Yin-Tung Wang, and Matthew Blanchard. 2005. The orchid grower, part 3. *Greenhouse Grower* (September): 96–100.

Lopez, Roberto, Erik Runkle, Yin-Tung Wang, Matthew Blanchard, and Tony Hsu. 2007. Growing the best phalaenopsis. *Orchids* 76 (3): 184–88.

Martin, John G. 1985. In search of red *Phalaenopsis*. *American Orchid Society Bulletin* 54 (4): 411–20.

Masaki, Chiba. 2002. *Phalaenopsis Species*. Sakado, Saitama, Japan: Phalaenopsis Species Publishing Society.

McKinley, Michael, ed. 2005. *Complete Guide to Orchids*. Des Moines, Iowa: Meredith Corporation.

McQueen, Jim, and Barbara McQueen. 1992. *Miniature Orchids: The World of Orchids*. Portland, Oregon: Timber Press.

Moses, John R. 1994. Development of semi-alba *Phalaenopsis*. *American Orchid Society Bulletin* 63 (9): 1000–1008.

———. 1980. *Phalaenopsis*: The search for pink. *American Orchid Society Bulletin* 49 (4): 363–71.

Moses, Mier. 2002. Send in the clowns. Harlequins: a look at the evolution of those crazy spotted phals. *Phalaenopsis, Journal of the International Phalaenopsis Alliance* 12 (1): 26–35.

Motes, Martin, Homer P. Norton, Mark Rose, Carlos F. Fighetti, and Dyle W. Frank. 1993. Red *Phalaenopsis* hybrids. *American Orchid Society Bulletin* 62 (3): 250–57.

Nash, Ned, and Isobyl La Croix. 2005. *Flora's Orchids*. Portland, Oregon: Timber Press.

Noble, Mary. 1994. *You Can Grow Phalaenopsis Orchids*, Rev. ed. Jacksonville, Florida: Mary Noble McQuerry.

Northen, Rebecca Tyson. 1996. *Miniature Orchids and How to Grow Them*. New York: Dover Publications, Inc.

———. 1970. *Home Orchid Growing*, 3rd ed. New York: Van Nostrand Reinhold Co.

Norton, Katherine. n.d. Birth of the Blues. http://orchidview.com/Birth_of_the_Blues.htm. Accessed November 2007.

O'Byrne, Peter. 2001. *A to Z of South East Asian Orchids*. Singapore: Orchid Society of East Asia.

OrchidWiz Encyclopedia 3.03. n.d. CD-ROM. Miami Shores, Florida: OrchidWiz, LLC.

Ott, F. Thomas. 2001. Modern white *Phalaenopsis*: origins and current status. *Orchid Digest* 65 (4): 148–54.

Rentoul, J. N. 1991. *Growing Orchids: The Hybrid Story*. Portland, Oregon: Timber Press.

Ritterhausen, Brian, and Wilma Ritterhausen. 2002. *The Practical Encyclopedia of Orchids*. London: Lorenz Books.

Runkle, Erik, Yin-Tung Wang, Matthew Blanchard, and Roberto Lopez. 2005. The orchid grower, part 1. *Greenhouse Grower* (July): 84–87.

Sessler, Gloria Jean. 1978. *Orchids and How To Grow Them*. Englewood Cliffs, New Jersey: Prentice-Hall, Inc.

Shaffer, Keith. 1960. *Phalaenopsis leuddemanniana* and its hybrids. *American Orchid Society Bulletin* 29: 493–94.

Sheehan, Tom, and Marion Sheehan. 1994. *An Illustrated Survey of Orchid Genera*. Portland, Oregon: Timber Press.

Smith, Frank. 1987. Spotted *Phalaenopsis*. *American Orchid Society Bulletin* 56 (3): 228–31.

Soon, Teoh Eng. 1995. *Orchids of Asia*. Portland, Oregon: Timber Press.

Stock, A. Dean. 2005a. Harlequin genetics: understanding pigment production and lack of pattern control. *Phalaenopsis, Journal of the International Phalaenopsis Alliance* 15 (3): 24–38.

———. 2005b. Peloric phals: they have a personality that most can do without. *Phalaenopsis, Journal of the International Phalaenopsis Alliance* 15 (1): 37–38.

———. 2005c. Ploidy pitfalls: when breeding for tetraploid reds it helps to know some basic genetics. *Phalaenopsis, Journal of the International Phalaenopsis Alliance* 15 (2): 16–19.

Sweet, Herman R. 1980. *The Genus Phalaenopsis*. Pomona, California: Orchid Digest Inc.

Szyren, Jan. 2003. Without high phosphorous: a new fertilizer proves itself with orchids. *Orchids* (June): 454–59.

Takasaki, Sheldon. 1989. Recent phalaenopsis breeding in the Hawaiian Islands. *American Orchid Society Bulletin* 58 (1): 8–15.

Teo, Chris K. H. 1985. *Native Orchids of Peninsular Malaysia*. Singapore: Times Book International.

Thornton, Frederick L. and Barbara A. 1967a. Observations on the dominant and recessive breeding characteristics of *Stauroglottis*, *Zebrinae*, *Polychilos*, and *Proboscidiodes* groups of the genus *Phalaenopsis*. *Orchid Digest* 31 (4): 122.

———. 1967b. Observations on the dominant and recessive breeding characteristics of *Stauroglottis*, *Zebrinae*, *Polychilos*, and *Proboscidiodes* groups of the genus *Phalaenopsis*. *Orchid Digest* 31 (8): 246–48.

———. 1967c. Observations on the dominant and recessive breeding characteristics of *Stauroglottis*, *Zebrinae*, *Polychilos*, and *Proboscidiodes* groups of the genus *Phalaenopsis*. *Orchid Digest* 31 (10): 306–309.

Tippitt, Bill. 1997a. Hybridizing *Phalaenopsis*, part 1. *Orchids* 66 (11): 1180–86.

———. 1997b. Hybridizing *Phalaenopsis*, part 2. *Orchids* 66 (12): 1291–97.

Tuskes, Paul, and Ann Tuskes. 2002. Culture of *Phalaenopsis* Species. *Orchid Digest* 66 (4): 165–93.

Ufford, Charles. 2005. The species challenge. *Phalaenopsis, Journal of the International Phalaenopsis Alliance* 14 (First Quarter): 19–36.

Vaughan, Lewis, and Varina Vaughn. 1973. An account of the moth orchids: the ascendancy of white *Phalaenopsis*. *American Orchid Society Bulletin* 42 (3): 231–37.

Wallenstein, Bob, and Lynn Wallenstein. 2000. Water Quality Issues for Slipper Orchid Growers. http://ladyslipper.com/waterq.htm. Accessed November 2007.

Wang, Yin-Tung. 1997. Phalaenopsis light requirements and schedule of flowering. *Orchids* (September): 934–39.

Wang, Yin-Tung, Matthew Blanchard, Roberto Lopez, and Erik Runkle. 2005. The orchid grower, part 2. *Greenhouse Grower* (August): 70–72.

Watson, James B., ed. 2002a. *Growing Orchids*, Rev. ed. Delray Beach, Florida: American Orchid Society.

———. 2002b. *Orchid Pests and Diseases*. Delray Beach, Florida: American Orchid Society.

Watson, W., and H. J. Chapman. 1903. *Orchids: Their Culture and Management*. New York: Charles Scribner's Sons.

White, Edward A. 1948. *American Orchid Culture*. New York: A. T. Mare Co., Inc.

White, Judy. 1996. *Taylor's Guide to Orchids*. Boston: Houghton Mifflin Co.

Index

Page numbers in *italic* include illustrations.

Opposite: *Doritaenopsis* Tying Shin Phoenix 'Golden Leopard' BM/TOGA. Photo by Marshall Ku.